UNCOVERING THE NEWS

A Journalist's Search for Information

Lauren Kessler
Duncan McDonald

School of Journalism
University of Oregon

Wadsworth Publishing Company
Belmont, California
A Division of Wadsworth, Inc.

Communication Editor   **Kristine Clerkin**
Editorial Associate   **Naomi Brown**
Production Editor   **Vicki Friedberg**
Designer   **Lisa S. Mirski**
Print Buyer   **Karen Hunt**
Copy Editor   **Steven Hiatt**
Cover   **Lisa S. Mirski**

Printed in the United States of America   34

1 2 3 4 5 6 7 8 9 10---91 90 89 88 87

Library of Congress Cataloging in Publication Data

Kessler, Lauren.
  Uncovering the news.

  Includes index.
  1. Reporters and reporting.   2. Research.
I. McDonald, Duncan.   II. Title.
PN4781.K47   1987   070.4'3   86-15930
ISBN 0-534-06954-1

To Jackson,
the newest information-gatherer
of our acquaintance;
and to several older ones,
Jane, Tom and Vanessa

Contents

7 | Institutional Knowledge 133

11

Whom Do You Trust? 219

Appendix: Identifying and Dealing with Ethical Issues 231

Foreword

When it comes time for reporters Tom Hamburger and Joe Rigert to negotiate how an article they've been working on will be written, here is how they do it: They get nose to nose and yell at each other until one of them faints. The one still standing sits down at the VDT and writes the article the way he intended all along. The other, once revived, is forced to react to what is already on the screen.

On days we are going to have a story conference or write a memo on where we are, each tries to arrive at the office before the other in order to write the first draft, thus making the laggard react to what's already on the table. That's led to 4 A.M. arrivals.

They've been working together on projects at the Minneapolis *Star and Tribune* off and on since 1984. Any onlooker might think these guys don't like to work together. That's wrong; they love it. They each have different strengths and they trust each other completely.

At 54, Joe has nearly 30 years in the business. He's the complete records hound and digger. If Joe can't find it out, it's because it hasn't happened. In addition, he can organize the massive amounts of data collected over a period of months in ways that would do any librarian or public accountant proud.

Tom, 33, has 13 years experience. Early in his partnership with Joe, Tom's idea of a filing system was to ask Joe where something was. Not so any more.

Tom is one of the very best interviewers, both by phone and in person, I've seen. And he is exceptionally good at coming up with creative and innovative tactics on projects.

Joe and Tom are the reporters who uncovered the minority contracts problems in Minnesota partially described in Chapter 2. The authors of this book use that series to show you how important it is to learn to go beyond the interview and become expert at finding and understanding records and documents.

That's true for reporters on projects, and it is true for reporters on daily deadlines. It is this ability to really find out what is going on that distinguishes the average reporter from the good and the good from the very best.

It is not a good mark for journalism schools, where I've toiled in classrooms as both teacher and student for more than a decade, that this kind of training comes so late to the smorgasbord of course offerings. It's been a relative handful of years that undergraduate journalism students have been exposed to social science tools, and typically this exposure has been restricted to such skills as polling and understanding statistics.

Such knowledge is often important. But more important is knowing where to look in the massive public record to document the claims and assertions of the people we interview or just to glean an understanding of how things work.

The most important impetus for this trend is the educational work of Investigative Reporters & Editors, a professional reporter organization that began in 1975. IRE has held conferences for professionals and journalism students in every region of the United States, bringing the best of America's most successful journalists to explain these skills to thousands of reporters interested in improving their own reporting abilities. This organization has also made possible *The Reporter's Handbook,* a more advanced guide to documents and records, which I played a part in producing when I was IRE's executive director.

Believe the authors of this book when they tell you how important it is for you to know more about reporting than just being able to invert the pyramid. You must learn to understand how things work before you can intelligently report on them, and looking at records is as good a road map as there is.

You may think that a course on records and documents just can't be much fun, but that's wrong. It is fun to learn how to dig out information that too many among us try to get simply by asking questions. This knowledge is a confidence builder. It arms you with a methodology that enables you to understand the daily activities that you must explain to readers, viewers or listeners.

Tom and Joe didn't have the good fortune of having this kind of book around when they were taking their courses. They've had to learn it the hard way.

You don't have to. Just continue to turn the pages. And welcome to the interesting and useful world of records and documents.

John Ullmann
Assistant Managing Editor/Projects
Minneapolis *Star and Tribune*

Acknowledgments

A number of busy people took time to help us in the preparation of this book. Our thanks to: University of Oregon reference librarian Ruth South for her meticulous reading of Chapter 4 and for her assistance in researching computerized databases; University of Oregon public affairs librarian John Shuler for his invaluable help with Chapters 5 and 7; Tom Hager for his help with Chapter 6 and for his suggestion for this book's title; Eugene Fire Department Captain Tim Birr and Deputy Police Chief John Rutledge for their insights on public safety matters discussed in Chapter 8; and to John McMillan, publisher of the Utica (NY) *Observer-Dispatch,* for his careful reading of and comments on Chapter 11.

Special thanks goes to John Ullmann, assistant managing editor of the Minneapolis *Star and Tribune,* for his thoughtful foreword to this book.

We also thank George Pica of the University of Missouri School of Journalism for his eagle-eyed review of our manuscript, as well as the other reviewers who took time to give us important counsel: Louis Alexander, University of North Carolina, Asheville; Roberta G. Applegate, Kansas State University; George Flynn, Fresno State University; Walter B. Jaehnig, University of Wyoming; Laurence B. Lain, University of Dayton; David B. Reddick, Methodist Hospital of Indiana; John N. Rippey, Pennsylvania State University; Lee Wilkins, University of Colorado; and Eugenia Zerbinos, Marquette University.

And for the record, it continues to be a pleasure to work with Wadsworth. The staff's close attention to detail and its constant concern about effective presentation impress us greatly. Many thanks to Kris Clerkin, our editor, to Vicki Friedberg, our production editor, and to Lisa Mirski, our book designer.

Lauren Kessler
Duncan McDonald
Eugene, Oregon

Why We Search

We live in a media-saturated society.

We scan the morning newspaper to check world events, tune in the car radio for company, leaf through a magazine while waiting for an appointment, relax in front of the television set after a hard day and gaze at the movie screen on Saturday night. We seek and sample the mass media's diversity every day, using different forms to satisfy different needs. The forms vary so widely—from a newspaper want ad to an episode of "Miami Vice," from an eye-in-the-sky traffic report to a "Star Wars" sequel—that we may forget the one similarity that overwhelms all the differences: information.

Information is at the heart of all mass media. The newspaper reporter follows its trail. The broadcast journalist pursues it. The magazine writer ferrets it out. The advertising agency account executive is after it, as is the public relations specialist. All need information before they can construct their messages, be they investigative stories or beer commercials. Of course, the messages differ; the forms and styles vary; the purposes are not the same. But at the core is information. And at the core of every mass communicator's job is information gathering.

THE TRADITION OF INFORMATION GATHERING

Even more important than writing is information gathering—for without information we have nothing to write about. That is why information gathering takes up more of the journalist's time than any other activity. Whether it is attending meetings, reading reports, checking documents or interviewing sources, journalists are constantly on the trail of precise, accurate information and have been since journalism's earliest days. The information-gathering tradition is a long and rich one.

- Journalists have long acted as the *public's eyes and ears,* attending governmental sessions, committee meetings, conferences and events on the public's behalf. Today C-Span's tireless cameras act as the public's eyes and ears in both the Senate and the House. But the tradition began more than 170 years ago when one early newspaper, the *National Intelligencer,* gained prominence by specializing in Congressional information gathering. Each day Congress was in session, the *National Intelligencer*'s two publisher-editors were in the gallery listening and taking notes. In those days before Minicams and tape recorders, the two newspapermen relied on the then-exotic skill of shorthand to capture debate and discussion. The result was accurate, sometimes verbatim, accounts of legislative action that were quoted widely in the young nation's other newspapers.

- Other journalists have specialized in thrilling *eyewitness* accounts, gathering information while it unfolded and communicating it with immediacy and drama. Long before Walter Cronkite covered NASA liftoffs, long before Edward R. Murrow reported the bombing of London, information-hungry journalists were on the scene telling their audiences what they saw, like this journalist who covered a New York City fire in 1835:

  Just came from the scene. From Wall street to Hanover Square, and from the Merchants' Exchange to the East River, all on fire. About 300 stores burned, and burning down—probably five millions of property lost. About 1000 merchants ruined, and several Insurance Companies gone. . . .

  Good God! in one night we have lost the whole amount for which the nation is ready to go to war with France! is it a punishment for our madness?

- Journalists have long acted as detectives, digging up information that others would rather have kept hidden from public view. TV journalist Geraldo Rivera made an impressive debut years ago with a fine piece of detective work—a story for WABC/New York on the scandalous conditions at a state run home for the mentally retarded. A hundred years earlier, another young reporter also began her career with fine detective work. Elizabeth Cochrane ("Nelly Bly"), on assignment for the New York *World,* went undercover to report on the ghastly conditions at a state insane asylum. In the 1970s, two young Washington, D.C., reporters helped change history by digging into the events surrounding the break-in at the Watergate office complex. In the early years of this century, another detective-reporter, Upton Sinclair, also helped change history when he uncovered unsanitary conditions in the meat packing industry, producing a classic book, *The Jungle*.

■ Journalists have a long tradition of acting as serious *researchers*, painstakingly documenting important stories by following paper trails, conducting solid interviews and piecing together evidence. In 1980 and again in 1985, a team of *Time* magazine reporters delved into America's toxic waste problem by studying government and corporate documents, commissioning opinion polls, conducting on-site inspections and interviewing hundreds of sources. Seymour Hersh, the dogged investigative reporter who broke the Vietnam My Lai massacre story in the 1970s, continued his serious work into the 1980s when he investigated the personal and professional relationship between Richard Nixon and Henry Kissinger. But these impressive modern-day reporters were merely following in the footsteps of journalistic researchers like Ida Tarbell, one of the original muckrakers for *McClure's* magazine around the turn of the century. Her meticulous research exposed the unfair business practices of John D. Rockefeller and his Standard Oil Company.

■ Mass communicators in the fields of advertising and public relations have a long track record as *data hounds*, commissioning surveys, ordering studies, culling motivational research, using government-generated statistics and supporting an array of pollsters and ratings services. The wealth of information they have gathered—from the first, unsophisticated Nielsen ratings and Gallup surveys of the 1950s to the refined demographic data of the 1980s—has made it possible to pinpoint, understand and reach specific audiences with various messages.

THE MASS MEDIA AS WATCHDOGS

However journalists have gathered the information vital to their craft, the result has been the development of the media's watchdog role. Accurate, in-depth information about institutions in society—from the federal government to a local hospital—make this guardian role possible.

Information gathering is thus the key to the most important, most honorable function of our channels of mass communication.

Set apart from other businesses by the protection granted in the First Amendment, the media have long thought of themselves as acting, at least in part, in the public interest. From Tom Paine's pre-Revolutionary War broadsides with their lofty political ideas to Ted Koppel's "Nightline" with its spirited debates on public issues, the mass media have set themselves up as societal watchdogs. They consider that their constitutional protection brings with it responsibility.

Exactly what that responsibility entails has been debated for centuries. One of the clearest explanations comes from a report written by a group of U.S. intellectuals in the years just after World War II. Dubbed the Hutchins Commission after its chairman, University of Chicago Chancellor Robert M. Hutchins, the group set forth what it saw as the responsibilities of a free press. The press, argued the commission in 1947, must provide a *truthful, comprehensive, intelligent* account of the day's events in a *context* that gives it meaning. It must act as a *forum* for expression on all sides of an issue. It must project a *representative picture* of the groups that make up American society, portraying the groups *fairly* and *without stereotypes*.

To report responsibly means to strive for the maximum amount of detailed, accurate information. It means continuous, persistent information gathering.

Consider how the quality of reporting suffers when journalists are *not* constant, tenacious information-gatherers. In late 1985, West Coast journalists met in Portland, Oregon, to figure out how they could have missed the "big story" at Rajneeshpuram, a controversial central Oregon commune established by followers of the Bhagwan Shree Rajneesh. These reporters had been following activities at the commune for four years. However, they were completely surprised when top commune officials disappeared and the Bhagwan charged them with a host of crimes from wiretapping to poisoning public officials. Why, the reporters asked themselves, did none of them have an inkling of the deep rifts in the commune, the fierce internal politics that erupted when the leaders left?

The answer is disturbingly simple: lack of consistent information gathering. The reporters—like their colleagues who cover Central America or the Middle East—descended on the scene periodically to report on individual events. The reporters left when the controversy of the moment died down. This "hot spot" reporting meant they had little time to nurture sources or develop an understanding of the commune, its politics or its people. The resulting coverage was fragmentary and disjointed. It often lacked context and depth, depending instead on superficial information and stereotypes. It was, by Hutchins Commission standards, irresponsible reporting. Because of sketchy, intermittent information gathering, the reporters missed the big story.

INFORMATION GATHERING IN THE INFORMATION AGE

We live in an information age in which more people than ever before are involved in creating, collecting, analyzing and disseminating information. The federal government alone employs more than 700,000 people whose primary job is to gather and evaluate information. Virtually every corporation, institution, agency, foundation, association, city and school district in the nation employs information specialists who create and help control the flow of information. The U.S. Government Printing Office, the largest publisher in the world, produces more than 50,000 informational books, brochures, pamphlets and documents each year.

We don't live just in an information age; we live amid an information glut. In a society so saturated with data, facts and opinions, the journalist's job is more challenging than ever. Information hunting is both easier and more difficult today than it has ever been before.

The sheer volume of data means today's journalist need never be at a loss for information and need never be dependent on a single source. Consider the recent controversy over using sulfites as preservatives in restaurant salad bars. The volume of information generated on the subject from government and private groups made information gathering easy in some ways. A public relations spokesperson for a major restaurant chain would not have had to use exhaustive investigative techniques to locate information. The Food and Drug Administration issued reports. Scientists at various research centers conducted experiments and published results. Powerful lobbying and citizens' interest groups became vocal. Various state legislatures debated the issue. Food industry representatives offered comments. Amid the riches of this information, the conscientious public relations practitioner could evaluate, question, probe and finally piece together a meaningful report based on numerous sources.

But the sheer volume of information also makes information gathering more difficult and more daunting. With so many documents to examine, so many people to interview, so many facts to evaluate and opinions to, balance, information gathering sometimes takes on herculean proportions. But it's not just the quantity of information that can be daunting; it's the problem of assessing its quality as well.

The information age is also the age of specialization, in which few people understand the big picture and many know its minuscule parts. Those who know its parts are isolated from one another and reinforce their isolation by creating a special language (jargon) that only they and their colleagues can understand. The journalist, often not truly an expert in anything, must attempt not only to understand the information generated by these legions of specialists, but also to try to draw together the facts into a coherent whole.

Take a "routine" story about a city budget. The journalist wants to learn why the city is asking for an increase, how the money will be spent, where it will come from and how the new budget will affect the lives of city residents. In gathering information for the story, the journalist must deal with a wide variety of experts who speak various "languages." These might include:

- The city planner, a professional public manager, who speaks *managementese*
- The elected mayor, a local businessperson, who speaks *politicsese*
- Budget committee members, who speak *financese*
- The city's union representatives, who speak *laborese*
- Various law enforcement officials, who speak *crimese*
- The city's airport manager, who speaks *aviationese*
- Public works personnel, who speak *engineeringese*
- Local merchants, who speak *businessese*

To deal with all these specialists and their reports, documents and opinions, the journalist must become a scrupulous researcher and a master translator.

This information age is also the age of digitalization and computer storage of information. For the journalistic researcher, computerized information brings both benefits and problems. As more and more information—from vital government documents to daily stock exchange reports—becomes available through electronic libraries (databases), journalists may find that information gathering is quicker, more efficient and more convenient. Without leaving their desks, they can tap into distant electronic storehouses of information and extract in minutes data that might have taken them hours, days or even weeks to get otherwise. Those who work far from the country's few information capitals and too many miles from a decent library can do just as thorough a reporting job as their big city colleagues. Geography makes no difference in the era of computerized information.

But computerization of information may also make the journalist's job more difficult, for with the new technology come additional costs and a need for special skills. Media organizations wanting to use their existing office computers to gather information have to budget funds for new hardware and software. They must also pay the ongoing costs of computerized searching. Journalists wanting to take advantage of the new technology have to learn another language—computerese—and become expert in a new set of skills.

There is also the nagging fear that computerized information is easier to hide from view, easier to tamper with, and simpler to destroy than piles of papers and documents—all of which would make the journalist's job that much more difficult. If information can be obscured, altered or zapped out of existence by a keystroke or two, journalistic researchers may be less than enthusiastic about the new technology.

For better *and* worse, the information age presents a new, tougher set of challenges for journalists. To meet these challenges, they need to appreciate the scope of available information and learn how to tap into its vastness. They need to know what's out there and how to get it—quickly, efficiently and confidently.

WELCOME TO UNCOVERING THE NEWS

Because information gathering is *the* skill basic to all varieties of mass communication, you are about to read an entire book devoted to its practice. Whether your career goals include print or broadcast reporting, advertising or public relations, the strategies, skills and information you are about to learn will be vital to your work. Here's what you can expect from the next 10 chapters.

In Chapter 2, "Searching and Reporting," you will learn about the close relationship between complete, effective information gathering and solid reporting. In fact, clear writing and coherent organization—both of which are essential to good journalism—are impossible without quality information. You will see that stories based on solid information tell the audience what it needs to know quickly and clearly and move crisply from one well-developed point to another. Stories based on flimsy information, on the other hand, are often a jumble of ideas that leaves the audience confused. You will read discussions of both as you begin to consider effective strategies for information gathering.

But before you start to learn the skills of information gathering, you should understand a few basics concerning the journalistic researcher and the law. Only by knowing your rights and understanding your responsibilities will you be able to perform your job competently and confidently. Chapter 3, "The Legal Minefield" is a brief introduction to the complex and fascinating world of press law. It covers three main areas: harm, access and privilege. Under *harm,* you will learn eight ways the law says reporters can hurt the people they gather information about, including libel, invasion of privacy and trespassing. Under *access,* you will learn about the laws that make the information-gatherer's job easier—for example, those allowing public access to records and requiring open meetings—and how to use the Freedom of Information Act to secure certain kinds of government documents and records. Under *privilege,* you will learn about the special protection some states give their journalists and how far that protection goes. You will also read about journalism's codes of conduct and cooperation, which do not carry legal force but which reflect the media's desire to act ethically.

Chapter 4, "Discovering the Library," will introduce you to that mainstay of journalistic research, the library. You have undoubtedly explored some of its riches in the course of your college career. Now it's time to delve deeper and learn how this important resource can supply you with everything from quick facts to in-depth background information. In this chapter, you will learn about those easy-to-use reference sources that simplify the information-hunter's job, from the familiar encyclopedia to the unexplored directory. You will learn how to gain access to the wealth of material in the library by using the various indexes that pinpoint books, magazines, journals and newspapers. Finally, you will learn what the major sources of information are in specialty fields commonly covered by journalists, from the arts to science and technology.

In Chapter 5, "Washington on File," you will learn about a special kind of library that knowledgeable journalists depend on for an amazing array of facts and figures: the government documents depository library. These libraries (or sections within larger libraries) house a wealth of information in the form of books, journals, reports and pamphlets published by the federal government. From Congressional committee proceedings to Census Bureau studies, from summaries of government-sponsored research to Department of Agriculture bulletins, government documents are a major source of information for the inquiring journalist. The key to finding the right document from among these riches is the index. In this chapter, you will learn how government information is organized and how to use the top indexes to locate the document you need. You will see how information from the federal government can enrich even the most local of stories.

What library has no building, no books and no librarians, yet can be enormously helpful in the journalist's quest for information? The

electronic library. In Chapter 6, "Electronic Libraries," you will learn about these vast storehouses of computerized information and what it takes to tap into them. You will see how the ordinary office computers commonly found on newsroom desks can become powerful information-gathering machines capable of extracting data from massive computers thousands of miles away. How can you log on with an online vendor to access a database? This chapter will tell you. You will also learn what information is contained in a number of journalistically relevant databases and see, in three sample searches, how journalists locate and use computerized information. But all is not perfect in the electronic universe. You will be introduced to some of the drawbacks of computerized information gathering, from the need to learn a new language to the problem of a new information elite.

In Chapter 7, "Institutional Knowledge," you will learn about the most prodigious, most prolific source of information in the world—the federal government. With its scores of agencies, boards, commissions, committees and departments and its more than 700,000 information specialists, the federal government is an expert on just about everything. But the complexity of its bureaucracy can make information gathering a tedious and time-consuming chore unless you know your way around some important government directories. In this chapter, you will experience four levels of searching for information—from basic federal government guides to specialized directories—as you follow a journalist researching a story. At the end of the chapter is a descriptive list of some of the many institutional sources that can provide the journalist with quality information.

Chapter 8, "Issues and Answers," concentrates on how to find information at the state, county, city and special district levels. Here you will learn how each governmental unit is organized and what kind of information each collects, as well as about the documents and the people most likely to have the information you need. The chapter examines information sources in the following areas: public safety, justice and corrections, education, social services, public works, labor, economics and finance, and the environment. For each of these areas commonly covered by journalists, you will learn about organization, services, personnel and paperwork—what you need to know to become a thorough information-gatherer on your home turf.

In Chapter 9, "Beyond the Press Release," you will learn how to get information from and about the business sector. If you think only an economics reporter or marketing executive needs to know information about the corporate world, the examples in this chapter will show you how wrong you are. Those who report on the environment, health, technology, science, education, politics—indeed, any number

of areas—often find that the key to understanding a story is understanding the economics behind the issue. In Chapter 9, you will learn about accessible federal documents that detail a corporation's financial health. You will learn about specialized reference works, trade press sources, industry group contacts and the public relations function.

Every day, journalists try to make sense of an increasingly complicated and specialized world that they themselves don't understand. How do they do it? In Chapter 10, "Experts and How to Find Them," you will learn one way: picking the brains of experts. But who are the experts, how do you locate them, and how do you deal with them? What interviewing techniques work? When are public relations departments helpful? You will find answers to these and related questions in this chapter. You will also learn strategies to help you get the most accurate information possible. You will learn how to use various kinds of experts in your work and why some sources are "problem experts."

At the end of the information trail, the journalist comes to perhaps the most difficult task of all—evaluating the information for authenticity. Documents sometimes lie; people may "misspeak"; experts are fond of contradicting one another. How is the journalist to know which information is accurate and which is not, which source is credible and which is not? In Chapter 11, "Whom Do You Trust?," you will learn strategies for confirming and verifying information. You will learn how journalists deal with conflicting evidence and what you can do to create the most credible story possible.

The Appendix is a discussion-based examination of some ethical issues in journalism. You are encouraged to do the readings suggested there and to think seriously about the questions posed in the discussion topics.

That's *Uncovering the News*. Welcome and dig in.

Searching and Reporting

2

LOS ANGELES (AP)—Actress Barbara Bain's dog was killed when a delivery person heaved a copy of the Los Angeles Times toward her front lawn and it landed on the animal, her agent said yesterday.

Agent Marty Blumenthal said the accident happened last week.

"They offered to make restitution, but how do you put a price on a pet you've had for 14 years?" Bain told the Los Angeles Herald Examiner.

The Times' circulation department declined to comment on the incident.

The news, we are told, is bits and snatches of information. It is the signal of an event. Often rushed and incomplete, it demands follow-up and more information.

That news can only be a partially assembled body of information creates a self-fulfilling prophecy: At some point, the information-gatherer will stop the search and present what is available. Determining that point is one of the issues examined in this chapter. The main one, however, is the quality of the search, which controls both story organization and presentation. Reporting and writing are weakened when basic, logical questions go unanswered.

Examine again the story of the unfortunate dog crushed by the day's news. Although the incident is tragic to the pet's owner, it is considered a "bright" in the news business. The unusual death becomes a vehicle for irony and humor and is used to break up the heavy tone of the news.

However, it is a story with a problem. It creates more questions than it answers, including:

1. *How big was the dog?*
   (Consider the implications if it was a Great Dane.)
2. *How heavy was the paper?*
   (For example, was it a hefty Sunday edition? Was it wet?)
3. *How was the paper thrown and from what distance?*
4. *How was the dog struck? Did it die immediately?*

Such questions may seem farfetched, but it's a good bet that readers will raise similar issues. The only definite pieces of information here are that the weapon was a newspaper and that the victim was an old dog—at least 98 years old in human terms.

Without this additional information, which seems fundamental and logical, this story is incomplete—an example of poor research and questioning. Without that information, even a brilliant writing style will not keep a reader from asking, "So what happened, anyway?"

Whether reporters work on a simple story or major ones with a labyrinth of issues, they must develop and follow a *search strategy*. The same is true for other media professionals. The public relations practitioner working on a speech or a corporate report must research carefully and then present a clear, concise body of information. An advertising executive researching a presentation in order to secure a new account must know corporate history and market performance if he or she is to suggest new ways to achieve higher product sales. All of these professionals need complete, understandable information—and they all have to search for it.

DEFINING THE ISSUE

Focus belongs in the media's blue-chip vocabulary stock, along with *completeness, fairness* and *conciseness*. Focus allows the journalist to isolate images, events and issues and to begin with a clean, solid foundation of information.

In deciding what information must be acquired, the journalist must define the key issue that will create the foundation of the story.

Often, that issue is the event itself. Journalists focus on the report of a happening; they try to explore it thoroughly and then look to causes and effects. In other words, they announce an event and then add detail and analysis. The eruption of Mount St. Helens in 1980 is a case in point.

The volcano erupts; the journalists announce that event. They survey its impact; they assess the damage. Then they analyze why it happened and investigate whether another occurrence can be better predicted in order to save lives. In further analysis, journalists wonder whether people were prepared to cope with a possible eruption, inasmuch as they had some warning that the volcano could erupt. So in the process of reporting an event, journalists also are developing related story ideas—stories that go beyond the immediacy of an event and inject analysis and human elements into the coverage.

But to begin, the eruption is reported. That is the basic issue. *Everything builds on it.* The force of the blast, its height, spread and duration are examined and reported. *Then more building is done.* Once the audience understands the dimensions of the blast, it is better prepared to learn its effects. The eruption has killed people; it has leveled and splintered massive stands of timber; it has swallowed a lake; it has turned rivers into torrents of mud.

A solid foundation of information has been created. Anything written about the eruption after this is tied to the original issue and all its contexts.

Identifying the key issue makes the journalist's work easier and more precise. Regardless of what point of a story is examined, the focus of that issue should be tightened so the search does not become too thin or spread out.

Search 1: A mayor is elected

Reporting election results generally is an easy task. The main issue is "Who got the most votes?" With certified results from the elections clerk, the story apparently is off and running.

But other questions help focus on the main issue and create secondary issues worthy of further research. Let's illustrate this with a series of questions and answers.

1. *Who was elected?*
   —Theresa Andrews, 37, is the new mayor of Agate City.

2. *How many votes did she get?*
   —According to the elections clerk, Andrews received 12,540 votes.

3. *How many votes did her opponent get?*
   —Louis Fenwick, the incumbent who had served seven consecutive terms, received 12,120.

4. *Was this result a surprise?*
   —*Surprise* is a controversial term to use in election reporting, especially because the term is usually based on a "guesstimate" of voter preferences. However, it would be safe to say that this election outcome would have at least surprised poll takers, because published polls had shown Andrews trailing Fenwick by as many as 45 percentage points. What *is* known is that these polls had been cited by Andrews as the cause for a lack of campaign contributions and volunteer help.

5. *What percentage of voters turned out?*
—More than 60 percent of registered voters turned out. This may be a city and state record.

6. *What impact will this vote have?*
—The first action may be the firing of the city manager, who actively opposed Andrews. Andrews also said she would investigate Fenwick's recent appointments to the city planning commission.

7. *Have the candidates commented?*
—Andrews has not. Fenwick says he wants a recount and claims he was the victim of campaign "dirty tricks."

These basic questions help journalists sort out issues and focus on the most immediate ones. This, for example, is the *basic* event:

> Theresa Andrews has narrowly defeated seven-term incumbent Louis Fenwick for mayor of Agate City.

Other levels of information include: (1) the actual votes and margin; (2) the victory's apparent contradiction of pre-election polls; (3) the record turnout; (4) the recount and allegations of dirty tricks; and (5) the long-term consequences of this election.

This logical focus allows journalists to search for information related to the *fact* of the victory, the *conditions* of that victory and its *impact*. Journalists must discover as much about the background of an issue before exploring further. Solid information also helps the reporter write a compelling lead paragraph, one that sets the tone for the story:

> Ignoring polls predicting incumbent Louis Fenwick's easy victory, Agate City voters yesterday turned out in record numbers and narrowly chose Theresa Andrews as their mayor.

The definition of the issue, as seen in the lead, suggests both the additional information needed and the possible organization of the story. First explain to readers how narrow the victory was: Andrews won with 50.8 percent of the vote; only 420 votes separated Fenwick and her. That fact helps explain why the incumbent is seeking a recount.

Second, talk to pollsters about the incredible disparity between their surveys and the voters' actual preference. Also, try to find out why this race stimulated a record voter turnout. For example, a quick check of precinct turnouts and votes will reveal if Andrews' predicted areas of strength did support her. None of this postelection analysis is going to make it any easier to predict outcomes, but it might help answer the question "How did she beat the incumbent?"

Creating primary focus provides another story level, to be used for follow-up and analysis. This level deals with the impact and its effects.

Like the Mount St. Helens story, these factors may not be obvious. They develop and become part of the event's aftermath.

However, the journalist must do first things first. Collecting too wide a body of information not only will confuse the story's organization but also will create time pressures on the writer, who may be hard-pressed to present a story in concise fashion.

Search 2: Pulling together distant but related events

A reporter receives a call from a funeral home about the death of a 19-year-old man. A recent graduate of a nearby rural high school, this young man has died of a heroin overdose. He was a star athlete in three sports and had been class president. After receiving this information (from both the funeral home and sheriff's deputies who found the body), the reporter remembered that some 10 months before, the principal of the high school had passionately urged the school board to institute a program of mandatory drug testing of its athletes.

Focusing on the death of this young man in the *context* of his school's unsuccessful attempt to do something about drug abuse adds *perspective* to routine event reporting. Two elements—the death and the plea for a drug abuse program—are linked. This relationship must be explored. Again, ask some questions to see where this issue is going:

1. *Was the cause of death officially determined?*
   —Yes. The medical examiner's report (a public record) indicated that the young man died of respiratory arrest linked to a massive injection of heroin. The deceased showed evidence of recent injections in the arms and thighs.

2. *Did he have a history of drug abuse?*
   —Yes. School officials reported that the young man was suspended for two weeks in his senior year for arriving at class in a disoriented, drug-induced state. In addition, police revealed that several months ago they were called by the youth's parents when he reportedly threatened them while under the influence of drugs. No arrests were made at the time, but a charge of driving while under the influence of intoxicating material had been pending in a local circuit court.

3. *How is his death related to the school's attempt to establish drug testing of its athletes?*
   —School board minutes (a public record, made available by the board clerk) reveal that the request was made because of an "alarming trend of drug abuse in the nation's schools among its athletes."

No mention of the school's problem was made. The board vetoed the request because of "difficulties in ensuring compliance." However, interviews with the principal, board chair and district superintendent should provide more background on this issue.

On the basis of these questions, it seems clear that the story of this tragic drug overdose should not be reported in a vacuum. It must be linked to the school's perception of a problem and its apparent inability to do something about it. In this case, the death is reported as a standard obituary, but it is quickly followed by a longer, analytical, issue-centered story on an example of adolescent drug abuse. Of course, the reporter must discover if the young man's death was an isolated incident or whether the principal feared that others on the school's athletic squads were involved with drugs—and why. Even national sources, such as the psychological division of Atlanta's Centers for Disease Control, can give this story a broader perspective.

In this search, the news has indeed signaled an event, but it also has provided a clue about a larger issue.

Search 3: Investigating advertising claims

A media buyer for a large advertising agency is intrigued by the claims of a large daily newspaper that its circulation has jumped by more than 10 percent in a single year and that it represents a good ad buy. The claim implies that great strides in reporting, graphics and design have attracted more readers. The job of the buyer, in representing a client who wants the best media exposure for the money, is to verify all these claims and get the best ad rate per thousand readers—called a "cost per thousand."

Several key questions will help the buyer focus on the main issue in this claim:

1. *Is this circulation figure true?*
   —Yes. According to figures from the Audit Bureau of Circulation, this paper's circulation has indeed risen by 10 percent.

2. *What is the reason for this climb?*
   —First, population figures for this area (found by researching statistics from the Census Bureau, the Labor Department and a nearby university center for population research) indicate that the area's population has remained stable. That would imply a bigger circulation promotion to increase what is called "household penetration." By contacting the state newspaper publishers association to

confirm the paper's claim, and by using a standard research tool of newspaper ownership and circulation—the *Editor and Publisher International Yearbook*—the media buyer discovers that a little more than a year ago, the newspaper corporation's afternoon paper (a money loser) folded. Subscribers to that paper were offered the morning paper instead. Doing some quick calculations, the buyer discovers that if all those subscribers had moved to the morning paper, that paper's circulation would have increased almost 20 percent. It now must be discovered how many of the "new" subscriptions were actually exchanges or tradeouts.

3. *So, is the paper's advertising rate a good buy for the agency?*
—According to the newspaper's rate card, the charge for a column inch of display advertising is $12. The buyer discovers this is a 20 percent increase over the previous year. Looking deeper, the buyer realizes that when both papers were offered in a *combination rate*, the column-inch charge was only $11—reflecting a combined circulation greater than that now claimed. While this may not look good, the buyer still must research ad rates at other publications and establish their cost per thousand readers. These figures may still put this publication in a competitive position. However, the media buyer now may have more leverage and may be able to challenge other claims, thereby enabling the client to get a more favorable rate.

In all these examples, questions have established basic issues. The questions have also pointed to necessary research. The information from this research suggests both its organization and its order of importance. However, these questions also create information that leads to more questions. That is why defining the issue is so important. If you begin with the most critical point of a story, your research will lead you to important and related issues.

Following those issues and finding their focal points are critical to polishing your story organization.

TRACKING THE ISSUE

After you identify the basic issue with preliminary questions, you must break down your research into several parts as you develop the story. A natural flow exists in this research pattern, once the main issue is identified:

1. Divide the issue into logical components.
2. Focus on the most significant point of each component.
3. Brainstorm sources that will provide information and that will corroborate information already obtained.
4. Evaluate information (for trustworthiness and reputation of source) and recheck information that is incomplete or suspicious.
5. Repeat steps 3 and 4 for all subissues.
6. Organize the information for presentation in order of issue significance and impact. Show the sources and provide attribution.

This process of information gathering could be criticized as too ideal. Media executives would say that it's not possible for journalists to do all this under the pressure of daily deadlines, space and time problems, and the economics of running a newsroom. This in-depth work is best suited to magazine reporters and others with more time and resources, they would add. Yes, it's hard to dispute these realities, but showing the ideal process also helps create a professional attitude that permeates and sharpens information gathering, presentation and editing.

Because of time pressures in acquiring and presenting the news, not all information can be given in a complete unit. Publication or dissemination of a story often raises other issues and opens other avenues of information. Always be on the alert for a follow-up.

ANATOMY OF A COMPLICATED SEARCH

When the Minneapolis *Star and Tribune* investigated abuses of a minority public works contract program in 1984, its decision to invest four months' time and resources was based on preliminary work establishing some basic issues in the search. After evaluating that work, the main issue emerged:

> Of the $179 million awarded to firms owned by women and minorities in Minnesota for public works projects in the past four years, how much of it went to "front" organizations actually controlled by male or white organizations that successfully subverted state requirements?

This broad issue naturally led to important subissues:

1. How could these front firms successfully compete for bids?
2. Did the state realize what was happening?

3. Did these fronts actually violate the law?

4. What action has been taken against such schemes?

5. What can be done to prevent future abuses?

The implication in these questions is that some abuse existed in the program. However, some evidence of that abuse was discovered in the newspaper's preliminary investigation. Those early findings allowed the paper to go ahead with the reporting and to develop important subissues.

To examine Question 1, the Minnesota journalists examined all contracts handed out to "minority" companies, reviewing government documents that revealed the true ownership of the firms, the amount of money paid to their subcontractors and the amount of control and experience of the minority business executives. They interviewed company and government officials.

The *Star and Tribune* discovered that some white-controlled firms installed a minority person as president with little responsibility or financial control. In one case, a man (white) listed his wife (who was one-fifth Chippewa) as head of a firm even though he retained control. Other companies entered into agreements to have new, minority-based firms with little construction skill bid for minority contracts and then supply the white-owned firms with lucrative subcontracts for labor and supplies. For example, in a $1.79 million contract given to a minority firm, all but $22,000 went to white-owned subcontracting firms.

To examine the next three questions, the paper looked at court cases and at contract rejections by the state's Women and Minority Business Enterprise to see how the state handled the problem of fronts. After discovering very little state surveillance or reaction, the paper was able to suggest corrective actions (Question 5).

This series reflected many of the search sources and strategies suggested in this book:

- Library materials and reference works
- Documents on file at depository libraries and in government agencies
- Outside experts contacted for evaluation of how the state was monitoring its program
- Special surveys
- Use of the Freedom of Information Act to obtain records from the Small Business Administration
- Personal interviews with officials and experts
- Visits to construction sites and contractors' offices

When the search appeared complete, the writing began. The series revealed that more than 25 percent of money intended for minority companies had actually been funneled to male or white firms through a system of fronts. Citing several well-developed case studies, the paper detailed how the fronting was done and how the law was violated. That was followed by an examination of how inept, understaffed agencies were unable to cope with such fraud. It showed, however, how Seattle successfully monitored its minority contracting program. It ended the series by having agencies explain how they would strengthen their programs. And the paper made it clear that it would return to this story soon.

Not many stories require the time or can permit the resources needed for such an intensive investigation. However, the process of defining and researching an issue remains the same, regardless of story importance or length. When that process isn't followed, or the right questions aren't asked, the story falls short.

Perhaps one way to help find the "right" issue is to examine stories that aren't quite successful. Look at stories in newspapers and magazines that leave you puzzled. Examine your reactions to broadcast stories that seem thin and disjointed. Ask yourself where you would go to find that missing information. *Be an editor.* It will make you a stronger reporter.

RECOGNIZING STORY DEFECTS

Reporters know all too well they are in trouble when pieces of their stories don't fit or are obviously missing. When that happens, writing becomes a nightmare. Writing around an issue because of incomplete information makes the omission more glaring. The story may look as if the reporter is trying to hide something, was too ignorant to ask about it, or is omitting it for ulterior motives.

Just who is this guy, anyway?

A common story defect emerges when a story lacks context or an "anchor" for credibility. Consider a story, written by a reporter for a university daily newspaper, about an ex-CIA agent who gave a speech denouncing that agency's secret actions in, as he said it, "destabilizing Third World countries." Never mind that the reporter failed to explain what "destabilizing" was and how it worked. Instead, wonder why the reporter never followed up on the *ex* in *ex-CIA.* According to the story, this speaker left the agency more than eight years ago! What has he been doing since then? What is he doing now? Under whose auspices was he brought to campus to give this talk? Is he now a freelance writer? A member of a think tank? We'll never know. Weak information and invisible context equals thin story. When the reporter failed to explain who this person is *now*, all the audience received was a speech from someone who was an employee of an agency almost a decade ago and who is now criticizing its supposedly secret operations of today. Two simple questions would have helped this story and its context:

- Who are you now?
- What have you been doing lately?

Well, your word is good enough for me

Consider this newspaper paragraph (slightly rewritten to deflect embarrassing attention from the publication):

> "We've gone from the worst to one of the top two or three schools in this area," says Bob Smith, executive director of the ——— Alumni Association. "And now we have the energy, leadership and enthusiasm to be number one in the East. All we need now are the resources."

Now consider this photo cutline, adjacent to the story:

> Bob Smith has made the ——— Alumni Association one of the top programs in the East.

Oh, really? Who said so? Mr. Smith? Fine. But that's his opinion. If he has anything to back that up—a survey, an accreditation report—then let the readers see it! The reporter should have asked the question and not just have accepted the source's word. In doing just that, even the photo caption lends credibility to a statement made by one self-serving source with absolutely no corroboration. It's a minor story but a major error. Consider also the implications of accepting one unverified source as the basis for an important story critical to the public welfare.

We know there's more to tell but
consider this the authoritative word for now

The Associated Press reported the 1985 arrest of Oregon commune leader Bhagwan Shree Rajneesh for allegedly trying to flee the country in the face of pending criminal indictments (which were not served until several days later). However, the wire service left out an important element: How did immigration officials know that the Bhagwan was trying to leave the country?

The first story came out early one morning (as news does, in bits and pieces), as the leader and an unknown number of his followers were arrested at the Charlotte, N.C., airport. The story did not say whether he was trying to board a private jet without a flight plan, whether his plane was forced down as he was heading to Bermuda or whether officials were tipped off to the secret exodus. Most grievously, the story did not even bother to report something like "officials did not reveal how they knew the Bhagwan was attempting to leave the country." Instead, by relying on a single source, who was not pressed for further information, the wire service reported:

> Bhagwan Shree Rajneesh was arrested early today in Charlotte, N.C., while trying to flee the country, a federal official said.

This is a perfect example of reacting to a major event with wholesale acceptance of the "official" *what* without questioning the *how* or *why*— or at least letting the reader know *why* the how and why can't be determined yet. As more disjointed reports trickled in (another feature of the news), it became apparent that a federal prosecutor in Oregon secretly requested the arrest because he feared the Bhagwan might leave (flee?) the country to avoid answering several secret grand jury indictments that the Bhagwan may or may not have known about.

When readers are forced to make too many inferences or to "fill in the blanks," they are dealing with information gathering that tells them: "This is all you're going to get, and we're not even going to suggest what questions remain unanswered. You figure it out."

Many of these holes disappear with a more thorough approach:

> Acting on information from a federal prosecutor in Oregon, U.S. customs agents this morning arrested commune leader Bhagwan Shree Rajneesh in Charlotte, N.C., for allegedly trying to leave the country.
> Although immigration officials did not reveal why they suspected the Bhagwan was trying to reach another country, they said the 53-year-old guru and several of his followers were taken into custody when their two chartered jets landed at Charlotte-Douglass International Airport.

Using proper attribution, describing sources, telling readers when information is incomplete or how attempts to find out more have failed will give a story more credibility. Reliance on a single source and acceptance of limited information when search time is up can lead to thin and official-sounding stories. Such influence even affects the headline writer, who viewed the first version of the Bhagwan story and wrote "Bhagwan arrested trying to flee country."

If professional writers jumped to these conclusions on the basis of limited information, what would the average person do?

DEVELOPING STORY IDEAS

Although one function of the news is to signal an event, it is *not* its most important one. Reporting an event under deadline pressure is a matter of speed, reaction and concentration. That may well be enough for the moment. But equally significant reporting examines themes, stringing events together and explaining them in a larger context. Developing this reporting skill is difficult; journalists must train themselves to see larger pictures. They need a broader base of information.

Developing story ideas makes the journalist think more deeply about the day's events and their relationship to important contexts. Such analysis comes from questioning journalists who look at the world and ask *Why?* and *What does this mean?* They look at stories and say *What is missing here?* and *Is more explanation needed?* Clearly, good journalists are curious; they need to explain things.

Curiosity can't be beat for tracking down a story that may have widespread interest. Say you have a headache. Or perhaps your muscles ache from your too-frequent (and too-intense) visits to the local fitness center. You need a pain reliever.

However, you want it to be aspirin free. At the drug store you see a widely advertised brand; its chief component is acetaminophen, pressed into 500-mg tablets. Next to that product is a non-advertised, generic version. The instructions and dosages are the same. However, the price is not—the generic version costs 60 percent less for the same number of tablets! You don't need to wear your reporter's hat to ask these consumer questions:

- Is the nationally advertised brand a better pain reliever? What do doctors and pharmacists say? Does this company make exclusive claims?

- Why is the advertised brand more expensive? How much of that price difference goes into product promotion?

- What company makes the generic product? What are its standards? Does it make any special claims?

■ Are generic drugs widely used? Why? Why are some drugs not available in generic form?

As you develop these questions and find sources who can answer them, you are developing a story idea that has a relationship to no event other than your upset at these massive price differences. Your curiosity has spawned an idea—and it may turn out to be news that people can really use.

As another example of natural questioning, consider 1985, a year called the most tragic in the history of airline travel. More than 2,000 people died in air accidents around the world. This naturally leads a reporter (and many air travelers) to ask *Why*? Were safety standards becoming lax? Was terrorism partly to blame? Was there a special problem with aircraft maintenance? Was weather a factor? These questions merit investigation.

However, reporters should be watchful for new and related information. Early in 1986, for example, the Federal Aviation Administration announced that it "appeared" that 1985 would be considered one of the safest years on record. That agency's measure is the number of fatalities per 100,000 departures for all scheduled airlines. The FAA said that rate was .080 in 1983 and .019 in 1984. It claimed that the rate for 1985 would be "very low." If that rate was low, then passenger boardings must have increased over previous years. That statistic may be of comfort to the gambler, but it should not dissuade the journalist from investigating the various *whys* of these crashes, the preventive maintenance and training activities of airlines, and the reliability of such statistics.

Some scholars and media critics are concerned about journalists' attempts at interpretive reporting. Getting away from event-centered news, some say, leads to the biased creation of news spawned by the reporters themselves. Mark Fishman takes this view:

> As journalists notice each other reporting the same news theme, it becomes established within a community of media organizations. Journalists who are not yet reporting a theme learn to use it by watching their competition. And when journalists who first report a theme see others beginning to use it, they feel their original news judgment is confirmed. Within the space of a week a crime theme can become so "hot," so entrenched in a community of news organizations, that even journalists skeptical of the crime wave cannot ignore reporting each new incident that comes along. Crime waves have a life of their own.*

*Mark Fishman, *Manufacturing the News* (Austin: University of Texas Press, 1980), p. 8.

Jumping on the bandwagon and creating thin issues, however, are not what this section is about. Creating a crime wave where none exists is nothing more than sensationalism. It is not helpful information. When you do have information that can be corroborated, that is useful, you are delivering an important commodity to your audience.

In developing story ideas, you are not expected to manufacture anything—you are supposed to let your curiosity lead you to real themes and connections. Be natural. Don't force anything.

A STORY IS JUST A PAUSE BETWEEN SEARCHES

The student journalist and the entry-level professional may be several years away from the research on major stories discussed in this and other chapters. Some may wonder why so many documents and sources are discussed. Our answer is that it shows you what is possible. It shows you where to go and how to get information. It reveals a process.

Whether you are reporting a city council meeting, a fire, or a school budget, or whether you are investigating financial kickbacks for city-controlled garbage franchises, you must satisfy yourself and your audience that the story is complete.

Don't cease your search until you have enough corroborated information on which to build a story. Yes, time pressures can force some journalists to produce stories based on what is available. However, that should not prevent them from returning to the story for a closer look.

When journalists challenge themselves to get enough information, perhaps audiences won't have to settle for incomplete "dead dog" stories. This enhanced version of the chapter's lead story does just that—inform:

> LOS ANGELES—Actress Barbara Bain's cocker spaniel was killed when a delivery person heaved a Sunday Los Angeles Times toward Bain's front lawn, striking the animal on its head.
>
> According to Bain's agent, Marty Blumenthal, the 11-lb. dog died instantly. A Times representative said the 3-lb. newspaper was tightly wrapped in plastic and thrown from a moving truck.

Such aggressive information gathering must exist at all story levels. If news is indeed the signal of an event, let's strengthen that signal and try to tell the whole story.

The Legal Minefield | **3**

Is the nation's press free? *Yes*. Is it protected from prior restraint of publication and from licensing? *Yes*. But can the press be prevented from obtaining information about a public organization? *Yes*. Can its representatives be jailed for protecting a confidential source of information? *Yes*.

Such apparent contradictions are not irreconcilable. The First Amendment* to the U.S. Constitution may appear to allow robust and unfettered expression, but this freedom is far from absolute. Compared with the press in countries like Chile, Libya or Poland, the U.S. media operate in a dreamworld where the state neither represses, tortures nor eliminates those with dissident viewpoints.

But such freedom has its boundaries. In a nation of complex regulations and conflicting rights, the press is in the midst of a seemingly endless debate concerning *privilege* versus *responsibility*. The persistence of such a conflict made sense to the Hutchins Commission, which noted in its 1947 statement on the social responsibility of the press that a free press cannot exist without meeting the responsibilities it owes to society.

It is vital that you understand both the rights and responsibilities of the press—what we call the "legal minefield" you must crisscross

---

*"Congress shall make no law respecting an establishment of religion, or prohibiting the free exercise thereof; or abridging the freedom of speech, or of the press; or the right of the people peaceably to assemble, and to petition the government for a redress of grievances."

as you search for and then report information. However, this chapter is not intended to be a complete overview of the legal principles affecting the press. This is best accomplished by a journalism course on the law of mass communications and careful attention to media law texts and journals, some of which are discussed at the end of this chapter. Instead, this chapter highlights important legal issues that journalists face as they pursue information. The discussion covers three areas: *harm*, *access* and *privilege*. It is followed by an examination of voluntary codes of cooperation, especially the Bar-Press Guidelines.

HARM

John Wade, dean emeritus of Vanderbilt Law School, has defined at least eight types of harm that reporters can inflict: defamation, invasion of privacy, trespassing, conversion, harassment, fraud, bribery and breaking confidences for profit.*

Defamation

Defamation is injury to one's good name; the offense is commonly called *libel*. Reporters know that provable truth in the absence of malice is the best defense against a charge of libel. A 1964 decision in the case of *New York Times* v. *Sullivan* expanded this defense by stating that only malicious writing "in reckless disregard of the truth" could be a legal cause of action if the complainant was a public figure. Today, the media and courts are engaged in heavy debate over who is a public figure, what constitutes malice and how to determine a reporter's "state of mind" in order to prove such malice.

Lest you think that libel is confined to "traditional reportage," consider these cases and their verdicts:

■   The Alton, Ill., *Telegraph* faced a $9.2 million judgment and bankruptcy proceedings when a contractor won his libel case. He claimed that two *Telegraph* reporters had defamed him in an unpublished memorandum to federal authorities linking him to a savings and

*"The Tort Liability of Investigative Reporters," *Vanderbilt Law Review* 37 (March 1984): 301–47.

loan association with reputed organized crime connections. Although the plaintiff settled for $1.4 million when the paper began to consider bankruptcy, the effect on the *Telegraph*'s reporting procedures was severe.

■ A U.S. Senate candidate won a $1 million verdict against *The Daily Oklahoman* for cartoons and editorials that he said defamed him during the campaign.

Legal journals and trade publications are full of stories about libel cases. And consider these statistics from the Libel Defense Resource Center: As many as 70 percent of libel cases in the United States were won by the plaintiffs (complainants) at the trial level, while more than 60 percent of those cases on appeal were awarded to the defendant. These figures show that libel cases are costly and time-consuming— even when the media win their cases.

Public perceptions of the media also play a role in such cases. According to the *Columbia Journalism Review*,

> What *has* changed dramatically is the willingness of juries to rule against the news media and to give away the farm in the process. According to the LDRC, before 1980 only one libel award had ever topped $1 million; since then, two dozen such "megawards" have been handed down, averaging more than $2 million each. In one remarkable case, a Texas appeals court overturned a $2 million award against the *Dallas Morning News*, asserting that the jury had found no evidence of defamation but had simply acted out of "passion and prejudice against newspapers."*

While nothing (short of a countersuit for harassment) prevents a person from suing for libel, proper information-gathering techniques will go a long way in not only discouraging such suits but winning them as well. It is important that you research carefully and secure corroborating information that will stand up in court. Delivering a story prematurely or choosing a narrow angle while ignoring evidence that disputes or changes your story is unprofessional—a trait not admired by libel juries.

Examine closely the libel cases reported in such publications as *The News Media and the Law*, and while you may see some of the "chilling effect" on free expression that the media fear, you will also see some incredible mistakes that have knocked down a journalistic house of cards.

*Michael Massing, "The Libel Chill: How Cold Is It Out There?," *Columbia Journalism Review* (May/June 1985): 31–43.

Invasion of privacy

Does the information you gather and publish establish truthful but embarrassing or hurtful facts about someone—facts not seen to be in the public interest? If so, you may face an invasion of privacy lawsuit. These cases have not been as plentiful as defamation actions, but some have been successful. Even where they have not—as in cases won on appeal by newspapers that published a story about a college student-body president who had a sex-change operation and a front-page close-up photo of an unclothed woman fleeing a motel room where her ex-husband had been holding her hostage—the media face severe public criticism when they seem to violate professional ethics.

The weight of public interest seems to be the main test in such cases. While reporting that vice-presidential candidate Thomas Eagleton received electroshock therapy for depression might be in the public interest, reporting on the private records of a prominent business figure might well be an invasion of privacy, as well as a violation of the Fair Credit Reporting Act.

Trespassing

Entering someone's property without permission of the owner or occupant can not only invite a lawsuit but an arrest as well. This is a serious issue; unfortunately, the movie image of reporters breaking into offices and rifling files is an established part of Hollywood fantasy. (Chevy Chase's 1985 movie "Fletch" depicted a reporter breaking and entering several times.)

Although a Florida court upheld a reporter's right to enter a fire-damaged home when invited by a fire department official, a Wisconsin court found a police officer liable for trespass for authorizing a reporter to enter a private building during a criminal investigation. In general, court decisions indicate that trespassing in pursuit of a story is asking for serious trouble.

Conversion

Interfering with or taking someone's property (for example, documents or records) can be illegal. The courts consider the significance and public interest of the information as well as the reporter's conduct. That partially explains why the Pentagon Papers case did not result in the conviction of reporters for receiving and using secret government documents on the conduct of the war in Vietnam. However, reporters are not often involved in cases of this stature. Be careful.

Other types of harm

The other harms that Dean Wade discusses are harassment, fraud, bribery and breaking confidences to profit the reporter. Fortunately, lawsuits involving these areas are uncommon, although they do embarrass the press and its mission. Still, it is important to recognize these potential pitfalls and to ensure that your conduct as a reporter is professional, honest and in the public interest.

ACCESS

Discovering records, getting access to them and gaining entry to meetings that are supposed to be public are important and often difficult tasks for the journalist. To give you an overview of the problem of access and some of the solutions to it, we discuss here the federal Freedom of Information Act, state public records laws and state open meetings laws.

Using the Freedom of Information Act

Since 1967, the federal government has been under legislative mandate to make available to anyone records, documents, forms and proceedings that are in the public interest. However, this act specifies certain exemptions—nine, to be exact. And, as some journalists and researchers have discovered, release of a document doesn't mean that it has survived the bureaucratic felt marker. Imagine trying to make sense of a released CIA memorandum like this:

FROM: ▀▀▀▀▀▀▀▀▀▀▀▀

TO: Director, ▀▀▀▀▀▀▀▀▀▀▀▀▀▀

SUBJECT: Allocation of ▀▀▀▀▀ and ▀▀▀▀▀▀▀▀▀
         (1) Your attention is directed to my directive of
▀▀▀▀▀ , in which I stated that ▀▀▀▀▀▀▀▀▀▀
▀▀▀▀▀▀▀▀▀▀▀▀▀▀
         (2) In accordance with policy stated in XO ▀▀▀▀
I must now direct you to ▀▀▀▀▀▀▀▀▀▀
▀▀▀▀▀▀▀▀

Although disclosure is presumed in this act, and although Congress demands an annual report of government compliance with it, the Freedom of Information Act (FoI) today is a battleground between journalists and bureaucrats where interminable delays and unreasonable search fees seem to be the main weapons.

The lesson learned by FoI-scarred journalists is to be persistent and to learn the bureaucratic maze well enough to know *what* to ask for and *where* to send the request. (Chapter 5 will help you identify potential federal sources of information.) In this section, we will explain the act and suggest ways to use it.

How the act works

Amendments in 1974 strengthened the Freedom of Information Act, legally establishing a bias in favor of disclosure of public information. But the act also presumes that the person requesting this information will (1) be as specific as possible in citing the information needed, (2) will direct the request to the appropriate agency and official and (3) will pay reasonable search and copy costs. Under the law, an agency has as many as 40 days to determine whether to comply with a request for information or to deny it on the basis of one of the nine exemptions.

In denying a request, an agency can assert that the document falls into one of the following categories: (1) classified documents affecting national security, (2) internal personnel rules and procedures of an agency, (3) records exempted by other statutes, such as Social Security records, (4) confidential trade secrets and financial information, (5) inter- or intra-agency records and memoranda generally only available to parties in litigation with that agency, (6) personnel and medical files, (7) investigatory records compiled for law enforcement purposes, (8) information for the use of an agency for the supervision and regulation of financial institutions, and (9) geological and geophysical information concerning wells, including oil deposits and water resources.

These exemptions are broader than those prescribed by many state public records laws. NBC News reporter Carl Stern, himself an attorney, has observed what he calls a 10th exemption. He calls it an " 'I don't want to give it to you so I won't give it to you' exemption."*

*For a fascinating look at how bureaucrats have learned to foil the FoI Act, see "Trashing the FoIA," *Columbia Journalism Review* (January-February 1985): 21–28.

Trouble areas

Two of the nine exemptions stand out as subject to abuse. Withholding records because of ongoing law enforcement investigations is one, while use of the "national security" catchall is the other. Under Executive Order 12356, which took effect in 1982, documents can stay classified "as long as required by national security classifications." In addition, previously unclassified information can be classified later. The implications of this change, which did not require congressional approval, are immense. It is conceivable that a federal agency could now request that an unclassified document be classified in order to withhold it from distribution. At present, the only way to challenge such a procedure is in the courts, which determine whether a document has been improperly classified. And time is on the bureaucrat's side.

You may be asking, "So what good is this act?" Persistence and pressure have worked wonders. There have been great success stories of journalists who have fought the system and won. For example, the CIA and FBI may be notorious for federal foot-dragging in this process, but journalists have found the Environmental Protection Agency and the Nuclear Regulatory Commission much more open and helpful. Our advice: Believe in the law. Read it all—5 United States Code §552— and presume that any non-judicial, non-legislative federal agency is fair game for your search. Know what you are looking for. And be patient.

How to use the act

Let's assume that you are investigating unprotected, perhaps even uncharted toxic waste sites in your state, and you are not getting cooperation from local and state authorities in your work. You believe, however, that these agencies have been in contact with the federal Environmental Protection Agency. Thinking that the FoIA would allow you to see copies of reports of the waste sites and of water/soil contamination in your area, you want to request these records for your review. What should you do? Here is a possible procedure.

1. Look in the *Congressional Quarterly*'s *Federal Regulatory Directory, CQ*'s *Washington Information Directory* or the *Federal Staff Directory* to get the names and phone numbers of the EPA's regional and national department heads, public information officers and freedom of information officers. The act mandates government agencies to name FoI officers to handle information requests.

2. Make some calls and write some letters to discover what type of information (types of reports, filings and so on) local and state

governments are supposed to submit about toxic waste sites and
suspected contamination. With that general and unthreatening information in hand, you can focus on what to request. Sometimes
you may run into surprising cooperation. You may also get some
interesting information orally and maybe even some reports without a formal request. Also, the documents librarian of your library
can help you sort through the *Federal Register*, which contains a
list of record types and records systems of federal agencies.

3. Draft your request to the agency's FoI service officer, using the
   sample letter in Figure 3.1. Be as specific as possible, and attach
   any information that will aid the search. As you can see from the
   sample letter, you may wish to say you will pay "reasonable"
   search and copy fees. It is best to send your request by certified
   mail so that you can prove receipt.

4. Although the law states that you are due an initial response within
   10 business days, many agencies will claim they are severely back-
   logged and unable to reply on time. If you do not get a satisfactory
   response within that time, either phone the agency to get a deadline
   from them or send them another letter. Tell the agency that because
   you have not received a reply, you will soon consider this a denial
   and will proceed to an appeal.

5. If you send an appeal letter because of non-response or actual denial of your request, fashion it after the sample letter in Figure 3.2.

6. If you still have received no satisfaction within 20 business days,
   you should consider having your organization file suit in U.S. District Court. (The law states that "the court may assess against the
   United States reasonable attorney fees and other litigation costs
   reasonably incurred in any case under this section in which the
   complainant has substantially prevailed.") At this point, we suggest
   you contact the FoI Service Center, a project of the Society of
   Professional Journalists/SDX and The Reporters Committee for
   Freedom of the Press. Its address is 1125 15th St., NW, Washington,
   DC 20005. You can call the Service Center at (202) 466–6312, or
   use the toll-free FoI Hotline, a 24-hour service for both FoI and
   libel questions, at 800–F–FoI–AID. Additional information can be
   obtained from the Investigative Reporters and Editors (IRE) group
   in Columbia, Missouri, at (314) 882–2042. With information from
   these sources on how (or whether) to pursue a lawsuit, you can
   make better decisions.

You may find the FoI Act a frustrating and burdensome law. But
consider what reporters would have without it: *almost nothing*. With
aggressiveness and proper digging, a reporter can make the FoI Act

Figure 3.1. *Sample FoI request letter*

Name of FoI Officer or Agency Official
Agency
Address
City, State, Zip Code

Dear ———:

This request is made under the federal Freedom of Information Act, 5 U.S.C. 552.

I am requesting copies of [here, clearly describe what you want. Be as specific as possible, listing names, places and periods of time if possible].

As you know, the FoI Act provides that if portions of a document are exempt from release, the remainder must be segregated and disclosed. Therefore, I will expect you to send me all non-exempt portions that I have requested and ask that you justify any deletions by reference to specific exemptions. I reserve the right to appeal your decision to withhold any materials.

If there are any search or duplication fees related to this request, please inform me before filling this request. As you know, the act permits you to reduce or waive the fees when the release of information is considered as "primarily benefiting the public." I believe that this request fits that category, and I therefore ask you to waive any fees.

As I am making this request in the capacity of a journalist [author, scholar, etc.] and this information is of timely value, I would appreciate your communicating with me by telephone, rather than by mail, if you have any questions regarding this request.

Thank you for your assistance. I look forward to your reply within 10 business days, as required by law.

Sincerely,

Name/Address /Phone

Figure 3.2. *Sample FoI appeal letter*

Name of FoI Officer or Agency Official
Agency
Address
City, State, Zip Code

Dear ——:

This is to inform you that I am appealing the denial of my request for information under the terms of the Freedom of Information Act, 5 U.S.C. 552.

On [date], I received a letter from [name] of your agency, denying my request for access to [describe the information sought]. I enclose a copy of this denial along with a copy of my original request.

[Set forth the reason for your appeal, citing as much evidence as possible. If the agency has given you some appeals guidelines, follow that format as much as possible.]

Please review this request and give me a reply within 20 business days, as required by law. I urge you to disclose the information I am seeking.

I am aware of my rights to file court action to secure these documents, and I am cognizant of the FoIA's provision for payment of plaintiff's attorney/court fees. I hope we can settle this matter short of such legal action.

Sincerely,

Name/Address/Phone

---

work. And increased lobbying in Congress by SPJ/SDX, IRE and The Reporters Committee could lead to amendments that would give FoI searchers more clout.

FoI-related access problems also exist in the federal depository library system. These problems include the sudden and unannounced reclassification of documents and the imposition of charges to secure previously free government information. These issues are discussed in Chapter 5.

FoI readings and sources

How to Use the FoI Act, published by the Reporters Committee for Freedom of the Press, Room 300, 800 18th Street, Washington, DC 20006.

Annual Report of the National Freedom of Information Committee of SPJ/SDX, 840 N. Lake Shore Drive, Suite 801W, Chicago, IL 60601. This report also deals with such topics as libel suits, shield laws and access to public reports and meetings.

FoI Digest, published by the Freedom of Information Center, School of Journalism, University of Missouri, Columbia, MO 65201. It contains excellent discussion of information-gathering issues at all levels.

The U.S. Department of Justice publishes *FoI Update* (a quarterly newsletter for government employees that contains interpretations of FoI law) and *FoI Case List* (an annual list of court cases involving the FoI Act).

Prologue is a quarterly publication of the National Archives. It contains valuable lists of recently declassified documents.

Stalking state and local government records

The federal Freedom of Information Act does not apply to state and local government policies on opening records and documents to public scrutiny. In fact, 11 years before passage of the federal law, more than 20 states had enacted some type of public records law. Today, all states and the District of Columbia have FoI statutes guaranteeing some right of public access to records.

That may look like a rosy picture. However, the reality is thorny with frustration, obstacles and court battles—with newsgathering organizations and citizens pitted against state and local officials looking for new, more narrow ways to interpret public records laws. Bureaucrats, it seems, produce tons of paperwork and records but are none too enthusiastic about sharing their "production."

Recent court decisions reveal how citizens and media organizations in various states have had to fight for the right to inspect records thought to be open. They have won the right, after lengthy court action, to review such items as

- A city's "police blotter" records and case reports (Wyoming)
- A township's cancelled checks, held by a bank (Pennsylvania)
- A city's fire inspection records (Kansas)
- Cost reports of nursing homes that receive federal Medicaid payments (Iowa)
- Applications for midwife licenses (Florida)
- Complaint and disciplinary files of a medical licensing board (Kentucky)
- Speeding tickets issued and lists of traffic violations (New York)

These cases show how the laws have received various interpretations, especially in terms of the (1) government bodies affected by public records legislation, (2) types of records covered and (3) types of records exempted.

Government bodies affected

A "public body, public funding" test is most often applied to determine whether an agency, commission or other body is covered by a public records access law. Check your state statutes (Figure 3.3 lists this legislation) to determine coverage. In general, assume that the law covers an agency wholly or partially supported by government funds—whether it is a state commerce department, county commission or mosquito abatement district.

While the statutes of some states seem to be comprehensive in their coverage, others may not be as broad and explicit. Check the legislative history of the law (the published hearings on the bill before it was enacted) and review administrative interpretations of the statute. Often, court cases have established the coverage of these statutes and the scope of any exemptions. Good sources for this type of information include the office of the state attorney general and your own organization's legal adviser.

The applicability of state FoI laws to the legislature and courts is not as clear. Most states have enacted separate statutes for their courts and lawmaking bodies. Some experts suggest that if your state does not expressly include these branches in its public records coverage, people seeking information in those areas "should argue that [these branches] fall within the definition of 'public agency' contained in the state's general FoI statute."*

Types of records covered

Although many states specifically refer to coverage of official or public *writings,* other states have also included recorded sound, films, tapes, photographs, maps and cards in their definition of *public record.* Check the interpretation of *record* in your state; it may be broader than you think.

Once you have identified the type of records you need, you face another hurdle: trying to determine which records can be *disclosed.* It seems reasonable that minutes of meetings, the records of police and fire departments, school budget information and opinions of the state attorney general would be covered by such legislation. But it's not that clear.

Unfortunately, most state laws do not specifically list what records can be disclosed. Some legislation *sounds* promising—for example, the Arkansas law (Sec. 12-2803):

> Public records are writings, recorded sounds, films, tapes or data compilations in any form (a) required by law to be kept, or (b) otherwise kept and which constitute a record of the performance or lack of performance of official functions which are or should be carried out by a public official or employer, a governmental agency, or any other agency wholly or partially supported by public funds or expending public funds.

That sounds comprehensive, but there is one complicating factor called the "public interest." Some records, various governments say, cannot be released because doing so would serve no broadly based public interest. If the logic of withholding documents from the public because releasing them would not serve the public's "best interests" escapes you, read on. Administrative, judicial and legislative exemptions to public records laws will give you a true reading of their strength.

Types of records exempted

This chapter would be interminably long if we listed all the exemptions to state public records laws. Here are some examples:

---

*Burt Braverman and Wesley Heppler, "A Practical Review of State Open Records Laws," *The George Washington Law Review* 49, No. 4: 731.

Figure 3.3. *State public records legislation**

ALABAMA Code, Section 36-12-40
ALASKA Statutes, Section 09.25.110
ARIZONA Revised Statutes, Section 39-121
ARKANSAS Statutes, Section 12-2801
CALIFORNIA Government Code, Section 6250
COLORADO Revised Statutes, Section 24-72-201
DELAWARE Code, Title 29, Section 10001
DISTRICT OF COLUMBIA Code, Section 1-1521
CONNECTICUT General Statutes, Section 1-15
FLORIDA Statutes, Section 119.01
GEORGIA Code, Section 50-18-70
HAWAII Revised Statutes, Section, 92-21
IDAHO Code, Section 9-301
ILLINOIS Statutes, Chapter 116, Section 201
INDIANA Code, Section 5-14-3-1
IOWA Code, Section 68A.1
KANSAS Statutes, Section 45-205
KENTUCKY Revised Statutes, Section 61.870
LOUISIANA Revised Statutes, Section 44:1
MAINE Revised Statutes, Title 1, Section 401
MARYLAND Code, Article 76A, Section 1-6
MASSACHUSETTS Laws, Chapter 66, Section 10
MICHIGAN Statutes, Subsection 4.1801 (1)
MINNESOTA Statutes, Section 13.01
MISSISSIPPI Code, Section 25-61-1
MISSOURI Revised Statutes, Section 610.010
MONTANA Code, Section 2-6-103
NEBRASKA Revised Statutes, Section 84-712

- Probation and parole records (Wyoming)
- Appraisal of real estate (Washington)
- Public employee personnel files (Utah)
- "Confidential" information under the state Toxic Substances Information Act (Virginia)
- Labor negotiations (Delaware)
- Applications for licenses to sell motor vehicles (Hawaii)
- Records of the state National Guard (Missouri)

The most common exemption seems to be for records concerning ongoing criminal investigations, although Illinois recently interpreted its law to make the acquisition of even common police blotter records difficult. Other common exemptions include trade secrets, certain busi-

NEVADA Revised Statutes, Section 239.005
NEW HAMPSHIRE Revised Statutes, Section 91-A:1
NEW JERSEY Statutes, Section 47:1A-1
NEW MEXICO Statutes, Section 14-2-1
NEW YORK Consolidated Laws, Public Officers Section 95
NORTH CAROLINA General Statutes, Section 132-1
NORTH DAKOTA Century Code, Section 44-04-18
OHIO Revised Code, Section 149.43
OKLAHOMA Statutes, Title 51, Section 24
OREGON Revised Statutes, Section 192.410
PENNSYLVANIA Statutes, Title 65, Section 66.1
RHODE ISLAND General Laws, Section 38-2-1
SOUTH CAROLINA Code, Section 30-4-10
SOUTH DAKOTA Codified Laws, Section 1-27-1
TENNESSEE Code, Section 10-7-501
TEXAS Revised Civil Statutes, Article 6252-17a
UTAH Code, Section 63-2-66
VERMONT Statutes, Title 1, Section 315
VIRGINIA Code, Section 2.1-341
WASHINGTON Revised Code, Section 42.17.250
WEST VIRGINIA Code, Section 29B-1-1
WISCONSIN Statutes, Section 19.31
WYOMING Statutes, Section 16-4-201

*This list is a beginning point of reference. Articles, chapters and sections of public records legislation often continue for many pages. Because new or amended sections may have been added since this list was compiled in 1985, no ending reference is given.

ness and appraisal information, and information that would compromise someone's privacy.

In addition to all these exemptions, most states today now provide for expunging (sealing) certain criminal records. Such sealing or destruction of criminal records may occur anywhere from the time of acquittal to several years after parole. The process may cover juvenile records, misdemeanor arrest records, first-time convictions and certain felony convictions. Some states provide for fines and imprisonment for unauthorized disclosure of these sealed records, and some courts have even held that publication of "old" convictions constitutes an actionable invasion of privacy. Check your state's laws closely.

Journalists should press for (1) a proper and reasonable opportunity to inspect records, (2) a reasonable and speedy appeal procedure in case of denial and (3) the imposition of only reasonable fees for searches and

Figure 3.4. *State open meetings laws**

```
ALABAMA Code, Section 13A-14-2
ALASKA Statutes, Section 44.62.310
ARIZONA Revised Statutes, Section 38-431
ARKANSAS Statutes, Section 12-2801
CALIFORNIA Government Code, Section 11120
COLORADO Revised Statutes, Section 24-6-4-1-02
DELAWARE Code, Title 29, Section 10004
DISTRICT OF COLUMBIA Code, Section 1-1504
CONNECTICUT General Statutes, Section 1-15
FLORIDA Statutes, Section 286.0105
GEORGIA Code, Section 50-14-1
HAWAII Revised Statutes, Section 92-1
IDAHO Code, Section 67-2340
ILLINOIS Statutes, Chapter 102, Section 41
INDIANA Code, Section 5-14-1.5
IOWA Code, Section 28A.1
KANSAS Statutes, Section 75-4317
KENTUCKY Revised Statutes, Section 61.805
LOUISIANA Revised Statutes, Section 42:4.1
MAINE Revised Statutes, Title 1, Section 401
MARYLAND Code, Article 76A, Section 7-15
MASSACHUSETTS Laws, Chapter 30A, Section 11A
MICHIGAN Statutes, Section 4.1800(11)
MINNESOTA Statutes, Section 471.705
MISSISSIPPI Code, Section 25-41-1
MISSOURI Revised Statutes, Section 610.010
MONTANA Code, Section 2-3-201
```

copying. No state sets a formal rate for searches, however, and many will waive the fees when the search is clearly in the public interest.

Learn your rights—and press your advantage.

Open meetings laws

Laws requiring public meetings of government bodies exist in all 50 states and the District of Columbia. (See the list of such statutes in Figure 3.4.) Although these laws are full of exemptions, their purpose is clear: to ensure that an informed public is aware of the deliberations and decisions of its government and that these decisions are made openly.

To understand these laws, a journalist must know (1) which governmental bodies are covered, (2) which ones are exempt from cov-

NEBRASKA Revised Statutes, Section 84-1409
NEVADA Revised Statutes, Section 241.010
NEW HAMPSHIRE Revised Statutes, Section 91-A:1
NEW JERSEY Statutes, Section 10:4-6
NEW MEXICO Statutes, Section 10-15-1
NEW YORK Consolidated Laws, Public Officers Section 95
NORTH CAROLINA General Statutes, Section 143-318.9
NORTH DAKOTA Century Code, Section 44-04-19
OHIO Revised Code, Section 121.22
OKLAHOMA Statutes, Title 25, Section 301
OREGON Revised Statutes, Section 192.610
PENNSYLVANIA Statutes, Title 65, Section 261
RHODE ISLAND Laws, Section 42-46-1
SOUTH CAROLINA Code, Section 30-4-10
SOUTH DAKOTA Codified Laws, Section 1-25-4
TENNESSEE Code, Section 8-44-101
TEXAS Revised Civil Statutes, Article 6262-17
UTAH Code, Section 52-4-10
VERMONT Statutes, Title 1, Section 311
VIRGINIA Code, Section 2.1-341
WASHINGTON Revised Code, Section 42.30.010
WEST VIRGINIA Code, Section 6-9A-1
WISCONSIN Statutes, Section 19.81
WYOMING Statutes, Section 16-4-401

*This list is a beginning point of reference only. New or amended sections may have been added after it was compiled in 1985.

erage, (3) what conditions or circumstances permit closed or executive sessions, (4) what notice is required to hold a public meeting and (5) what sanctions exist for violations.

Coverage

Most state and local boards, commissions, councils and agencies are covered by open meetings laws. However, these laws do not necessarily apply to advisory groups of governing bodies or to private groups to whom a state or local agency may have contracted services. Assume that a public body performing some public business and receiving some public funds is under the law. If it is not, it should be covered by a specific, statutory exemption to the law, not by some administrator's whim.

Exempt groups and proceedings

All open meetings laws specify certain exemptions, such as salary negotiations and matters of collective bargaining, personnel issues, sale or lease of real property, discussion with attorneys about pending litigation, parole or prison release hearings, sale or purchase of securities, political caucuses and juvenile court hearings. Some states close meetings of judicial fitness commissions, public employee relations commissions and prisoner review boards.

Examine your state law carefully to find out what groups and proceedings are exempt. In addition, your state attorney general's office has published opinions and interpretations about "appropriate" closure of meetings.

Closing a meeting

Under what conditions may officials close a "public" meeting? Does the governing body have to cite its reason for closure and vote on a closure motion? Can a final decision be made during these closed sessions, or does the decision have to be voted on during a public session? Are media representatives permitted to attend these closed sessions in exchange for an agreement not to discuss the substance of the discussions? These are questions you should ask—and find clear answers for. Legislative history and judicial interpretations in your state will provide helpful information.

Some states do not allow final action to be taken during closed sessions. When final action is improperly taken or where a meeting is improperly closed, the reporter should complain to the governing body that he or she intends to report what is going on at the closed session. This objection usually causes immediate review of the proposed closure. However, it can also lead to the barring of the reporter from the meeting—eventually moving the entire discussion to the courts.

Notice required for public meetings

Many states require public notice of forthcoming meetings. Some states set no specific requirements for advance notice for regular meetings; others prescribe notice of a week to 10 days. In the case of *emergency* meetings, a term not generally well-defined, 24 hours' notice may be sufficient, especially if the media and interested parties receive notice by phone. This is an obvious area for abuse; watch for an epidemic of emergency gatherings.

Alaska has taken the emergency meeting one step further by allowing conference telephone calls for last-minute gatherings. Virginia courts had approved this practice, too, but the state's General Assembly passed a law in 1984 making this form of meeting illegal.

Also watch for creative "non-meetings." City council members organizing regular coffee klatches and county commissioners going on "retreats" may be violating the law if they discuss public business and make decisions.

Sanctions

Check to see if your law has teeth. In Hawaii and Maine, for example, violation of the open meetings statute could send an official to jail for a year. In New York and other states, action taken during an improperly called or improperly closed meeting can be declared void. In addition, some states require the government body to pay reasonable attorney's and court fees if citizens must go to court to halt violations of public meetings laws.

The serious information-gatherer should fight every time a public body attempts to close even a portion of its gatherings to the people. In the authors' experiences, many public officials are not fully aware of the provisions of their state's open meetings law. These officials have also tended to interpret the law broadly to permit closed sessions when a public meeting, with proper notice, is obviously warranted.

As both a citizen and representative of the public who has the right to know the public's business, be ready to challenge and complain. (We remember one incident in which a nervous group of city councillors, unsure of their knowledge of the open meetings law, turned to the newspaper reporter seated in the council chambers and asked if their next business item—hiring a new assistant city manager—could be discussed in private.)

THE SHIELD OF PRIVILEGE

Do people who gather information professionally for public dissemination have more rights than ordinary citizens? Do they have the right to protect confidential sources from disclosure? Can they be protected from a judicial citation for contempt of court if they refuse to answer a subpoena to reveal information gathered but not published? These questions continue to be debated in state legislatures and in various courts. After much discussion and controversy, 26 states* have decided to give some statutory privilege to journalists. This section will examine the concept of privilege and give you some guidelines for its use in your role as information gatherer.

Why protection is necessary

A reporter's need to protect the confidentiality of his or her sources and to be protected from unreasonable search and seizure of information and related materials is of paramount importance in journalism today. Journalists fear they will lose sources of valuable information if those sources begin to think that the journalists can, in effect, act as agents of law enforcement and the courts. These sources demand absolute confidence, or else the flow of information will cease.

Despite their understanding of a reporter's need to grant confidentiality, many editors today demand that a reporter share secret sources with someone else in the newsgathering chain to ensure the sources exist. This is a predictable fallout from the Washington *Post*-Janet Cooke debacle of 1981, in which a series that won a Pulitzer Prize for feature reporting (later withdrawn) was actually based on a composite of characters. Some of the sources Cooke claimed she relied on did not actually exist. In addition, many courts, citing the concept of "everyman's evidence," want to know why the information gathered by a journalist (a citizen with evidence) should *not* be used to help determine guilt or innocence in a criminal case. These issues have created clashes between journalists and the courts, with journalists spending time in jail and news organizations paying heavy fines for not cooperating with the courts.

Defenders of special privilege for journalists cite the media's watchdog function, saying that an occasional guarantee of confidentiality is necessary if the journalist is to expose wrongdoing and provide information helpful to the public. In trying to defend his privilege, Los Angeles *Herald-Examiner* reporter Bill Farr spent 46 days in jail in 1970, and New York *Times* reporter Myron Farber was jailed for 40 days in 1978—with the *Times* also paying $285,000 in contempt fines.

In recent years, however, such long jail terms have been rare; this may be due to the increase in shield laws, the courts' acceptance of

*As of 1985, the following states had some type of press shield legislation: Alabama, Alaska, Arizona, Arkansas, California, Delaware, Illinois, Indiana, Kentucky, Louisiana, Maryland, Michigan, Minnesota, Montana, Nebraska, Nevada, New Jersey, New Mexico, New York, North Dakota, Ohio, Oklahoma, Oregon, Pennsylvania, Rhode Island and Tennessee.

some concept of privilege and the courts' rejection of prosecutors' pleas for help when they appear to be simply on fishing expeditions.

The real drive for shield legislation began in 1972, when the U.S. Supreme Court ruled in the case of *Branzburg v. Hayes* (408 US 655) that journalists had no inherent constitutional privilege to keep sources secret. It added, however, that its ruling would not prohibit a state legislature from providing some sort of shield law for journalists.

As more states passed legislation, it became clear that such protection provided a qualified shield—that is, while the shield could not completely override Sixth Amendment protections offered to a defendant in a criminal case, courts would increasingly look at the public interest of a story and grant some form of privilege accordingly. For this reason, it is important that you examine your state's shield law and judgments handed down by courts. Here are some protections to look for and to argue for:

1. *That the person or job description covered be given a broad definition.* In the early days of press shield legislation, magazine writers and TV broadcasters were sometimes exempt from coverage. Even today, the status of freelancers and reporters for the alternative press as protected journalists could be in jeopardy. A recent California ruling held that unless a freelancer had a publishing contract in hand, he or she would not qualify as a journalist. The Oregon statute, on the other hand, uses a broad definition of *journalist* as any "person connected with, employed by or engaged in any medium of communication."

2. *That exemptions to the law be narrow and specific.* New Mexico's law was watered down in 1982 after a state court ruled the act unconstitutional in 1976. Now its law allows the district court to rule if disclosure is necessary "to prevent injustice." That open-ended language provides little protection to the journalist. Two common statutory exemptions exist in many states with shield laws: They do not protect the journalist who the court believes has committed or is about to commit a crime, nor do they protect the journalist from revealing the source of allegedly defamatory information, when that information is sought to defend a defamation suit.

3. *That subpoenas seeking information or sources be specific and narrow.* The greatest strength of a shield law or a qualified privilege is its ability to create compromise between a judge, prosecutor and media. Judges are becoming more sensitive about overly broad subpoenas. A judge is more likely today to ask if attorneys have exhausted all avenues of gaining information before seeking help from a journalist.

However, the problem has not been solved, even though the courts have become more reluctant to compel a journalist to testify. The Society of Professional Journalists' Freedom of Information Committee continues to fill its files with stories of reporters jailed for contempt for refusing to testify or to answer a subpoena.

How to view the idea of privilege

Journalistic privilege is far from absolute. Although some states recognize a form of privilege, such exemptions will not keep you from the witness stand or from jail if the court feels your refusal to cooperate is trampling a defendant's Sixth Amendment rights. Add to that the lack of a federal shield law, and you can see the need to develop a long-term strategy to protect and strengthen information gathering.

Our advice is to learn exactly what your state shield law provides. If there is no such law, learn what precedents have been set in relevant court cases. A call to your state attorney general's office is a good start; interviews with your state newspaper publishers association, broadcasters association, legal advisers to the media and university law professors also will be helpful.

When dealing with a source who wants to remain confidential, decide immediately if you can make such an agreement. Are you satisfied that this source is not leading you on with false information that will trap you later? Are you willing to go to jail over this issue, or can you try harder to discover corroborating information from a source who can be identified? Find out how your news organization feels about confidential sources. Will it back you up?

This is an emotional issue. It is also confusing. In 1984, a New York court held, for example, that a reporter could not be compelled to reveal the source of a sealed grand jury report that was leaked to the reporter. On the other hand, an Ohio appeals court said that while a reporter might be able to protect a source, any tapes, notes or other materials that might ensure a defendant's right to a fair trial must be turned over to the court.

Ultimately, you must look at your role in information gathering and reporting as giving you rights—and responsibilities—beyond those of an ordinary citizen. By providing information in the public interest, you deserve some consistent protection that will not harm your ability to secure confidential information. Fight for it.

Search and seizure

Another aspect of journalistic privilege deals with the right not to have your notes, tapes, films and other materials seized in a court-authorized search. Such an issue was raised in the 1979 case of *Zurcher* v. *Stanford Daily* (436 US 547), in which the U.S. Supreme Court held that a police search of a college daily newspaper was legal under the Fourth Amendment because it provided evidence necessary to a case.

Since that decision, nine states have passed laws to protect the media from these "third-party searches."* Such a limited response by the states is disheartening, which might explain why some newspapers and broadcast stations have recently adopted policies of discarding negatives, prints and videotapes not published or broadcast.

Once again, the media should act swiftly to ensure that search warrants are not handed to police officials on fishing expeditions. The warrant should specify exactly what is sought and the purpose for its discovery. The media should try to persuade judges to require exhaustion of all other avenues of evidence discovery *before* turning to the media. Such a position is consistent with the theory behind shield laws, which is why some states have added restrictions against search and seizure to their privilege legislation.

CODES OF CONDUCT AND COOPERATION

The media also employ codes of conduct and cooperation. These codes do not carry any legal force but do reflect the media's desire to act in a professional and moral way. Codes of conduct or ethics have been in existence since 1923, when the American Society of Newspaper Editors adopted its Canons of Journalism Ethics. Three years later, Sigma Delta Chi (later the Society of Professional Journalists) created its Code of Ethics, with this statement of purpose:

> We believe in public enlightenment as the forerunner of justice, and in our Constitutional role to seek the truth as part of the public's right to know the truth.
>
> We believe those responsibilities carry obligations that require journalists to perform with intelligence, objectivity, accuracy and fairness.

*As of 1985, California, Connecticut, Illinois, Nebraska, New Jersey, Oregon, Texas, Washington and Wisconsin.

Codes have also been adopted by the Associated Press Managing Editors Association, the National Association of Broadcasters and the Public Relations Society of America. These codes have been criticized because they obviously lack enforcement power. This criticism reveals a basic irony of the U.S. media system: It is unconstitutional to license journalists, but the system is harassed because of its inability to control the conduct of members.

Codes of cooperation, however, show real interaction between the media and their various sources. Two major ones involve hospitals and justice organizations. These codes help information-gatherers because they reflect an established agreement on what is in the public interest and what is an invasion of privacy or harmful to the public interest.

Because of its importance, we will focus on the Bar-Press Guidelines, which arose from a 1968 Advisory Committee on Fair Trial and Free Press of the American Bar Association. This group produced what has been called the Reardon Report. Here is a typical set of guidelines, dealing with what can be disclosed about a criminal case.

What can generally be disclosed before trial

1. The arrested person's name, age, residence, employment and marital status. (This information might also be given if police are searching for a suspect.) In most states, however, names of juveniles (those under 18) are not released unless they are involved in a capital crime.

2. The charge.

3. The amount of bail or any release conditions.

4. The identity of and biographical information about the complainant or victim. (Obviously, media are urged to consider the effect of harassment or coercion against this individual. For example, most newspapers do not publish the name of a rape victim, even though no law prevents them from doing so.)

5. The circumstances of the arrest, including any pursuit, resistance and use of weapons.

6. The identity of the arresting agency as well as the type and length of investigation.

7. A photograph of the accused or arrested individual.

Information not appropriate for pretrial release

1. The contents of any admission or confession, or the fact that such an admission or confession has been made
2. Speculation or opinion about the guilt, innocence or character of the suspect
3. Results of fingerprint or polygraph exams, ballistics tests or laboratory work
4. Precise descriptions of items seized or discovered during an investigation
5. Prior criminal charges and convictions of the suspect
6. Statements about anticipated testimony of witnesses
7. Opinions about evidence or argument in the case

If these voluntary guidelines seem too restrictive, then consider what has happened in their absence and what still can happen despite their presence.

Before osteopathic physician Sam Sheppard was arrested in 1954 for the murder of his wife, Ohio newspapers and television stations were filled with "testimony" from law enforcement officials, potential witnesses and others as to the doctor's presumed guilt. What followed during the trial (better described as a journalistic circus) was unfettered abuse of the defendant's fair trial rights. When Dr. Sheppard's murder conviction was overturned more than 10 years later, the press was notified that courts would use citations for contempt to prevent future abuses. Such solutions as voluntary guidelines to balance press and defendant rights seemed logical and necessary.

But the media carnival that followed the 1984 "subway vigilante" case of Bernhard Goetz shows what can happen when such pretrial guidelines are not followed. In a gloomy day for journalistic ethics, ABC-TV obtained from "an undisclosed source" Goetz's videotaped confession, made to an assistant district attorney while in police custody. Several of his statements were broadcast (and subsequently published) before the trial's start, including these: "I decided I was going to kill 'em all, murder 'em all, do anything. . . . You can accuse me of a lot of things, okay? Because I know in my heart what I was. They didn't die, well, that's what God wanted, if there is a God. That I knew in my heart I was a murderer." Several police officers were interviewed, and they also revealed some of Goetz' statements.

Such examples, which reflect strong public interest in particular criminal cases, nonetheless lead to legal challenges of the fairness of police and court proceedings. Why, some would ask, do media organizations act sometimes like prosecutors? Inevitably, both the media's zeal and their suspicion that vital information is being withheld result in conflict with courts and law enforcement officials.

Such conflicts are part of the give-and-take of a free press in a free society. We urge you to consider fairness and professionalism as you gather information for publication. Statutes, court decisions and ethical codes will affect your strategy—but your personal vision and moral sense will provide the most consistent direction.

IMPORTANT SOURCES

We suggest that you examine the following periodicals and books for information about the legal issues relevant to information gathering.

The News Media and the Law. This magazine on legal issues affecting the media is published four times yearly by The Reporter's Committee for Freedom of the Press, 800 18th St., NW, Washington, DC 20006. It and supplementary publications are sent to people who make a tax-deductible contribution of $20 or more to the committee.

Media Law Reporter. This hefty weekly publication of The Bureau of National Affairs (1231 25th St., NW, Washington, DC 20037) is a compilation of court cases involving media issues. It is expensive (almost $500 a year), but it keeps the journalist up-to-date with judicial opinions and case summaries; it also has a good topical index. Here is a small portion of its coverage: national security restraints, privacy, pretrial restraints, obscenity statutes, public figure definition, retraction, protection of sources, the Fairness Doctrine, trespass and disclosure of unpublished information.

Mass Communications Law. This excellent work by Gillmor and Barron (West Publishing, 4th ed., 1984) covers all legal issues affecting the media and gives case excerpts and cogent commentary.

Mass Media Law. University of Washington Professor Don Pember gives strong narrative focus to media legal issues. Although he doesn't excerpt cases as much as Gillmor and Barron do, his discussion is perceptive and practical.

The Reporter and the Law. Lyle Denniston, a veteran reporter covering the U.S. Supreme Court for the Baltimore *Sun*, wrote this book in 1980 (Hastings House Publishers). His direct, insightful views of reporters' roles and responsibilities should be required reading.

West's Law Finder. This handy legal publication manual is an unabashed promotion of the large legal library of West Publishing (Box 64526, St. Paul, MN 55164), but it is extremely helpful in sorting through the various digests and manuals that make up a law library. The *Law Finder* briefly explains what is contained in the various court reporters, digests and encyclopedias, and gives handy tips on how to use them.

Discovering the Library

4

Put yourself in the place of these journalists. They need accurate information quickly. Where should they go?

- Journalist A, a general assignment reporter for a daily newspaper, has just been told to cover a speech scheduled for that evening. Joe McGinniss is making a previously unannounced visit to a nearby university to discuss his latest book. Journalist A needs complete and accurate biographical background for McGinniss.

- Journalist B, a television reporter, is putting together a feature segment about the week 40 years ago during which a series of fires destroyed five square blocks of downtown. To put this locally significant day in context, Journalist B wants to know what was happening in the nation and the world that week.

- Journalist C, a magazine writer, is beginning a story about the phenomenal growth of health clubs across the nation. As part of the preliminary research, Journalist C wants to compile a list of some of the major clubs in Los Angeles, Denver, Cleveland and Philadelphia.

- Journalist D, a speech writer in a corporate public relations department, is working on a "state of the corporation" address for the chief executive officer. Journalist D needs to know how other companies in the same industry fared last year.

Answer: The four journalists should make a beeline to the reference section of their local libraries. Journalist A will be guided to the needed information in *Biography Index*. Journalist B needs to look up the week in question in *Facts on File*. Journalist C should settle in with a stack of out-of-state phonebooks. Journalist D can peruse *Moody's Manual of Investments* and selected corporate annual reports.

These journalists can make use of one of the most basic, most easily accessible information resources available. Smart journalists understand how vital library research can be to complete, accurate reporting.

"I'm sort of a library nut," says Barry Mitzman, KCTS-TV (Seattle) producer for public affairs programming. "When I'm on a story, the library has traditionally been my first stop. I have never worked on a story that didn't involve good, solid time in the library."

"I've used the library at all stages of my work," says St. Paul (MN) *Pioneer Press* features editor Ken Doctor. "First I go there to get story ideas, then background, then potential sources. The place is full of phenomenal sources."

But a disturbing number of working journalists rarely darken the doors of their local libraries. Why not?

No time, they say. Deadline pressure, they insist. Sometimes they're right; often they're not.

Going to a nearby library to research an issue or gather background on a person may be a far more efficient and accurate way to gather information than sitting in the office and making phone calls. If time is tight, it makes sense for reporters to go directly to the reputable, documented, verifiable sources they can find in the library. But many don't.

Some don't understand what a library has to offer. They think of it as an overheated mausoleum stacked high with outdated books and stodgy journals, a place useful for academics and scholars but irrelevant to harried journalists. Perhaps the first and last time they trudged through a library was as students researching term papers.

Many journalists don't understand how to use a library. They've never learned how libraries are organized. With the exception of referring to the card catalog and *Readers' Guide to Periodical Literature*, they don't know how to find information in the library. Because they know neither the system nor the guides to the system, they see library research as tedious and time consuming.

In a way, they're right. Even conducting simple research—gathering biographical data on a visiting author, for example—can seem interminable when the researcher doesn't know where to go. But it's the researcher's fault, not the library's. Library research can be fast and efficient if reporters understand *what* materials are housed in a library and *how* to find them.

WHAT'S IN THE LIBRARY?

Not all libraries are created equal, but they all contain at least some of the same kinds of materials, and almost all depend on the same organizational system (the Library of Congress numbering system). A major university library may have 7 million volumes and the local branch of your city library barely 7,000, but they have much more in common than you might think. Whether you are stalking the library at Harvard or Hicksville, you will find these categories of sources relevant to journalistic research:

■ *Reference material.* From directories of corporations to lowly phonebooks, reference materials can be invaluable sources for the journalistic researcher. So numerous that they could fill a modest library by themselves, reference books bring together facts from a vast number of sources and arrange them for fast and convenient use. Although they cover thousands of different topics, reference books serve the information hunter in two basic ways: Either they supply information directly, like dictionaries, encyclopedias and almanacs, or they point the way to where the information can be found, like directories and indexes. Some reference tools do a little of both.

■ *Published books.* Journalists wanting background information, historical context, authoritative details or additional sources can turn to their library's collection of published books. Books can provide the depth and documentation journalists need for certain projects, but books do have their limits in journalistic research. Unlike reference tools, they may require a hefty investment in time. The information may be too specialized or expressed in mind-boggling jargon. Because most books take years to be written, an additional year to be published, and another six months to find their way to the library, they don't contain the recent information or breaking news that journalists often need.

■ *Magazines and journals.* Periodicals are so numerous and so varied that few library collections do more than scratch the surface. The federal government alone publishes 30,000 magazines and newsletters. Journalists can use periodicals for relatively quick reference and background work. They can use magazine and journal articles to check recent developments, help put local issues in a larger context, compile lists of relevant sources to be contacted or stimulate ideas for future projects. Periodicals can be classified according to their intended readership. Consumer magazines, the most popular of which are found on newsstands, are directed to general or nonexpert audiences. Trade publications are published for those involved in specific occupations, such as dentists or dog groomers. Scholarly, academic or research journals are published by and for experts in a variety of disciplines from art history to zoology.

■ *Newspapers.* Newspapers can be indispensable sources of both timely and historical information. Journalists who need to trace the origins of a controversy, research a current problem, compile a list of potential sources, put a local issue in context, or take a national issue and give it a local slant can consult newspapers. University libraries carry local, regional, national and international newspapers. City libraries often have decent collections of regional papers. A newspaper's own library, sometimes called a *morgue* because it houses already published ("dead") stories, is also a source.

■ *Government documents.* The U.S. government is a major source of information for the journalistic researcher. Almost 1,400 libraries across the country—designated depository libraries—select titles from the more than 25,000 new publications issued annually by the government. Even small libraries outside the depository system carry some government documents. Both the scope and the depth of information available are awesome. Government-gathered statistical data—from the number of salmon caught commercially to the number of children inoculated against measles—can be vital to the journalist. Agency and department reports, congressional committee hearings, debate transcripts, and thousands of pamphlets, newsletters and journals all provide journalists with detailed, specialized information they probably could not find elsewhere. A host of special catalogs and indexes are available to help the researcher locate material. (See Chapters 5 and 7 for complete discussions of the information resources of the federal government.)

■ *Special collections.* Many libraries, especially university libraries, contain special collections of material. The letters, notes and diaries of people important to the history of the region may be housed in a special collection. A library might contain unpublished material relating to the operation of local organizations. Maps and charts of the region may constitute another special collection. These collections generally have their own guides and directories. Historical collections are of particular value to journalists looking to understand issues of the past and how they relate to contemporary concerns.

HOW TO FIND FACTS FAST

Some library research involves finding facts quickly. Knowing what reference tools are available is a big step toward becoming an intelligent, effective information-gatherer. But there are so many that you will need a guide. Mary Barton and Marion Bell's *Reference Books: A Brief Guide,* published by Enoch Pratt Free Library, is an inexpensive paperback that ought to be part of any journalist's personal library. Eugene P. Sheehy's *Guide to Reference Books* has been updated by several recent supplements. Reference librarians are superior sources themselves.

What follows is a description of a number of important reference books relevant to the journalistic researcher. In general, these books are direct sources of information, not indexes to information (see pages 69–74 for a guide to some useful indexes).

Encyclopedias

Encyclopedias contain brief, readable articles on a profusion of subjects. Many of the important articles are written by specialists and contain illustrations and bibliographies. Although journalists must go far beyond these volumes for detailed, up-to-date information, they can gain a quick overview of the subject by reading an entry in one of the leading encyclopedias. With this basic understanding, the researcher can then formulate more specific questions and use more sophisticated reference tools.

The most overlooked feature of encyclopedias is the index volume, the researcher's guide to the entries in the other books. Another underused volume is the yearbook that updates the encyclopedia. These volumes carry obituaries, chronologies of the year's events and other timely material.

Chambers's Encyclopaedia. First published in the late 1850s and most recently updated in the late 1960s, this 15-volume British encyclopedia is famous for its clear, accurate entries on a wide variety of international subjects.

Collier's Encyclopedia. Bright, colorful and profusely illustrated, *Collier's* offers basic, easy-to-read information.

Encyclopedia Americana. A useful, general encyclopedia, the *Americana* is noted for its articles on American places, even small ones, and on American organizations and institutions. Its glossaries of technical terms, texts of documents and illustrations are valuable to researchers.

The Encyclopaedia Britannica. Probably the most famous encyclopedia—and the one preferred by many researchers—the *Britannica* comes from the United States, not Britain, and is in its 15th edition. This most recent edition, a 30-volume set, is highly innovative. Ten volumes, containing more than 100,000 short entries, are designed for researchers looking for one fact or the answer to a single question. The remaining volumes provide lengthy, readable articles written by authorities.

Foreign encyclopedias. For reasonably detailed information about people, places, events and topics related to other countries and not covered or covered insufficiently in English-language encyclopedias, multilingual researchers should refer to top foreign references. *La Grande Encyclopédie* (France), *Brockhaus Enzyklopädie* (Germany), *Enciclopedia Italiana di Scienze, Lettere ed Arti* (Italy) and *Enciclopedia Universal Ilustrada Europeo-Americana* (Spain) are examples.

Specialty encyclopedias. Most people think of encyclopedias as general reference tools, but a number of highly specific encyclopedias are available. Covering major subject areas such as philosophy, psychology, education and biology, these encyclopedias can be valuable quick references for journalists who need to be "instant experts" in unfamiliar fields. Some of the major specialty encyclopedias are discussed in the "Discovering Specialty Sources" section of this chapter, where they are listed under their subject area.

Almanacs

You're beginning a story on grain exports, and you need to know how many hectoliters make a bushel. You're researching the background for an article on violence and American politics, and you want to know which U.S. elected officials have been assassinated since 1865. You're researching a story on an upcoming change in your state's compulsory school attendance law. For context, you want to know the age limits imposed by the other 49 states.

You can get the answers to these and countless other questions—from who won last year's pingpong championships to who heads the Republic of Vanuatu—in those wonderful compendia of important and trivial facts known as almanacs.

Facts on File. A week-by-week compilation of significant news of the day, *Facts on File* records world events as reported in a number of metropolitan dailies.

Information Please Almanac. A yearly compilation of facts and figures, this highly readable almanac includes numerous graphs and charts as well as special descriptive articles on the year's developments in certain fields.

Statistical Abstract of the United States. A digest of data collected by the federal government's statistical agencies, this book is an information gold mine. Charts and tables concerning virtually every aspect of American life provide rich details. For more on this and related government documents, see Chapter 5.

World Almanac and Book of Facts. This invaluable and justly famous reference is a yearly compendium of facts, figures, lists, charts and miscellany.

Dictionaries

Working journalists know how important dictionaries are to achieving precise, accurate use of the language. This is one reference they keep handy and use often.

Abridged dictionaries. Used for quick reference, these dictionaries don't attempt to list every known word and don't give detailed etymological information for those they do. Bookstores are filled with a wide variety of adequate paperback or hardcover dictionaries. *The American Heritage Dictionary of the English Language* is highly regarded.

Unabridged dictionaries. Offering not only a guide to spelling, definition, pronunciation, syllabication and usage, these impressive tomes include derivations, quotations and illustrations as well. The following are considered reliable sources: *Webster's New International Dictionary of the English Language, Webster's Third New International Dictionary, Funk & Wagnalls New Standard Dictionary.* For information on the history of words, nothing beats the *Oxford English Dictionary on Historical Principles.*

Special word dictionaries. Writing a story on the death of the city's oldest greasy spoon diner and want to know hash house lingo of the 1930s? Use *The Dictionary of American Slang* or *Dictionary of Slang and Unconventional English.* Looking for a workable substitute for the word *report,* which you discover you've used three times in two sentences? Refer to *The Synonym Finder* or *Webster's Dictionary of Synonyms.* Other special word dictionaries include those for rhyming words, antonyms and commonly misspelled words.

Specialty dictionaries. Journalists often need to decipher the "foreign" languages (aka *jargon*) used in various unfamiliar fields. Dictionaries covering everything from architecture to zoology help demystify professional and academic fields. Some of them are listed under their respective fields in the "Discovering Specialty Sources" section of this chapter.

Atlases

Maps can answer questions no other reference tool can. (What highway connects two towns? Where is the county line?) They can present complex ideas in simple, graphic terms. (How do the countries of the world compare according to the average caloric intake of their populations?) Atlases are compilations of maps with related material.

The Encyclopaedia Britannica World Atlas International. This authoritative work includes topographic and political maps, comparative tables and country-by-country summaries as well as all the usual maps.

Rand McNally Commercial Atlas. Annually updated, it includes large, clear maps and is noted for its detailed treatment of the United States.

The Times Atlas of the World. This famous five-volume set published by the *Times* of London is known for both the accuracy and the beauty of its maps.

Biographical dictionaries and indexes

A reporter covering a speech, planning an interview or attempting to sort out all the characters in the latest boardroom drama needs to get accurate biographical information quickly. Fortunately, biographical sources abound. In fact, there are so many that they have their own guide, *Biographical Dictionaries and Related Works,* which lists nearly 5,000 works. Here are a few of the more important ones.

Biography Index. Published quarterly, it indexes biographical material found in current English-language books and 1,500 periodicals.

Contemporary Authors. Continually updated, this multivolume reference includes biographical sketches of both famous and obscure living authors. Personal information, education, jobs and publications are included.

Current Biography. A good, basic source for biographical information on anyone prominent in the news of the day, this reference tool is published annually. Photographs often accompany the entries.

Dictionary of American Biography. If you're looking for biographical data on prominent deceased Americans, this is the place to go. Accurate, well-written entries are followed by bibliographies.

The New York Times Obituary Index. This easy-to-use index directs journalistic researchers to obituaries published through 1968 in the *Times.*

Who's Who in America. Fashioned after the successful British *Who's Who,* this biographical dictionary offers brief sketches of notable living Americans. Published every other year, the book includes current addresses for its subjects. The same publisher issues *Who's Who of American Women.*

Specialty biographical references. Your local library may have any number of specialty "who's whos" listing and describing people involved in various industries and occupations. *American Men and Women of Science* and *Directory of American Scholars* are two examples.

Directories

Probably the least-used and most potentially valuable sources on the reference shelves are directories. They can be used in two ways: to provide answers to specific questions and to open the doors to further research.

The Directory of Directories. This important reference tool is a guide to business and industry directories, professional and scientific rosters and other such lists. Each of the almost 8,000 entries includes the directory name, the address of its publisher, a description and information about updates.

The Foundation Directory. This bulky volume lists more than 7,000 non-profit foundations. Each entry includes the foundation's address, date of establishment, purpose, activities, as well as data on its finances.

Encyclopedia of Associations. More than 12,000 U.S. organizations in a wide spectrum of fields are listed in this important reference book. Each entry includes the organization's address, the name of its leading official, date of founding, function, number of members and publications issued.

Polk's city directories. R. L. Polk Co. of Detroit compiles and publishes directories for more than 1,400 cities. Generally issued annually, each directory contains the name, address, telephone number, marital status, occupation and place of employment of all adult city residents. For area businesses, entries include the names of owners, partners or corporate officers.

Telephone books. City and university libraries often stock a wide variety of out-of-town (and out-of-state) telephone directories. For tracking down people and compiling lists of sources, there is no better or more valuable tool.

Specialty directories. Many professional fields—medicine, academia and business, for example—have their own directories. Locate them by looking up the profession in the *Directory of Directories* index.

Books of miscellany

Sometimes a journalist just has to know when the first plastic automobile license was made or who holds the rope skipping record or which state celebrates Mecklenburg Day. For these and other odd questions, consider the following books of curious facts.

The American Book of Days. Historical and religious holidays, birthdays, anniversaries, festivals, celebrations, jubilees and other assorted red-letter days are listed in this fascinating reference book.

Famous First Facts and Records. A collection of thousands of factual "firsts"—from the first advertising agency to the first zipper—this quirky book covers politics, sports, science, business, education, the military and hundreds of other areas.

The Guinness Book of World Records. If you need to know the tallest, strongest, heaviest, fastest, oldest or most any other superlative, this is the place to find it.

The Reader's Encyclopedia. A compilation of facts for the literati, this book includes information on books and authors, fictitious characters, literary and mythological allusions and assorted works of art.

HOW TO FIND BOOKS AND ARTICLES

Finding a book or a magazine article is a simple research task for those who understand indexes. Information hunters gain easy access to the wealth of material in the library and elsewhere by using these guides. There's no mystery to an index. It's merely a systemized list that pinpoints an item and tells you where to find it.

But there are two tricks to using indexes efficiently. The first is to know what the index indexes. Two hours spent poring over *Reader's Guide to Periodical Literature* trying to find a listing for an article published by a research journal is two hours wasted. Each index is a guide to specific material, although some indexes overlap. The periodicals indexed are almost always listed in the front of the volume.

The second trick is learning to think like an indexer. This happens naturally as you use an index and become familiar with its listings and categories. The important thing to remember is that your name for something may not be the indexer's name for it. Suppose you're researching a story on displaced homemakers and their decision to return to school. You look up *displaced homemaker*. Nothing. You look up *college enrollment*. Nothing. The absence of these headings doesn't necessarily mean that there's no material. Perhaps the indexer thought to list articles about this trend under *education, university* or *women*. Experiment.

What follows is a discussion of some major indexes and their relevance to the journalistic information-gatherer.

Books

Books, as you know, can be tremendously helpful sources of background information. Although a TV reporter on a two-hour deadline would not have the leisure to leaf through a book, many other journalists are able to take the time. How would they go about finding the book they needed?

The familiar card catalog or the more modern microfiche or on-line catalogs are the indexes to all the books housed in that library. Whether you're looking for a particular book by its title or author or just hunting for anything on a given subject, these are your primary guides. Each listing offers information about the book (title, author, publisher, date of publication, number of pages, number of illustrations, index) and the shelf number assigned to that book in that library.

Suppose your library doesn't have many books dealing with the subject you're researching. You know there must be books out there—books you can borrow through interlibrary loan—but you don't know the titles or authors. Obviously, the card catalog can't help. Where do you go?

The first place to look is OCLC (Online Computer Library Center), a network of public, university and government libraries that have agreed to share resources. All the books owned by all the libraries—most U.S. libraries belong to OCLC—are in a central database accessible through your library's computer. If the book is anywhere in the system, it can be found quickly and, in most cases, borrowed. The OCLC computer is simple to use and generally accessible to library patrons.

Another place to look is the yearly three-volume reference set *Books in Print*. The author, title and subject volumes list almost all the books in print in the United States. A final place to look for information about a book not in your home library is *The National Union Catalog* (NUC). This is a massive index of all the books housed in the nation's premier library, the Library of Congress. Because there are more than 80 million books listed in the NUC, the number of volumes is dauntingly large. But if you have a fair idea of when the book was published, the NUC, with its five-year cumulative indexes, is not difficult to use.

Newspapers

Daily newspapers can be the journalist's most timely source. They offer succinct reports and include a wealth of potential sources. How do journalists go about finding the articles they need?

Newspaper indexes are one solution. The New York *Times,* Washington *Post, Christian Science Monitor* and *Wall Street Journal* all have their own indexes organized by subject. Some are easier to use than others, but all are professionally compiled and frequently updated. They can be enormously helpful, assuming that your local library subscribes to these newspapers. If so, your library undoubtedly receives microfilm copies, not the newsprint editions.

These individual indexes are guides to four of this country's best daily newspapers, but what about the more than 1,700 other U.S. dailies? How accessible are they to the researcher? "Not very" is unfortunately the answer. Most are not individually indexed. Those that are, often have been indexed intermittently by amateurs, with the indexes available only to the libraries in or close to the city of publication.

The bright spot is *Newsbank,* a monthly service that both indexes (in book form) and provides (on microfiche) articles from more than 100 of the nation's larger dailies. *Newsbank*'s indexers look for articles covering particular subject areas like education, employment, environment and business. The index, a popular one in libraries, points the researcher to the location of the article on a microfiche card.

Periodicals

Articles in magazines and journals are often excellent sources of information for the journalist. Longer and more detailed than newspaper accounts, they generally contain more timely information than books.

Indexes make them readily accessible. In the "Discovering Specialty Sources" section of this chapter, you will find the names of indexes and abstracts of periodicals in specialized fields like business and medicine. What follows is a brief discussion of indexes for general interest publications.

For magazine articles published from 1980 on, the best source is the *Magazine Index,* a microfilm subject and author index that is updated monthly. It indexes more than 400 consumer magazines from the familiar *Time* and *Newsweek* to the more exotic *Lapidary Journal* and *Archery World.* Magazines reflecting all varieties of hobbies, sports and interests are included. Because the *Magazine Index* indexes just about every publication found in *Readers' Guide to Periodical Literature*—plus hundreds more—the researcher looking for material from 1980 on need refer only to the *Index.*

For articles published before 1980, the familiar *Readers' Guide to Periodical Literature* is the index to use. Published twice monthly (except for monthly issues in July and August), this subject and author guide began in 1900. It indexes more than 170 general interest and non-technical magazines, If you are looking for an article published earlier than 1900, refer to *Poole's Index to Periodical Literature,* which indexes periodicals published from 1802 to 1908.

DISCOVERING SPECIALTY SOURCES

General interest sources—books, newspapers and magazines—have several vital functions in the information-gathering process. They provide journalists with background about an unfamiliar subject. They introduce the important issues and players. They help point the direction for further digging. But they are the beginning, not the end, of the research trail.

When journalists need detailed, specialized information, general interest sources just don't suffice. Reading about Alzheimer's disease in *Time* magazine may help the journalist understand the basic issue, a necessary first step in researching a story. But a journalist who doesn't take the second step—consulting specialty publications in medicine and gerontology—is doing a slipshod job of information gathering.

Articles in specialty publications bring the journalist face to face with primary material and the people who generate it. The advantages of this kind of information are obvious: It is authoritative and current. The one disadvantage is obvious, too: Jargon often makes these articles difficult to understand. They are written by and for specialists who talk to one another in a code that an enterprising journalist can and must break. Fortunately, help is available. Most fields have their own dictionaries and encyclopedias to help the journalist through the maze. These reference tools are also valuable background sources in themselves.

What follows is a list of major sources in seven specialty fields commonly covered by journalists. Some of the indexes are available through computer databases and may be easier and quicker to use in this form (see Chapter 6).

The arts

Art Index. It indexes magazines, museum bulletins and annuals—currently more than 130—devoted to architecture, archaeology, painting, sculpture, ceramics, graphic arts, photography and film.

The Music Index. This monthly subject index gives researchers access to articles in more than 200 music-related periodicals published in the United States and abroad.

Guide to the Performing Arts. This is an index of articles on theater, television and dance.

A Biographical Dictionary of Film. More encyclopedia than dictionary, this reference book contains critical essays on 900 international film directors, producers and actors.

The Dance Encyclopedia. A combination of brief articles and long, signed pieces, this encyclopedia covers dancers, dances and dancing with special attention to native folk dance.

Encyclopedia of World Art. This 15-volume set includes more than 7,000 full-page plates and hundreds of essays on all of the visual arts.

The Oxford Companion to Music. A collection of more than 10,000 articles, this reference tool covers the history, composition, performance and performers of music.

The Oxford Companion to the Theatre. This encyclopedia includes articles on actors, producers, dramatists, individual theaters and theater history.

Business and economics

Business Periodicals Index. Issued monthly, this is a subject index to more than 120 periodicals in accounting, advertising, banking, business, finance, insurance, labor, marketing, taxation and related fields.

The McGraw-Hill Dictionary of Modern Economics. A dictionary of terms and a directory of organizations concerned with economics, this reference work also includes bibliographies of book and periodical articles.

Encyclopedia of Banking and Finance. This authoritative work contains articles on money and credit, banking history and practice, securities and other related topics.

Economic Almanac. A compilation of statistical and other data in the field of economics and business, this book (published irregularly) includes information on prices, productivity, trade, manufacturing, agriculture, transportation and various industries.

Moody's Manual of Investments, American and Foreign. A detailed compilation of current data—material is updated by semi-weekly supplement sheets—this vital reference work consists of five annual volumes covering transportation, public utility, municipal and government, bank and finance, and industrial securities.

Poor's Register of Corporations, Directors and Executives. This annual reference book has three parts: (1) a list of 35,000 corporations and their directors, (2) a list with brief biographical data of more than 70,000 directors and executives and (3) a list of industrial products and the companies selling them.

The Directory of High Technology Corporations. This is the place to look for corporate and financial information on more than 1,600 publicly held high-tech firms in computer technology, electronics, aerospace, telecommunications, biotechnology, optics, lasers and related fields.

Thomas' Register of American Manufacturers. Published annually, this guide is arranged according to products, with manufacturers of each product listed geographically.

Education

Current Index to Journals in Education. More than 300 education and education-related journals are indexed monthly.

Education Index. Indexing books, pamphlets and some government publications as well as journal articles, this guide concentrates on material related to teaching, educational trends and administration. It does not go beyond the late 1960s.

Standard Education Almanac. A compilation of statistical data related to education, this annual offers material on enrollment, financing, degrees and other subjects.

International Yearbook of Education. Published by UNESCO, this annual offers information on the condition of education in more than 80 countries.

The Encyclopedia of Education. International in scope but primarily concerned with all levels of education in the United States, this multivolume reference work contains more than 1,000 signed articles.

Encyclopedia of Educational Research. Each article in this book attempts to synthesize and interpret recent studies in the field.

American Universities and Colleges. A survey of U.S. higher education, this book contains a few broad articles on educational issues as well as an information-filled directory of universities and colleges.

Health

Index Medicus. The most comprehensive guide to journals in the medical sciences, this index is issued monthly and cumulated annually.

Biological Abstracts. Offering both citations and summaries of research, this index covers biology, basic medical sciences, microbiology, immunology, public health and many other related subjects.

American Medical Directory. This register of U.S. physicians lists each physician's name, address, medical school, specialty, subspecialty, type of practice and the year he or she was licensed.

Dorland's Illustrated Medical Dictionary. This standard reference contains almost 2,000 pages of medical terms from *anaphylaxis* to *zygoma*.

Psychiatric Dictionary. Terms in psychiatry and allied fields are defined in brief articles.

Physicians' Desk Reference. Known as the *PDR*, this annually published volume lists more than 2,000 prescription drugs with information on dosage, effects and precautions.

Encyclopedia of Biological Sciences. A comprehensive guide to the broad field of biological sciences, this reference tool is designed for intelligent non-experts.

Politics

The Literature of Political Science. This broad-based guide directs the researcher to periodical indexes, abstracts, book reviews, U.S. government and U.N. publications and other sources.

Public Affairs Information Service Bulletin. Published weekly, this is a subject guide to periodicals, pamphlets, documents and other material related to public administration, international affairs and social conditions.

Index to Legal Periodicals. This guide to law-related material indexes about 300 legal periodicals.

The American Political Dictionary. This reference work contains definitions and important information on general topics such as civil liberties, the legislative process and foreign policy.

Black's Law Dictionary. The standard in the field, it defines legal terms and concepts ranging from those of feudal law to ones appearing in recent court opinions.

Book of States. This book contains an overview of each state, including information about leading officials. (Note: Many states issue their own directories offering detailed information about the state's political organization and elected and appointed officials.)

Who's Who in American Politics. Particularly useful for information on local or minor officeholders, this book provides data on more than 12,000 current political figures.

International Yearbook and Statesman's Who's Who. This is an annual compilation of material about international organizations and countries and their politicians.

(Note: A major source of information about politics, politicians and the political process is the U.S. government itself. Government documents and other government sources are discussed in Chapters 5 and 7.)

Science and technology

Applied Science and Technology Index. Published monthly, it indexes more than 200 of the top U.S. and British scientific and technical periodicals.

McGraw-Hill Encyclopedia of Science and Technology. A 15-volume set that includes more than 7,000 articles, this reference tool offers comprehensive coverage of the physical, natural and applied sciences.

Van Nostrand's Scientific Encyclopedia. More than 16,000 science, engineering, mathematics and medical terms are explained.

Asimov's Biographical Encyclopedia of Science and Technology. Compiled by prolific science and science fiction writer Isaac Asimov, this volume includes biographical sketches of more than 1,500 scientists from ancient times to the present.

World Who's Who in Science. This book includes brief biographical sketches of some 30,000 notable scientists of all periods.

Scientific and Technical Societies of the United States. A directory of societies, this volume contains information about the history, aims, membership, research funds, awards and publications of some 1,000 groups.

Social issues

Sources of Information on the Social Sciences. An extensive guide to sources in sociology, psychology and other social sciences, this book offers detailed bibliographies and annotated lists of reference works.

Sociological Abstracts. This source indexes and abstracts a wide range of periodical literature dealing with sociological topics.

Psychological Abstracts. Classified by subject, this reference tool indexes and abstracts books, journal articles, dissertations, monographs and reports.

A Modern Dictionary of Sociology. This work defines terms and concepts in sociology and other social sciences.

Encyclopedia of Psychology. This book contains more than 5,000 entries written by authorities in the respective fields.

Encyclopedia of Social Work. Both an encyclopedia and a directory, it includes articles on social work and related topics, as well as biographies of those prominent in the field.

SEARCHING

Reading about the riches of the library is one thing; making use of them is another. Good researchers not only know what's available, they develop a search strategy to help them use the library's resources efficiently. Strategies vary from journalist to journalist and from story to story, but most have two common elements:

1. The search goes from the general to the specific, using reference guides such as encyclopedias and almanacs to build a basic core of knowledge, then moving to more detailed, specialized sources to deepen that knowledge.

2. The search is based on specific questions the journalist formulates at the start of the search and throughout the process as new information is discovered. These questions help break a story into its component parts and guide the researcher to specialized references.

Let's put these strategies into action and see how some of the sources discussed in this chapter can help the working journalist.

An unknown person or group has just bombed a local women's health clinic that performs abortions. The media have, of course, covered the event as breaking news. Now you—as a newspaper, broadcast or magazine reporter—have the chance to do an in-depth story on the rising tide of violence against these legal medical facilities. You will delve into police records (see Chapter 8). You will undoubtedly conduct interviews with a wide range of authorities (see Chapter 10). You may consult various government documents (Chapter 5) and institutional sources (Chapter 7). But the core of your knowledge, and documented answers to some of your questions, will come from solid library research. Consider some of the sources you might use:

- *General reference tools.* To discover how many abortions are performed in the United States, you will want to refer to the *Information Please Almanac, World Almanac and Book of Facts* or *Statistical Abstract of the United States.* To trace violence against women's clinics, you might thumb through *Facts on File.* To locate potential sources for your story, you could use any number of directories from *The Foundation Directory* and *Encyclopedia of Associations* to local telephone books.

- *Books.* Books concerning the ongoing controversy over abortion might offer helpful background information, provide the necessary context and target expert sources.

- *Newspapers and magazines.* To put your local incident in context and explore some of the component issues of the abortion controversy, you will certainly want to refer to newspaper and magazine stories. *Newsbank* is probably your best bet. You might also refer to the separate indexes for the New York *Times,* Washington *Post* and *Christian Science Monitor,* assuming your library subscribes to these papers. The *Magazine Index* should point you to a number of articles in general consumer magazines.

- *Specialty sources.* Building on the basic knowledge you've accumulated thus far, you're ready to break the story into its component parts. Suppose you need background information on the medical side of the story? *Index Medicus* will guide you to pertinent articles. You can explore some of the legal questions through articles referenced in the *Index to Legal Periodicals*. *PAIS Bulletin* might steer you to articles dealing with abortion as a social concern. Is abortion big business? Perhaps you can find out by reading articles referenced in the *Business Periodicals Index*.

Moving from the general to the specific, consulting specialty sources targeted to the component parts of the story, you can use the library quickly and efficiently. And with a well-conceptualized story idea, a simple search strategy and a working knowledge of the library, you are well on the road to producing a solid piece of journalism.

Washington on File 5

The conscientious and curmudgeonly editor I. F. Stone of *I. F. Stone's Weekly* always seemed to sniff out the tough stories other journalists missed: political duplicity, bureaucratic waste, military adventurism, racial inequities. From 1953 to 1971, he regularly exposed and documented government malfeasance in his renowned Washington, D.C., newsletter. Was he a supersleuth with inside connections? A dogged muckraker who spent the wee hours in dark alleys meeting with his own "Deep Throat"?

No. In fact, Stone didn't even consider himself an investigative reporter. Neither did he have a special pipeline into the government. Where did his consistently provocative material—material his contemporaries at the New York *Times* and Washington *Post* never seemed to have—come from? Government documents.

Because he had hearing difficulties, Stone developed the habit of reading transcripts of congressional hearings and committee meetings rather than attending them. He combed the *Congressional Record* daily and spent hours perusing other documents. One of his basic operating principles was, "A government always reveals a good deal, if you take the trouble to find out what it says." Stone took the trouble—and proved his principle week after week.

Documents produced by the government are not only excellent sources of information about the government itself, as I. F. Stone found, but also about the nation, its people and their numerous activities.

Consider these recently published stories. Their sources are noted in brackets:

- Violent criminals or thieves victimized roughly one in four American households last year. [Report by the Bureau of Justice Statistics, Department of Justice]
- A diet containing less red meat, less refined sugars and more fiber can help prevent certain cancers. [Report from the National Cancer Institute, National Institutes of Health]
- At least 102 aircraft near misses went unreported to the public in 1983 and 1984 as a result of "creative categorization" by the Federal Aviation Administration. [FAA regional reports secured through the Freedom of Information Act]
- Fewer than half of the women awarded child support payments actually received the full amount they were due. [Study conducted by the Census Bureau, Department of Commerce]
- Some terminally ill patients are not properly advised about their participation in experiments involving unapproved drugs and therapies. [Senate subcommittee hearings]

We hear about how much the Defense Department pays a contractor for a screwdriver. We read about a senator making a sizable income from speaking engagements. We learn how much real estate a presidential candidate's spouse owns. We discover that a major corporation is declaring bankruptcy. Government documents are the original sources for all these stories. Intelligent, thorough information gathering is impossible without them.

Why are documents such a vital source for the journalist?

- They are written, tangible evidence upon which a reporter can base a story—and defend it.
- They contain details that no single person could possibly know or remember.
- They cover a scope of activities far greater than the knowledge of any single person.
- Some contain such a variety of information from such a vast array of sources that it would take the journalist months to gather the same data.
- Others contain verbatim accounts that could not be obtained unless the reporter was physically present.
- Many are issued at regular intervals, making historical comparisons possible without trusting to sometimes faulty memory.

But for all their advantages, documents are hardly neutral sources of information. They are compiled and written by people—people whose careers, egos and political and economic aspirations may affect the character of a report. The Federal Aviation Administration story mentioned earlier is a good example. On the same day that FAA chief Donald Engen issued a public report concluding that "near midair collisions decreased by 50 percent over the last four and a half years," consumer advocate Ralph Nader released a series of documents obtained through the Freedom of Information Act contradicting that claim. Reports from three of nine regions showed that more than 100 midair near misses were not counted in the FAA chief's report, because they were categorized under other headings like *operational errors*.

Bureaucrats, administrators and officials all want to look good. Committees, bureaus, divisions, agencies and departments all want to look efficient and productive. Everyone would like to report progress. Everyone would like to report that problems don't exist, aren't as bad as we thought, or are almost solved. Reporters need to develop and nourish a healthy skepticism that allows them to see the possible pitfalls of depending on information obtained through any single source, including documents. Just because something is published and has the imprimatur of the U.S. government doesn't guarantee its complete accuracy. On the other hand, history has proved I. F. Stone right. The government does reveal much about itself (even when it doesn't want to or intend to) through its documents.

WHAT ARE FEDERAL GOVERNMENT DOCUMENTS?

Anything published by any agency of any branch of the federal government in whatever form for whatever purpose is considered a government document. Some documents, like a White House manual on how to efficiently manage office personnel, are designed for internal use but might be available to the public on request. Others, like the technical specifications for the MX missile, are classified "top secret" and are only available to those with that level of security clearance. Still others, like a Department of Agriculture bulletin on backyard gardening, are created specifically for public dissemination. A vast array of documents don't fall into any of these categories but instead constitute an ongoing record of the activities of various arms of the government. Not created specifically for the public, they are nonetheless readily available and are often of great public interest. Transcripts of congressional hearings and committee reports are examples.

With such an all-encompassing definition of what constitutes a document, it is little wonder that the U.S. government is considered the world's largest publisher. Its yearly output includes books, magazines, newsletters, manuals, maps, charts, reports, studies, speeches, circulars, proceedings, proclamations, hearings, decisions, bills and laws—so many and so varied that no one really knows how many there are.

Most agencies keep no central file on the publications they produce. And although all unclassified government publications are mandated by law to go to the Government Printing Office's Library Division— there to be indexed and listed in the *Monthly Catalog of United States Government Publications*—apparently many don't make it. In 1978, government researchers surveyed 74 federal departments and agencies to measure their publications output. They estimated that 102,000 separate publications were issued during an 18-month period. During the same 18-month period, the government's official listing of "all" documents, the *Monthly Catalog,* contained 66,000 titles.

WHERE TO FIND GOVERNMENT DOCUMENTS

In the early 1800s, with an eye toward opening up the government's business to its citizens, Congress mandated that various documents be printed and distributed to institutions outside the federal establishment. By the 1850s, this mandate had been translated into the Federal Depository Library Program, a national network of designated government document storehouses. Today the network includes 50 regional depository libraries, which receive every unclassified government publication received by the Government Printing Office and deemed of interest to the public. More than 1,300 other depository libraries, many of which are associated with colleges and universities, choose from among 25,000 new publications every year.

For many information-gatherers, a depository library will be the most convenient place to locate government documents. Figure 5.1 lists all 50 regional depositories. To find the location of other depository libraries in your area, call the regional library nearest you. Better yet, go to your local library and look through the American Library Association's *Directory of Government Documents Collections and Libraries,* a guide to all libraries (whether designated as depositories or not) with significant government document holdings. The book lists thousands of private, corporate, public and academic libraries, briefly describing the documents collection held by each.

Suppose your nearby government documents collection doesn't include the material you need. What do you do? It depends on why the material isn't there. If the document has been publicly disseminated but just doesn't happen to be part of your local library's collection, you can most probably locate it through the regional depository. Ask your local documents librarian for assistance. If the document is unclassified but has not routinely been distributed within the depository system, you have these choices:

- Mail-order it from the Office of the Superintendent of Documents, U.S. Government Printing Office. Ask your local government documents librarian for a mail-order form.
- Buy it directly from the issuing federal agency.
- Contact your congressional representative and ask him or her to send the document to you.
- Locate the document using the Freedom of Information Act (see Chapter 3).

Regardless of where you locate the document, the first step is to identify it. Knowing its name and publication information about it is essential to finding it. But with literally millions of publications in existence, the task seems impossible. Fortunately, both the federal government and private enterprise recognize the problem and publish a variety of indexes and guides. They are your keys to Washington on file.

HOW TO FIND DOCUMENTS

Indexes to government documents may look intimidating, but they are easy to use if you know two things: what kinds of documents the particular index covers and what system it uses. Here is an explanation of the nine indexes most important to journalistic information gatherers with specific examples of their use. When you become familiar with these guides, the vast world of federal documents will be open to you.

Monthly Catalog of United States Government Publications

First issued in 1895, later revamped in 1976, and just recently made available via computer (see Chapter 6), the *Monthly Catalog* is the government's official index to all its publications. The only index in

Figure 5.1. *Federal Depository Library Program*

The Federal Depository Library Program provides government publications to designated libraries throughout the United States. The regional depository libraries listed below receive and retain at least one copy of nearly every federal government publication, either in printed or microfilm form, for use by the general public. These libraries provide reference services and interlibrary loans; however, they are *not* sales outlets. You may wish to ask your local library to contact a regional depository to help you locate specific publications, or you may contact the regional depository yourself. Remember that there are more than 1,300 other, smaller depository libraries.

Arkansas State Library
One Capitol Mall
Little Rock, AR 72201
(501) 371–2326

Auburn Univ. at Montgomery Library
Documents Department
Montgomery, AL 36193
(205) 279–9110, ext. 253

Univ. of Alabama Library
Documents Dept.—Box S
University, AL 35486
(205) 348–7369

Dept. of Library, Archives and Public Records
Third Floor—State Cap.
1700 West Washington
Phoenix, AZ 85007
(602) 255–4121

University of Arizona Lib.
Government Documents Dept.
Tucson, AZ 85721
(602) 626–5233

California State Library
Govt. Publications Section
P.O. Box 2037
Sacramento, CA 95809
(916) 322–4572

Univ. of Colorado Lib.
Government Pub. Division
Campus Box 184
Boulder, CO 80309
(303) 492–8834

Denver Public Library
Govt. Pub. Department
1357 Broadway
Denver, CO 80203
(303) 571–2131

Connecticut State Library
Government Documents Unit
231 Capitol Avenue
Hartford, CT 06106
(203) 566–4971

Univ. of Florida Libraries
Library West
Documents Department
Gainesville, FL 32611
(904) 392–0367

Univ. of Georgia Libraries
Government Reference Dept.
Athens, GA 30602
(404) 542–8951

Univ. of Hawaii Library
Govt. Documents Collection
2550 The Mall
Honolulu, HI 96822
(808) 948–8230

Univ. of Idaho Library
Documents Section
Moscow, ID 83843
(208) 885–6344

Illinois State Library
Information Services Branch
Centennial Building
Springfield, IL 62706
(217) 782–5185

Indiana State Library
Serials Documents Section
140 North Senate Avenue
Indianapolis, IN 46204
(317) 232–3686

Univ. of Iowa Libraries
Govt. Documents Department
Iowa City, IA 52242
(319) 353–3318

University of Kansas
Doc. Collect.—Spencer Lib.
Lawrence, KS 66045
(913) 864–4662

Univ. of Kentucky Libraries
Govt. Pub. Department
Lexington, KY 40506
(606) 257–3139

Louisiana State University
Middleton Library
Govt. Docs. Dept.
Baton Rouge, LA 70803
(504) 388–2570

Louisiana Technical Univ. Library
Documents Department
Ruston, LA 71272
(318) 257–4962

University of Maine
Raymond H. Fogler Library
Tri-State Regional Documents Depository
Orono, ME 04469
(207) 581–1680

University of Maryland
McKeldin Lib.—Doc. Div.
College Park, MD 20742
(301) 454–3034

Boston Public Library
Government Docs. Dept.
Boston, MA 02117
(617) 536–5400 ext. 226

Detroit Public Library
Sociology Department
5201 Woodward Avenue
Detroit, MI 48202
(313) 833–1409

Michigan State Library
P.O. Box 30007
Lansing, MI 48909
(517) 373-0640

University of Minnesota
Government Pubs. Division
409 Wilson Library
309 19th Avenue South
Minneapolis, MN 55455
(612) 373-7813

Univ. of Mississippi Lib.
Documents Department
University, MS 38677
(601) 232-5857

Univ. of Montana
Mansfield Library
Documents Division
Missoula, MT 59812
(406) 243-6700

Nebraska Library Comm.
Federal Documents
1420 P Street
Lincoln, NE 68508
(402) 471-2045
(*In cooperation with
University of Nebraska-
Lincoln*)

University of Nevada Lib.
Govt. Pub. Department
Reno, NV 89557
(702) 784-6579

Newark Public Library
5 Washington Street
Newark, NJ 07101
(201) 733-7812

**University of New
Mexico**
Zimmerman Library
Government Pub. Dept.
Albuquerque, NM 87131
(505) 277-5441

**New Mexico State
Library**
Reference Department
325 Don Gaspar Avenue
Santa Fe, NM 87501
(505) 827-2033, ext. 22

New York State Library
Empire State Plaza
Albany, NY 12230
(518) 474-5563

**University of North
Carolina at Chapel Hill**
Wilson Library
BA/SS Documents Division
Chapel Hill, NC 27515
(919) 962-1321

**University of North
Dakota**
Chester Fritz Library
Documents Department
Grand Forks, ND 58202
(701) 777-2617, ext. 27
(*In cooperation with North
Dakota State Univ.
Library*)

State Library of Ohio
Documents Department
65 South Front Street
Columbus, OH 43215
(614) 462-7051

**Oklahoma Dept. of
Libraries**
Government Documents
200 NE 18th Street
Oklahoma City, OK 73105
(405) 521-2502

Oklahoma State Univ. Lib.
Documents Department
Stillwater, OK 74078
(405) 624-6546

Portland State Univ. Lib.
Documents Department
P.O. Box 1151
Portland, OR 97207
(503) 229-3673

State Library of Penn.
Government Pub. Section
P.O. Box 1601
Harrisburg, PA 17105
(717) 787-3752

Texas State Library
Public Services Department
P.O. Box 12927—Cap. Sta.
Austin, TX 78753
(512) 471-2996

Texas Tech. Univ. Library
Govt. Documents
Department
Lubbock, TX 79409
(806) 742-2268

Utah State University
Merrill Library, U.M.C. 30
Logan, UT 84322
(801) 750-2682

University of Virginia
Alderman Lib.—Public Doc.
Charlottesville, VA 22901
(804) 924-3133

Washington State Library
Documents Section
Olympia, WA 98504
(206) 753-4027

West Virginia Univ. Lib.
Documents Department
Morgantown, WV 26506
(304) 293-3640

**Milwaukee Public
Library**
814 West Wisconsin
Avenue
Milwaukee, WI 53233
(414) 278-3000

**St. Hist. Lib. of
Wisconsin**
Government Pub. Section
816 State Street
Madison, WI 53706
(608) 262-4347

Wyoming State Library
Supreme Ct. & Library Bldg.
Cheyenne, WY 82002
(307) 777-6344

existence that attempts (although unsuccessfully) to be inclusive, it covers documents issued by all three branches of government.

Published monthly, the catalog cumulates annually. Unlike some other indexes, the annual cumulations are not later arranged in three- or five- or 10-year indexes. This practice makes looking for documents somewhat tedious unless you know the year of publication. If, for example, you are looking for a Department of Interior report on the Navaho Indians, but you have no idea whether it was published last year or as long as 10 years ago, you may have to look through 10 individual indexes to locate it.

This shortcoming in the indexing system has led commercial publishers to create additional guides that simplify the use of the *Monthly Catalog* and help overcome its inadequacies. The guides below are obviously dated but still useful for locating documents of historical interest. More recent editions will undoubtedly be published.

- *Cumulative Subject Index to the Monthly Catalog of U.S. Government Publications, 1895–1899*

- *Cumulative Subject Index to the Monthly Catalog of U.S. Government Publications, 1900–1971*

- *Cumulative Personal Author Index to the Monthly Catalog of U.S. Government Publications, 1941–1975*

Finding a document in the *Monthly Catalog* is a two-step process. First, look in one of seven indexes organized either alphabetically or numerically according to author, keyword, title, subject, report number, stock number or classification number. Which index you use depends on what information you already have. Commonly, an inquiring journalist uses the subject index, looking up a general heading to find a list of specific documents dealing with that subject. In the index, each document is named and identified by a number, but no other information is included. You scribble down the number. That's the end of step one.

Step two: Use the number to locate a description of the document in the catalog itself. The *Monthly Catalog*s are organized numerically and arranged sequentially according to the numbers given each document in the indexes. Go to the shelf and find the volume that includes the number you are looking for. The span of numbers included is listed on the spine of each volume. Remembering that this portion of the catalog is organized numerically, not alphabetically, find the number you scribbled down. There you will find a listing that includes author, title, issuing agency and the information you need to either locate the document in the depository library or order it from the government.

Figure 5.2 details all the information you will find in a *Monthly Catalog* entry.

Now let's search. Your state legislature is hotly debating the licensing of midwives. Your newspaper has assigned you to write a story on the pros and cons of having midwives deliver babies. Being a savvy researcher, you know the federal government must have published something on this subject. You go to a recent *Monthly Catalog* subject index volume and look under the heading *midwives*. You find what you're looking for nearby under *Midwifery—United States—Statistics*. You write down the accompanying number. (See Figure 5.3.) Going to the numerically sequenced catalog volume, you find the document. Reading the entry, you note the large dot signifying that the document has been distributed to depository libraries. (See Figure 5.4.) You may continue to search through indexes for other months or use the annual index.

Congressional Information Service Index

Compiled by a private firm with a reputation for excellence, *CIS/Index* indexes and abstracts most documents generated by Congress, including House and Senate reports, special publications, executive reports and committee hearings. The index is issued monthly, cumulates first quarterly, then yearly, then every four or five years. These long-term cumulative volumes make the index less tedious to use than the *Monthly Catalog*. The outstanding feature of the CIS system is that every document listed in the index is available on microfiche from CIS. Libraries routinely order certain documents. All others are available on request.

CIS/Index is organized somewhat like the *Monthly Catalog* with an alphabetically arranged index volume that gives you a reference to a listing in a numerically arranged abstracts volume. The CIS indexing system, however, is much broader in scope. The subject and name index, for example, allows you to look for the document according to the subject of the document or hearings, the subject discussed by individual witnesses, names of authors, names of subcommittees and official and popular names of laws and bills. There are additional indexes for titles of publications, bills, reports, documents and hearings, and print numbers.

Let's search. You're a magazine writer working on a story about the problems working parents have in finding decent, affordable day care for their children. One of the avenues you want to pursue is the federal government's response to this pressing problem. Perhaps some

Figure 5.2. *Sample* Monthly Catalog *entry*

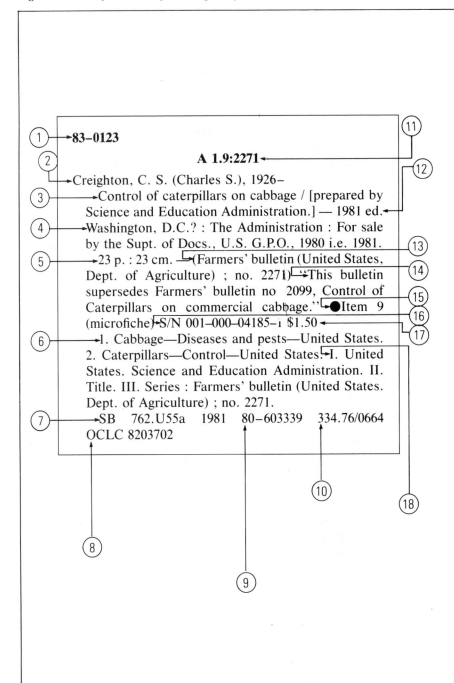

1. MONTHLY CATALOG ENTRY NO.—The entry number is assigned after the records are arranged alphanumerically by the Superintendent of Documents classification number. The first two digits establish the year; the last four digits locate the record in the Catalog.

2. MAIN ENTRY—A main entry may be a personal author, a corporate author, a conference, uniform title, or the document title, as established by the Anglo-American Cataloging Rules.

3. TITLE PHRASE/STATEMENT OF RESPONSIBILITY—Title phrase and author statement are recorded from the title page or its substitutes. Material in bracket is supplied from other prominent sources.

4. IMPRINT—The imprint contains place of publication, issuing agency, and date of issue. Includes name of distributor if different from issuing agency.

5. COLLATION—Collation notes pages, illustrations, and size.

6. SUBJECT, HEADINGS (Arabic numerals)—Headings are selected from the Library of Congress subject headings. Some Natl. Agricultural Library and Natl. Library of Medicine subjects may be used. Natl. Libr. of Med. subjects will be indicated by an asterisk (*). Natl. Agri. Lib. subjects will be indicated by a dagger (†).

7. LIBRARY OF CONGRESS CLASS NO.—This is given when it is available from the Library of Congress.

8. OCLC NO.—This is the number assigned by the OCLC to identify this record in the database.

9. LIBRARY OF CONGRESS CARD NO.—Included when it is available from the Library of Congress.

10. DEWEY CLASS NO.—Dewey class is given when it is available from the Library of Congress.

11. SUPT. OF DOCS. CLASS NO.—This is the number assigned by the GPO Library to identify the document cataloged.

12. EDITION—The edition is recorded from information in the document.

13. SERIES STATEMENT—This identifies the series title and number.

14. NOTES—Notes include additional bibliographic information about the publication, including funding information for technical reports.

15. ITEM NO.—This document was distributed to depository libraries requesting this item number. Microfiche indicates the document was distributed as such.

16. STOCK NO.—This is a Government Printing Office sales stock number. It is used only in ordering from the Superintendent of Documents.

17. PRICE—GPO sales price.

18. ADDED ENTRIES (Roman numerals)—When the Government publisher is not a main entry, it is included with added entries.

Figure 5.3. *Excerpt from* Monthly Catalog *index*

Midwifery U.S. Statistics

Midwives — United States — Statistics.
Midwife and out-of-hospital deliveries, United States, 1978–79 : an analysis of the demographic characteristics and pregnancy history of mothers and birth weight of babies delivered in a non-hospital setting or by a midwife in a hospital., 84-12893

Migrant agricultural laborers — Housing — United States.
Conducting MSPA housing inspections., 84-17578
Conducting MSPA housing inspections : resource book /, 84-17579

Migrant agricultural laborers — United States.
Farm labor wage issues /, 84-2331

Migrant labor — United States.
Conducting MSPA housing inspection : test book /, 84-19647
Conducting MSPA housing inspections : task book /, 84-19646

Migration, Internal — United States.
Analysis of migration characteristics of children served under the migrant education program : report to the Congress /, 84-5248

Migration, Internal — United States — Statistics.
1980 census of population., 84-14210

Migration, Internal — United States — Statistics — Periodicals.
Geographical mobility., 84-11936

Mildew.
Stop mildew on buildings!, 84-16754

Military architecture — United States.
Architecture : earth-sheltered buildings., 84-20874

Military art and science — Bibliography — Periodicals.
Military review., 84-985

Military art and science — Handbooks, manuals, etc.
Soldier's manual and trainer's guide, MOS 15J : operations/fire direction specialist, skill level 2/3/4., 84-20636

Military art and science — History — 19th century — Congresses.
Proceedings of the 1982 International Military History Symposium : "The impact of unsuccessful military campaigns on military institutions, 1860–1980" /, 84-18811

Military art and science — History — 20th century — Congresses.
Proceedings of the 1982 International Military History Symposium : "The impact of unsuccessful military campaigns on military institutions, 1860–1980" /, 84-18811

Figure 5.4. *Example of* Monthly Catalog *entry*

Government Publications — June 1984

NATIONAL CENTER FOR HEALTH STATISTICS
Health and Human Services Dept.
Washington, DC 20202

84-12893
  HE 20.6209:21/40
Taffel, Selma.
 Midwife and out-of-hospital deliveries, United States, 1978–79 : an analysis of the demographic characteristics and pregnancy history of mothers and birth weight of babies delivered in a non-hospital setting or by a midwife in a hospital. — Hyattsville, Md. : U.S. Dept. of Health and Human Services, Public Health Service, National Center for Health Statistics : Washington, D.C. : For sale by the Supt. of Docs., U.S. G.P.O., 1984.
 iv, 43 p. : ill. ; 28 cm. — (Vital and health statistics. Series 21, Data from the national vital statistics system ; no. 40) (DHHS publication ; no. (PHS) 84-1918) "February 1984." Includes bib-liographical references. ●Item 500-E S/N 017-022-00836-0 @ GPO ISBN 0-8406-0285-5 : $2.00
 1. Childbirth — United States — Statistics. 2. Midwives — United States — Statistics. 3. Birth weight — United States — Statistics. 4. Hospitals, Gynecologic and obstetric — United States — Statistics. 5. United States — Statistics, Medical. 6. United States — Statistics, Vital. I. National Center for Health Statistics (U.S.). II. Title. III. Series. IV. Series. V. Series: DHHS publication ; no. (PHS) 84-1918. [DNLM 1. Birth weight — United States — Statistics. 2. Delivery — United States — Statistics. 3. Midwifery — United States — Statistics. 4. Nurse midwives — United States — Statistics. 5. Pregnancy — United States — Statistics. W2 A N148vu no.40] HA211.A3 no. 40 83-600276 [RG530.3.U5] 312/.1/73 s [362.1/982 ¢2 19] OCLC 09894520

---

congressional group held hearings or issued a report, you think. You go to a recent index volume of *CIS/Index* and look up the subject *Day care,* where you find an intriguing listing: *Working parents problems and needs.* (See Figure 5.5.) The number after the listing tells you where to go in the abstracts volume. The first number directs you to volume *3* of the accompanying abstracts. The remaining numbers constitute the CIS code for the document itself and are used to list the document in the abstracts volume. In that numerically organized volume, you quickly find what you're looking for. (See Figure 5.6.) Because

Figure 5.5. Index page excerpt from CIS/ Index

Davies, Richard W.

Davies, Richard W.
Ark wilderness areas estab and expansion, **1** S311-3.1

Davis, Billy G.
Fla food stamp program audit rpt, **1** S161-4

Davis, Calif.
World hunger situation, US intl and domestic educ programs, **3** H961-9

Davis, Carolyne K.
Infant mortality causes and incidence; maternal and child health services review, **1** H361-7.3

Davis County Savings Bank, Iowa
Fed crop insurance program ops and mgmt, **1** S161-3.3

Davis, Devra L.
Pesticide regulation and pesticide food residue tolerance rules revision, **2** H361-17.6

Davis, Donald W.
Oil and gas dev in Gulf of Mexico, environmental and socioeconomic effects, **1** H561-1.3

Davison, Robert P.
Natl parks dev projects threatening fish and wildlife habitats, Fed funding prohibition, **3** S321-5.2

Dawkins, Maurice A.
Youth employment and educ incentive program estab, **3** H341-19.8
Youth summer employment minimum wage estab, **1** S541-3.3

Dawn
Mich children and families, unemployment impact and assistance programs, **3** H961-4.1

Dawn Enterprises, Inc.
Ethanol fuels production and use, tax incentives, **2** H781-8.2

Dawsey, John F.
SBA loans to small businesses in communications industry, regulations revision, **2** H721-5.4

Dawson, Robert K.
Port and inland waterway user fees estab, **3** S361-17.2

Day care programs
Child day care programs, parental needs and options, **3** H961-5, **3** H961-8
Child food assistance programs, impact on home day care services; "Condition of Child Care in the U.S. in 1984: The New Reality vs. the Old Status", **2** H341-5.3
Day care in public schools grant program, FY85-FY87 authorization, **1** H341-3
Low-income women's employment and employability problems, **3** J841-4
Pa educ programs review and Fed funding needs, **1** H341-1.1
School and day care meal programs revision, **1** S161-2
Women's Bur programs oversight, **2** H401-10.3
Working parents problems and needs, **3** H961-6

Figure 5.6. *Excerpt from* CIS/Index *abstracts volume*

H961-5 CHILD CARE: BEGINNING A NATIONAL INITIATIVE.
Apr. 4, 1984. 98-2.
iv + 109 p. $4.00
S/N 052-070-05966-4.
CIS/MF/4
•Item 1009-B-10;
1009-C-10.
Y4.C43/2:C43/11.
MC 85-5644.
LC 84-604081.

Hearing before the Select Committee on Children, Youth, and Families to examine the extent and nature of child day care needs, and options regarding public and private sector response.

Includes submitted statements and an article (p. 98–109).

H961-5.1: Apr. 4, 1984. p. 4–51. *Witnesses:* **KAMERMAN, Sheila B.,** prof. Columbia Univ School of Social Work; fellow, Center for Advanced Study in the Behavioral Sciences.
ZIGLER, Edward F., head, psychology section, Yale Child Study Center; dir, Bush Center in Child Dev and Social Policy, Yale Univ.
TOMPKINS, Rachel, dir, Children's Def Fund.
Statements and Discussion: Characterization of child care services used by working mothers (related articles, p. 14–23); perspectives on public and private sector child care assistance efforts; concerns about lack of affordable child care, focusing on problems of low-income families.

H961-6 WORKING FAMILIES: ISSUES FOR THE 80's
Apr. 13, 1984. 98-2.
iv + 97 p. $3.75
S/N 052-070-05971-1.
CIS/MF/4
•Item 1009-B-10;
1009-C-10.
Y4.C43/2:F21/4.
LC 84-604098.

Hearing in Hamden, Conn., before the Select Committee on Children, Youth, and Families to examine problems of working parents, including child care needs.

Includes submitted statements, correspondence, and articles (p. 81–97).

H961-6.1: Apr. 13, 1984. p. 5–8. *Witnesses:* **WOLFARTH, Ms. LAGASSE, Gil CRUZ, Amy COOPER, Theresa ZAMPI, Corey,** all four participants, Peer Outreach program.
Statements and Discussion: Explanation of Peer Outreach program addressing family relationship problems.

H961-6.2: Apr. 13, 1984. p. 9–24
Witnesses: **MILSTEIN, Merilee,** commr. Conn Permanent Commission on the Status of Women.
BUCKNELL, Susan, exec dir.
Statements and Discussion: Review of needs of working parents; perspectives on various child care initiatives.

CIS has all the documents it indexes on microfiche, you know you'll be able to locate this one either immediately in the library or through the CIS system.

American Statistics Index

ASI is the most comprehensive guide to statistical material from the federal government (including that amazing compendium, the census). Published by CIS, it identifies, indexes and abstracts statistical publications from the executive and legislative branches and from other federal entities. These include 800 periodicals, some of which are available at depository libraries; others can be ordered through ASI Microfiche Library or CIS Periodicals on Microfiche. *ASI* is issued monthly and cumulates both quarterly and annually. It is also accessible via computer. (See Chapter 6.)

Like *CIS/Index* and the *Monthly Catalog*, *ASI* has an alphabetically arranged index volume where the researcher can look up a document by its subject, name, category or title. A report number index is numerically organized. The subject index is probably the handiest for most people. The index listing identifies the document by name and gives it a number. That number guides you to an entry in the numerically organized abstracts volume, where you can learn more about the document and get the information you need to find it in the library's hardcover or microfiche collections or to order it from the CIS or *ASI* services.

Ready for a search? Your state is about to pass stricter drunken driving laws, and the news director at your TV station has asked you to put together a story on the dimensions of the drinking and driving problem. You are particularly interested in the correlation between traffic deaths and alcohol and figure that some government agency must have conducted or commissioned a study. Because it's statistics you want, you head for *ASI*.

In the subject and name index, you look up *Drunk drivers* and are directed to *Driving while intoxicated*. The first listing, an article about fatal accidents and the presence of alcohol (or drugs) in the blood, looks promising. (See Figure 5.7.) The number following the title directs you to an entry in the numerically organized abstracts volume. (See Figure 5.8.) You read the brief description and decide the article is of interest. The general listing tells you which publication contains the article, its date and volume number, and the information you need to locate it in the library or order it.

Figure 5.7. *Excerpt from* ASI *index*

Index by Subjects and Names

Disasters
see also Storms
see also Volcanoes

Discrimination
see Discrimination in
employment
see Sex discrimination

Discrimination in employment
Women's pay equity based on
comparable worth, and labor
force participation and earnings differentials by selected
characteristics, 1984 conf papers, 11048-181

Diseases and disorders
Developing countries disaster
preparedness and summary
sociodemographic, political,
and economic data, country
rpt series, 9916-2
NIH publications, 1984, annual
listing, 4434-2
see also Alcohol abuse and
treatment
see also Blood pressure
see also Cardiovascular
diseases
see also Circulatory diseases
see also Diabetes
see also Digestive diseases
see also Drug abuse and
treatment
see also Eye diseases and
defects
see also Food and waterborne
diseases
see also Hearing and hearing
disorders
see also Mental health and
illness
see also Mental retardation
see also Mobility limitations
see also Musculoskeletal
diseases

**Domestic and International
Business Administration**
see Bureau of Industrial
Economics
see International Trade
Administration

Domestic relations
see Child abuse and neglect
see Families and households
see Marriage and divorce

Domestic violence
see also Child abuse and
neglect

Domestics
see Household workers

Drinking water
see Water supply and use

Drivers licenses
see Licenses and permits

Driving while intoxicated
Accidents (fatal), drug and alcohol presence in blood of
drivers killed for men aged
15–34, 1982–83, article, 4042-
3.503
Accidents, injuries, and
deaths, by circumstances and
characteristics of persons and
vehicles involved, 1983, annual rpt, 7764-13

Drought
Developing countries disaster
preparedness and summary
sociodemographic, political,
and economic data, country
rpt series, 9916-2

Drug abuse and treatment
Abuse of drugs, indicators in
selected metro areas, research
results, data collection, and
policy issues, June 1984 conf,
semiannual rpt, 4492-5

Figure 5.8. *Excerpt from* ASI *abstracts*

4042
PUBLIC HEALTH SERVICE:
GENERAL
                Current Periodicals

4042-3 PUBLIC HEALTH
    REPORTS
Bimonthly. Approx.
110 p. PHS 84-50193.
•Item 497. GPO: $21.00
per yr; single copy
$5.00. ASI/MF/4
S/N 017-020-80001-0.
·HE20.30:(v.nos.&nos.)
MC 85-957.
                LC 75-642678.

ARTICLES:

JANUARY/FEBRUARY 1985
Vol. 100, No. 1

4042-3.502: Cardiovascular Fit-
ness Program: Factors Asso-
ciated with Participation and
Adherence
By Jerrold Mirotznik et al. (p.
13–18). Report on sociodemographic and health characteristics of persons who participated
and did not participate in fitness
programs after being evaluated
for risk of coronary heart
disease.

Based on a 1979 study of 215
clients of the 92nd Street Young
Men's-Young Women's Hebrew
Assn Coronary Detection and
Intervention Center in NYC. Includes 5 tables showing regression results.

4042-3.503: Drugs in Fatally In-
jured Young Male Drivers
By Allan F. Williams (p. 19–25).
Report on presence of alcohol,

marijuana, and other drugs in the
blood of male drivers killed in
traffic accidents. Based on a
1982–83 study of 440 California
males, aged 15–34, who died
within 2 hours of an accident
for which they were judged
responsible.

Includes 6 tables showing
drivers, by age, vehicle type,
number and type of drugs
detected, and blood alcohol
concentration.

4042-3.504: Estimates of Preg-
nancies and Pregnancy Rates
for the U.S., 1976–81
By Stephanie J. Ventura et al.
(p. 31–34). Report on number,
rate, and outcome of pregnan-
cies, by age and race of mother,
selected years 1976–81. Data are
from NCHS sources. Includes 2
charts and 2 tables.

4042-3.505: Age Variation in
Use of a Contraceptive Service
by Adolescents
By Susan Gustavus Philliber et
al. (p. 34–40). Report on con-
traceptives use, sociodemographic characteristics, and sexual and pregnancy history of
women aged 21 and under visiting an adolescent health service in the Washington Heights
area of NYC, 1977–82. Data are
from records of 4,318 patients.

Includes 6 tables showing patients by selected characteristics, and regression results relating characteristics to reason
for 1st clinic visit, contracep-
tives use, and whether pregnant
at 2nd or later visit.

Index to United States Government Periodicals

Although this commercially published reference tool indexes fewer than 200 of the government's thousands of periodicals, it is nonetheless a helpful guide because of its unusual scope. The choice of periodicals is eclectic, ranging from highly technical journals like *Cancer Treatment Reports* to non-technical magazines for specialized audiences like *Black News Digest*. The publications are selected, says the publisher, because they contain substantive articles of lasting research or reference value. Often, this is just the kind of material a journalist needs for background.

All the publications indexed are listed on the inside cover of each volume, and those available in depository libraries are identified with large dots. Periodicals not in a library's collection may be available from the issuing department or agency. In any case, articles from all the indexed periodicals are available through Microfilming Corporation of America. Ordering information appears in the beginning pages of each volume.

Using this index is a simple, one-step process because it has no accompanying abstracts volume. The alphabetically arranged author and subject index is issued in quarterly volumes and annual cumulations. The researcher need only look up the author or subject to find a full citation for the article.

Let's search. You're a freelancer doing work for a magazine directed to retirement-age readers. You're pursuing a story on exercise and aging. Does regular exercise really add to the quality of life? You know that the federal government, with its specialized bureaus and vast resources, must have studied this issue. You try a recent volume of the *Index to United States Government Periodicals*. Under the subject heading *Aging,* you find a listing for an article entitled *Exercise, vitality and aging* in the April–May 1984 issue of *Aging* magazine. A quick check with the inside cover tells you that *Aging* is distributed to depository libraries. You're set.

Government Reports, Announcement and Index

In 1970, the National Technical Information Service (NTIS) was established to simplify and improve public access to scientific and technical reports produced by federal agencies and their contractors. An agency within the Department of Commerce, NTIS is the central source for reports about U.S. government-sponsored research in both the physical and social sciences. NTIS currently has more than 1.2 million titles, all of which are available for sale. Unlike many other government documents, they are not distributed for free to depository libraries because NTIS is obligated by law to recover its costs from users. The index to NTIS' considerable holdings is *GRA&I*.

Issued semi-monthly, *GRA&I* consists of both index and abstract volumes. The index itself comes in six sections: two subject/keyword volumes, two contract/grant number volumes, a personal author index and a corporate author index. Using *GRA&I* involves the familiar two-step index-to-abstracts process. But in the *GRA&I*, the item listed in the index is followed by not one, but three sets of numbers. The first numbers are needed if you intend to order the document from NTIS. The middle set of numbers guides you to the issue number and abstract number of the abstracts volume. The final set is a price code.

Let's search. You're a television reporter covering the aftermath of an important environmental story. Last week you reported on a local herbicide spill that involved dioxin contamination. The story unfolded quickly and was necessarily treated superficially. Now you have time to give your viewers the in-depth information they need to understand the problem. You want to find out what scientific studies have shown about the dangers of dioxins. Because so many studies are funded to some degree by the government, you go to *GRA&I* to guide you to research accumulated by NTIS.

In the keyword index volume, you find multiple listings under *Dioxins*. The title "Dioxin: A Cause for Concern" looks promising. You note the middle set of numbers (see Figure 5.9), which guides you to the correct abstracts volume and then quickly locate the item in the abstracts volume (see Figure 5.10). Perhaps you have time to send for the study. Perhaps you want to pick up the phone and interview the authors at the University of Wisconsin.

CIS United States Serial Set Index

The *Serial Set* is an excellent historical source for journalists interested in tracing the evolution of congressional action. A grab bag of documents from the House, Senate and various executive branch agencies, it contains more than 325,000 individual titles spanning 1789–1969. (After 1969, *CIS/Index* or the *Monthly Catalog* will be your guide.) The congressional reports, manuals and directories, as well as annual reports from federal executive agencies, are bound into more than 14,000 separate serial set volumes. The key that unlocks these volumes is the *CIS U.S. Serial Set Index*.

This index has 12 parts, each covering a specific span of years (as few as 10 or as many as 60). Each part contains three volumes: an

Figure 5.9. *Excerpt from* GRA&I *keyword index*

DIOXINS

Air Force Health Study (Project RANCH HAND II). An Epidemiologic Investigation of Health Effects in Air Force Personnel Following Exposure to Herbicides. Baseline Morbidity Study Results.
AD-A138 340/5   11-*430,439*
PC **A16**/MF **A01**

Air Force Engineering and Services Laboratory Herbicide Orange Monitoring Program.
AD-A143 260/8   22-*456,761*
PC **A04**/MF **A01**

Mutagenicity of 2,3,7,8-Tetrachlorodibenzo-p-Dioxin and Perfluoro-n-Decanoic Acid in L5178Y Mouse-Lymphoma Cells.
AD-A145 260/6
25-*464,173*   Not available NTIS

Cytosol Receptor for 2,3,7,8-Tetrachlorodibenzo-P-Dioxin: Mediator of Two Distinctive Pleiotropic Responses.
AD-P001 976/0   04-*410,385*
PC **A02**/MF **A01**

Starvation-Like Syndrome and 2,3,7,8-Tetrachlorodibenzo-P-Dioxin: New Ideas on the Mode of Action at the Whole Animal Level.
AD-P001 977/8   04-*410,386*
PC **A02**/MF **A01**

Receptors for 2,3,7,8-Tetrachlorodibenzo-P-Dioxin: Their Inter- and Intra-Species Distribution and Relationship to the Toxicity of this Compound.
AD-P001 978/6   04-*410,387*
PC **A02**/MF **A01**

Dioxin: A Cause for Concern.
PB84-104199   01-*400,453*
PC **A02**/MF **A01**

Determination of Dioxin Levels in Carbon Reactivation Process Effluent Streams.
PB84-137710   06-*418,044*
PC **A07**/MF **A01**

Destruction of PCB-Contaminated Soils with a High-Temperature Fluid-Wall (HTFW) Reactor.
PB84-168796   11-*431,443*
PC **A02**/MF **A01**

Review of Literature on Herbicides, Including Phenoxy Herbicides and Associated Dioxins. Volume 3. Analysis of Recent Literature on Health Effects.
PB84-207703   18-*447,079*
PC **A16**/MF **A01**

Review of Literature on Herbicides, Including Phenoxy Herbicides and Associated Dioxins. Volume 4. Annotated Bibliography of Recent Literature on Health Effects.
PB84-207711   18-*447,080*
PC **A05**/MF **A01**

Containment of Dioxin Emissions from Refuse Fired Thermal Processing Units: Prospects and Technical Issues.
PB84-217090   21-*455,529*
PC **A06**/MF **A01**

DIPHENYL COMPOUNDS

Amine Terminated Bioaspartimides, Process for Preparation Thereof, and Polymers Thereof.
PAT-APPL-6-561 702
11-*430,655*   PC **A02**/MF **A01**

Figure 5.10. Excerpt from GRA&I *abstracts*

Field 6—BIOLOGICAL AND MEDICAL SCIENCES
Group 6E—Clinical Medicine

400,452

PB84-102532 PC **A02**/MF **A01**
Health Effects Research Lab., Research Triangle Park, NC.
Outbreak of Waterborne Giardiasis Associated with Heavy Water Runoff Due to Warm Weather and Volcanic Ashfall.
Journal article,
B. G. Weniger, M. J. Blaser, J. Gedrose, E. C. Lippy, and D. D. Juranek. 1983, 7p EPA-600/J-83-056
Pub. in American Jnl. of Public Health, v73 n8 p868–872 1983. Prepared in cooperation with Oregon Dept. of Human Resources, Portland; Colorado Univ., Denver. School of Medicine; Veterans Administration Hospital, Denver, CO. and Montana State Dept. of Health and Environmental Sciences, Helena.

From mid-June through early August 1980, an outbreak of gastrointestinal illness in Red Lodge, Montana affected approximately 780 persons, as estimated from attack rates of 33 percent and 15 percent in urban and rural residents, respectively. Giardia lamblia was identified in stool specimens from 51 percent of 47 persons with a history of untreated gastrointestinal illness and in 13 percent of 24 specimens from asymptomatic persons. The epidemic curve was bimodal with peaks in mid-June and mid-July. Each peak occurred about three weeks after an episode of very heavy water runoff resulting from warm sunny weather and snow darkened by ashfall from the Mt. St. Helens volcanic eruption of May 18, 1980. Unfiltered and inadequately chlorinated surface water was supplied by the city water system. Which was implicated as the vehicle of transmission in the outbreak. Water systems providing unfiltered surface water are more likely to become contaminated during periods of heavy water runoff.

400,453

PB84-104199 PC **A02**/MF **A01**
Wisconsin Univ.-Madison, Sea Grant Inst.
Dioxin: A Cause for Concern,
T. Stolzenburg, and J. Sullivan. c1983, 25p WIS-SG-83-141, NOAA-83101101
Grant NA80AA-D-00066

There are conflicting reports in the public media regarding the danger to people posed by dioxins, particularly 2,3,7,8-TCDD — which is usually identified as 'the most toxic chemical ever made.' The UW Sea Grant Institute has produced this booklet to help answer some of the most common questions about dioxins — what they are, why they are a problem, whether they pose a danger to the public health, and what is being done about the problem — in the belief that an informed approach to the dioxin problem is the best way to find the proper solution for it. (Copyright(c) 1983 Board of Regents University of Wisconsin System Sea Grant Institute).

A–K subject index, an L–Z subject index and a numerical list of documents. The items listed in the index are followed by a code that tells you how to locate the document in one of the serial set volumes.

Now for the search. Suppose you're a newspaper reporter doing a major series on how the government has responded to the needs of the mentally ill. For historical context, you want to look at records of previous congressional action. You go to the *CIS U.S. Serial Set Index*. In the subject index of Part XII (1959–69) under *Mental Health,* you find an item titled "Protecting constitutional rights of mentally ill." (See Figure 5.11.) Reading the code below, you note that the document is a Senate report from the second session of the 88th Congress and can be found in serial volume number 12616–1. (See inset, Figure 5.11.) In the appropriate serial set volume, you find the report, a 64-page document full of just the kind of information you're looking for. (See Figure 5.12.)

Congressional Record Index

The *Congressional Record (CR)*, issued daily when Congress is in session, is not, as many think, a verbatim account of what is said on the floor of the House and Senate. In fact, a recent study found that 70 percent of what is in *CR* was never uttered in Congress. It is, instead, reprints of articles, editorials, book reviews, tributes and assorted trivia inserted into the *Record* by members of Congress. The 30 percent that does represent congressional speeches, debate and discussion may or may not be published verbatim. By law, members of Congress are allowed to edit their remarks—presumably for grammar and construction, not substance—before they reach *CR*.

The *CR* has four sections: the proceedings of the House, proceedings of the Senate, extensions of remarks and a daily digest including highlights of the legislative day, and summaries of each chamber's action and a schedule for the next day. Each of the four sections— identified by the letters *H*(ouse proceedings), *S*(enate), *E*(xtensions) and *D*(igest)—is paged continuously and separately during each session. This daily record of Congress has a fortnightly index, the *Congressional Record Index,* which is just beginning to appear on microfiche. The hardbound edition of *CR,* normally two to three sessions behind in publication, is accompanied by a master index organized differently from the fortnightly edition.

The fortnightly index comes in two parts: a subject/individual index to the proceedings and debates, and a history of bills and resolutions index arranged by chamber and according to bill or resolution number.

Figure 5.11. *Excerpt from subject index of the* CIS U.S. Serial Set Index

Mental Health

Mental retardation facilities and community health centers
construction act of 1963
S.rp. 180 (88-1) 12533
Mental retardation facilities and community mental health centers
construction act amendments of 1965
H.rp. 678 (89-1) 12665-5
Mental retardation facilities and community mental health centers
construction act of 1963
H.rp. 694 (88-1) 12543; H.rp. 862 (88-1) 12544
Printing additional copies of Judiciary Committee hearings on
Constitutional rights of mentally ill and Wiretapping and
eavesdropping legislation
H.rp. 1915 (87-2) 12431
Protect constitutional rights of persons who are mentally ill
H.rp. 1833 (88-2) 12619-4
Protecting constitutional rights of mentally ill
S.rp. 925 (88-2) 12616-1
Providing care and treatment for returning United States nationals
who became mentally ill in foreign country
S.rp. 1143 (86-2) 12233
Providing for care and treatment of returning nationals of U.S. who
became mentally ill in foreign country
H.rp. 1624 (86-2) 12245
Supplemental appropriations for activities of Health, Education, and
Welfare Dept., related to mental retardation
H.rp. 1041 (88-1) 12545
Supplemental appropriations for Health, Education, and Welfare
Department's activities related to mental retardation
S.rp. 814 (88-1) 12536
Voluntary admission of mental patients to District Training School
H.rp. 23 (89-1) 12665-1
Voluntary admission of patients to D.C. institution for mentally
retarded
H.rp. 118 (90-1) 12753-1
Voluntary admission of patients to District institution providing care,
etc., of mentally retarded persons
H.rp. 165 (91-1) 12837-1

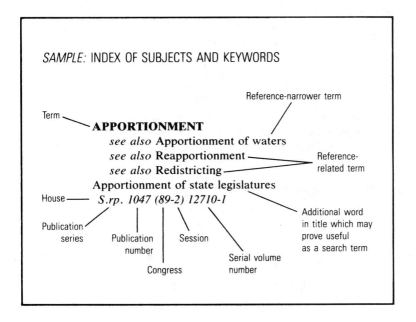

SAMPLE: INDEX OF SUBJECTS AND KEYWORDS

Reference-narrower term

Term

APPORTIONMENT
    see also Apportionment of waters
    see also Reapportionment
    see also Redistricting
    Apportionment of state legislatures
House —— *S.rp. 1047 (89-2) 12710-1*

Reference-related term

Publication series

Publication number

Session

Congress

Serial volume number

Additional word in title which may prove useful as a search term

Figure 5.12. Document from the U.S. *Serial Set*

Calendar No. 900

88TH CONGRESS 2d Session	SENATE	REPORT No. 925

PROTECTING THE CONSTITUTIONAL RIGHTS OF THE MENTALLY ILL

FEBRUARY 27 (legislative day, FEBRUARY 26), 1964.—Ordered to be printed

Mr. EASTLAND, from the Committee on the Judiciary, submitted the following

REPORT

[To accompany S. 935]

The Committee on the Judiciary, to which was referred the bill (S. 935) to protect the constitutional rights of certain individuals who are mentally ill, to provide for their care, treatment, and hospitalization, and for other purposes, having considered the same, reports favorably thereon, with an amendment, in the nature of a substitute, and recommends that the bill, as amended, do pass.

AMENDMENT

Strike out all after the enacting clause and insert in lieu thereof the following:

SHORT TITLE

SECTION 1. This Act may be cited as the "District of Columbia Hospitalization of the Mentally Ill Act."

DEFINITIONS

SEC. 2. As used in this Act—

(1) the term "mental illness" means any psychosis or other disease which substantially impairs the mental health of an individual;

(2) the term "mentally ill person" means any person who has a mental illness;

(3) the term "physician" means an individual licensed under the laws of the District of Columbia to practice medicine, or an individual who practices medicine in the employment of the Government of the United States or of the District of Columbia;

(4) the term "private hospital" means any nongovernmental hospital or institution, or part thereof, in the District of Columbia, equipped and qualified to provide inpatient care and treatment for any individual suffering from a physical or mental illness;

(5) the term "public hospital" means any hospital or institution, or part thereof, in the District of Columbia, owned and operated by the Government

99–010

The index listing will give you a letter—*H, S, E* or *D*—to guide you to one of *CR*'s four parts and a number indicating the page containing the item within that part.

Let's search. Suppose you're a magazine journalist researching an in-depth profile of Oregon's powerful senator Bob Packwood. You want to find out what Packwood had to say about the major issues facing Congress. Let's say you're particularly interested in his remarks concerning the Equal Rights Amendment. In the subject/individual index under *Packwood, Bob,* you find a reference to *Women: constitutional amendment on equal rights.* The code tells you to look on page 534 of *CR*'s Senate section. (See Figure 5.13.) This you do, finding Senator Packwood's remarks on introduction of the Equal Rights Amendment in the Senate. (See Figure 5.14.)

CIS Federal Register Index

The *Federal Register* (*FR*) is a key information source for those concerned with government regulatory activities and programs. Issued every working day, it consists of the rules, proposed rules, notices and announcements promulgated by all federal regulatory agencies. These documents provide public notice of actions, meetings, reports and decisions for all areas of regulatory concern. Cumulatively, the *FR* documents both the substance and reasoning behind regulatory actions. In 1984, CIS began publishing the *CIS Federal Register Index,* your guide to the *FR.*

The index, issued weekly and cumulated both quarterly and semi-annually, has four sections: a subject/name index, an index using the U.S. Code of Federal Regulations number, one using the federal agency docket number and a chronological listing by agency. Chances are good that you will be using the subject/name index. Each listing gives you all the information you need to find the document in the appropriate *FR* volume. (See Figure 5.15.) For research that requires regulations issued before 1984, the journalist must rely on the *FR*'s own self-contained index.

Weekly Compilation of Presidential Documents and Public Papers of the Presidents of the United States

For those who want comprehensive documentation of presidential actions and activities without setting foot in Washington, D.C., there are no better sources than the *Weekly Compilation* and *Public Papers.*

Figure 5.13. *Excerpt from the* Congressional Record Index

PACKWOOD, BOB

Appointments
Committee on Commerce, Science, and Transportation, S7
Committee on Finance, S8
Committee on Small Business, S8

Bills and resolutions introduced by
Employee Educational Assistance Extension Act: enact (see S. 249), S386
Merchant marine: marine safety and seamen's welfare laws (see S. 46), S90
National Transportation Commission: create (see S. 48), S90

Bills and resolutions introduced by, as cosponsor
Broadcast services: marketplace competition (see S. 55), S90
Federal Supplemental Compensation Act: extend (see S. 106), S92
Fishing industry: capital construction funds (see S. 254), S386
Mortgages: continue to issue bonds (see S. 137), S93
Women: constitutional amendment on equal rights (see S.J. Res. 10), S95

Remarks by, on
Employee Educational Assistance Act: enact (S. 249), S443
Merchant marine: improve international transportation system (S. 47), S248•
——safety and seamen's welfare laws (S. 46), S288
National Transportation Agency: consolidate ICC, FMC, and CAB functions (S. 48), S290
Women: constitutional amendment on equal rights (S.J. Res. 10), S534, S536

Texts of
S. 48, National Transportation Agency, S291
S. 249, Employee Educational Assistance Act, S444

PAKISTAN, ISLAMIC REPUBLIC OF

Reports
Visit by Kirk Douglas to Pakistan, USIA, E66

PALESTINE LIBERATION ORGANIZATION

Articles and editorials
News That's Hard To Find, E63

PALM BEACH, FLA.

Remarks in House
Free enterprise: proclamation to increase public awareness, H194

PALM BEACH GARDENS HIGH SCHOOL

Remarks in House
McConkey, Dale: commend activities to increase public awareness of free enterprise, H194

PANAMA, REPUBLIC OF

Communications from
Transfer of property: report, S38 (EC4)

PANAMA CANAL COMMISSION

Communications from
New records system: proposed, S384 (EC114), H83 (EC19)
Overobligation of funds: report, S38 (EC1)

Figure 5.14. *Senator Packwood's remarks on ERA, excerpted from the* Congressional Record

CONGRESSIONAL RECORD — SENATE

The **PRESIDING OFFICER.** Does the Senator yield back his time.

Mr. TSONGAS. Mr. President, I reserve the remainder of my time, but I do not expect to use it unless the Senator from Oregon says something outrageous and I feel compelled to respond.

Mr. PACKWOOD. Mr. President, as the Senator from Massachusetts has indicated, we start today with 55 cosponsors. In addition, I have had other Senators indicate to me that they will vote for the equal rights amendments, although they are not now cosponsors. I am sure that the Senate will be faced with this issue, if not immediately, very soon in this session because I expect the House of Representatives will pass it and send it to the Senate.

Mr. President, today I am proud to recommence in the Senate the effort to insure equal rights for women and men. Fifty-three Senators join my colleague from Massachusetts, Senator TSON-GAS, and me in reintroducing the equal rights amendment. Already, on January 3, the ERA was reintroduced in the House of Representatives with 221 cosponsors. It is a matter of time, not lack of dedication or principle, before the ERA becomes an integral part of the law of our land.

The equal rights amendment is a fundamental statement of our democratic ideals. But, unfortunately, history demonstrates that fundamental rights have often been achieved only by virtue of long-term concerted efforts. The Magna Carta and our bill of rights are themselves the result of persistent struggles to guarantee basic rights and freedom from abuse by the Government. The more recent civil rights movement and the struggle for women's suffrage are poignant reminders that equal rights have not been readily granted to blacks or women. Difficult though the course, however, the goals have been achieved: 60 years of tenacity and courage by women and men led to the adoption in 1920 of the 19th amendment granting women the right to vote. Three years later, ERA was first introduced in the Congress. From 1923, ERA was introduced every year until it passed both Houses in 1972. Then, between 1972 and 1982, 35 States, representing 72 percent of the U.S. population, ratified ERA.

The struggle has been long, but it has also endured. And it will continue with courage, diligence, and persistence until ERA is a reality. Women and men committed to equal justice will not rest until the equal rights amendment is adopted as part of the U.S. Constitution.

Figure 5.15. CIS Federal Register Index

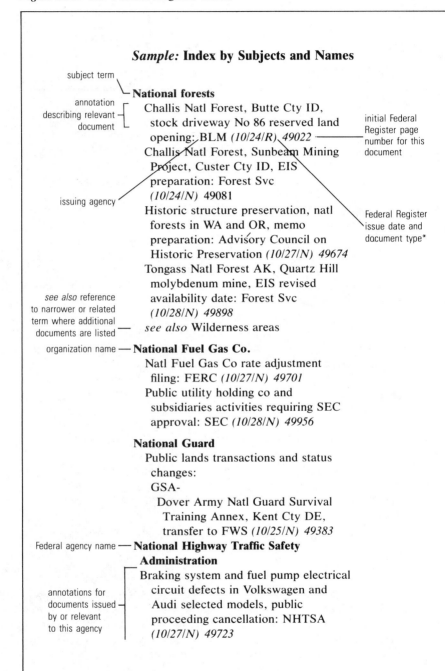

***Sample:* Index by Subjects and Names**

subject term

National forests

annotation describing relevant document

Challis Natl Forest, Butte Cty ID, stock driveway No 86 reserved land opening: BLM *(10/24/R) 49022*

initial Federal Register page number for this document

Challis Natl Forest, Sunbeam Mining Project, Custer Cty ID, EIS preparation: Forest Svc *(10/24/N) 49081*

issuing agency

Historic structure preservation, natl forests in WA and OR, memo preparation: Advisory Council on Historic Preservation *(10/27/N) 49674*

Federal Register issue date and document type*

Tongass Natl Forest AK, Quartz Hill molybdenum mine, EIS revised availability date: Forest Svc *(10/28/N) 49898*

see also reference to narrower or related term where additional documents are listed

see also Wilderness areas

organization name — **National Fuel Gas Co.**

Natl Fuel Gas Co rate adjustment filing: FERC *(10/27/N) 49701*

Public utility holding co and subsidiaries activities requiring SEC approval: SEC *(10/28/N) 49956*

National Guard

Public lands transactions and status changes:

GSA-

Dover Army Natl Guard Survival Training Annex, Kent Cty DE, transfer to FWS *(10/25/N) 49383*

Federal agency name — **National Highway Traffic Safety Administration**

annotations for documents issued by or relevant to this agency

Braking system and fuel pump electrical circuit defects in Volkswagen and Audi selected models, public proceeding cancellation: NHTSA *(10/27/N) 49723*

Motor vehicle-related fatalities through
1990, projections availability: NHTSA
(10/24/PR) 49076
Tire labeling and marking rqmts,
exemption approval of B F Goodrich
Co: NHTSA *(10/25/N) 49403*

Federal program name ── **National Toxicology Program**
Color and food additive FD&C Red
No 3 carcinogenesis bioassay, Natl
Toxicology Program peer review mtg:
FDA *(10/25/R-CX) 49233*

act name ── **National Traffic and Motor Vehicle Safety
Act**

annotation describing
document issued under ── Tire labeling and marking rqmts,
act's authority   exemption approval of B F Goodrich
Co: NHTSA *(10/25/N) 49403*

Index terms not
used by CIS Federal   **National Wildlife Refuge System**
Register index   *see* Wildlife refuges ── see references to
   Natural disasters   alternative terms
   see Floods ── where relevant
   documents are listed

State name ── **Nevada**
Airport construction public lands lease
appl by Wells NV: BLM
(10/28/N) 49934
Electric power project, White Pine
Project NV, draft EIS availability:
BLM *(10/26/N) 49556*

annotations for
documents relevant to ── Public lands transactions and status
State and specific   changes: BLM
localities   Clark and Nye Counties NV public
   lands classifications vacated
   (10/28/N-CX) 49932
   Douglas and Lyon Counties NV
   lands, reconveyance to US and
   opening to mining *(10/28/N) 49933*

Issued weekly since 1965, *Weekly Compilation* includes the texts of proclamations, executive orders, addresses, remarks, communications to Congress, letters, messages and telegrams and transcripts of news conferences. Acts approved by the president, nominations submitted to the Senate, a digest of other White House announcements and a checklist of White House press releases are included as supplemental materials. These are all *public* documents. Presidents often donate their *private* papers to specific libraries, or they may establish libraries of their own. Since the Carter administration, *Presidential Papers* has been a cumulative, permanently bound republication of the *Weekly Compilation*. Before 1977, it was an edited version of this material.

The indexes to both sources are easy to use. In the back of each issue of the *Weekly Compilation* are subject and name cumulative indexes to that issue and previous issues up to the end of the quarter. Quarterly, semi-annual and annual indexes are issued separately. The index gives you the *Weekly Compilation* volume and page number, making short work of your research. The index for *Presidential Papers* is in the back of each volume and is arranged either by subject or by category, depending on the type of presidential activity or document. Like an index in the back of any book, it cites the page within that volume where the material can be found.

THREATS TO ACCESS

Journalists must have ready access to the official documents chronicling the political life of the country. Without that access, an important component of the U.S. system of checks and balances—the watchdog media—cannot operate. Without that access, citizens have little chance of informed participation in the workings of their nation's government.

The Federal Depository Library Program was established more than 130 years ago to open an information channel between the government and its people. Now that channel is becoming clogged. Journalists—and all those committed to the free flow of government information—should be concerned about the following developments:

- The Freedom of Information Act is being seriously undermined by the very bureaucrats assigned to make it work. By making improper use of one of the legal exemptions, by delaying processing, by charging high fees and by arguing that the documents requested are of no apparent public interest, Washington bureaucrats are managing to thwart journalists' successful and timely use of the FoIA.

■ Government documents that used to be accessible to the public because they were unclassified or declassified are being reclassified to exclude all eyes except those of designated government officials. Some of these newly classified documents have been available to the public for years.

■ Access is threatened by a seemingly attractive plan to cut government expenditures by requiring federal agencies to recover their costs of providing information from users. Individual information seekers would have to pay for government publications and reports that used to be free. Although this plan excludes federal depository libraries, which would continue receiving documents at no expense, it nevertheless would have an impact on them. In fact, the effects are already being felt, although the plan is not yet officially under way. Depository libraries no longer receive a wide variety of government publications that they used to receive for free. Those publications are now only available through the pay-as-you-go NTIS system. The information still exists—but it is far less accessible.

■ Ironically, the computerization meant to increase the accessibility of government information is currently having the opposite effect. While the government is busy creating databases, many depository libraries have been left behind. Some simply can't afford the computer terminals necessary to access the new databases. Others can't afford to train their librarians to use the new systems. A recent study of depository libraries found little on-line searching of government documents databases and limited access to on-line terminals.

Still, the information access picture is brighter in the United States than virtually anywhere else in the world. The sheer volume of government information is staggering. Its variety, scope and depth are awesome. The intelligent information-seeker will take the time to learn how to tap into this important resource.

Electronic Libraries

6

Meet the modern mass communicator:

- He peruses a recent Supreme Court decision, delves into the financial records of a major corporation, locates an important piece of medical research, checks on the progress of a bill in the state legislature and reads the latest federal agency news brief.
- She tracks a competitor's media buying patterns, studies readership response to several dozen magazines, checks last night's Nielsen ratings, refreshes her memory about a rival agency's successful ad campaign back in 1980 and reads a market research summary for a new product.

They do all this without running to the library, waiting for the mail, shuffling papers or rifling through reports. They never leave their offices or, for that matter, get up from their desks.

How? They boot up, log on and tie in to an electronic universe where vast stores of information flash around the world at the speed of light, appearing almost instantaneously on the screen of their desktop computers. They use these small, relatively inexpensive office machines to perform their primary task as mass communicators: information gathering.

MASS COMMUNICATION AND THE INFORMATION REVOLUTION

Computerized newsrooms, publishing companies and ad agencies are hardly futuristic. Everyone—from backcountry editors to Madison Avenue moguls—is sitting in front of terminals to write ad copy, edit articles and figure payroll accounts. During the past 15 years, computers have revolutionized how mass media workers handle information.

But the most important part of the information revolution has yet to hit the majority of newspapers, magazines, broadcast stations and ad agencies. Right now, most journalists use their computers to process, store and retrieve information only within the electronic boundaries of their own office systems. A reporter writes a story on the terminal and sends it to an editor's screen. The editor reworks it and sends it on to the typesetting system. All the information stays within the same network. The terminals, which are physically connected to one another ("hard-wired"), talk only to each other.

But with only modest extra expense, these same computers could talk to massive electronic storehouses of information hundreds or thousands of miles away, extracting important information and whisking it back in seconds. Communication between distant computers is the next phase of the information revolution. But most media industries have been slow to catch on.

Consider today's information-gatherers. They wait for the morning mail to bring reports, documents and studies. They drive to the library to pore over reference books and journals. They spend hours on the phone tracking down a piece of information. All this, when sitting on their desks is a machine that could link them to more information than they could use in thousands of lifetimes as a journalist. Lack of information about the electronic world coupled with an unhealthy awe of the technology keeps many journalists from moving into the future.

What are the advantages of using computers to help gather information?

- *Time*. Time is the journalist's most precious commodity—and most often cited excuse for superficiality. It's deadline pressure, say all varieties of mass communicators, that keeps us from doing the complete, in-depth job we'd like to do. Enter the information-gathering computer. Assuming the journalist has the option of driving to a decent library with solid reference and government documents sections—and many journalists don't—a desktop computer plugged into an electronic information-gathering network makes it possible to do the job both faster and more thoroughly. Think of the time saved by not having to hunt for material in the library or not waiting for certain federal agencies to send requested documents. Consider how the computer can shorten the information lag. While many computerized libraries are updated daily or weekly, the local library may receive only quarterly or annual updates of certain information. Library acquisition of some government and

legal documents typically runs months (or even years) behind because of production and distribution schedules. These same documents may be available almost instantaneously via the computer.

- *Accessibility.* Dedicated journalists make time to travel to the library.
  After an hour of hunting, they find just the article, book or document they need for their story, only to discover that it is checked
  out, misplaced or at the bindery. The same information in a computerized library is always available. Not only can many people
  read the material at the same time, but most computer libraries
  stay open almost 24 hours a day. And what of the journalists who
  don't work near well-stocked reference, law or government documents libraries? Are they doomed to write ill-researched stories
  and superficial reports? Not if they are hooked into an electronic
  information-gathering network. The reporter for the *Dead Moun-
  tain Echo* can access the same information as the journalist for the
  New York *Times*. An even more compelling advantage is that some
  information is simply not available through any source other than
  a specialized computer service.

- *Convenience.* Searching for material via computer is frequently the
  most convenient information-gathering method. You stay at your
  desk while the information comes to you. You allow the computer's
  tireless, single-minded energy to dig through masses of information
  that would take you hours (days, weeks) to sort through. Instead
  of poring over four separate indexes, each covering only three years
  of material, you use a computer service that does the combined
  search for you—in minutes. Instead of looking up three related
  topics, cross-referencing them, and culling what you find, you instruct the computer to combine topics and find common references.

LEARNING THE LINGO

You don't have to be a computer wizard to participate in the coming
phase of the information revolution, but you do have to understand a
few concepts and learn a little jargon. Unless you are one of those who
delight in talking Pascal, peripherals and parallel ports, it helps to think
of the computerized information-gathering process in human rather
than machine terms. Think of your desktop computer as an extension
of yourself as information-seeker. It can make telephone calls, ask
questions and take notes. Think of the distant computer that stores
masses of information as a library with newspapers, magazines, books,

reference materials and documents—preserved not as ink on paper but as electronic impulses. By using existing phone lines, your computer calls the distant computer library. There it finds an electronic librarian who asks what information you're seeking and then, at the speed of light, gets it for you. Your computer, also at the speed of light, copies down the material.

Let's complete the picture with a minimum of jargon. Your computer may be a *microcomputer* (also known as a *PC,* for *personal computer*) or, if it's connected to an office system, a *minicomputer.* The name does not describe the machine's physical size but rather its power. How much information can it store at one time? How quickly can it perform certain tasks? Can it do several tasks simultaneously? A microcomputer is the least powerful type of computer, but it is still powerful enough to use as an information-gathering tool.

The device that allows your computer to use telephone lines to call a distant computer is known as a *modem.* It translates the electronic impulses that make up your computer's vocabulary into signals that can be carried by phone lines, then changes them back into electronic impulses for the benefit of the distant computer.

The distant electronic storehouse of information is called a *database,* and it can vary in the amount of information it contains—just as libraries vary in size—from a few hundred items to many millions. But unlike a library that may sprawl through many large rooms and up several floors, it is amazingly compact. A computer the size of your bathroom can store more information than a good-sized university library.

Databases most helpful to journalists come in two basic forms: *bibliographic* and *full-text.* A bibliographic database is an enormous index (or set of indexes) that provides the information necessary to locate the actual material. This kind of database can tell you who wrote what article published in which issue of what journal. It might even give you a two-sentence summary of the article. But if you want to read the article itself, you need to plug into a full-text database. There you will find the entire contents of selected magazines, newspapers, reference books, reports and documents.

Several companies lease the rights to a variety of individual databases, making dozens or even hundreds of them available by calling one phone number. These companies are called *on-line vendors,* and they offer what are known descriptively as *encyclopedic database services.* DIALOG is the largest of such services with nearly 200 databases and more than half a million users. The databases, which provide bibliographic data, citations and abstracts, are organized into these categories: business/economics, chemistry, agriculture and nutrition, medicine and biosciences, energy and environment, science and technology, patents, law and government, current affairs and directories. BRS, another popular vendor, supplies 75 databases—some bibliographic, some full-text—in the areas of business, medicine, science, education, the social sciences and general reference works. SDC/ORBIT offers 80 databases in roughly the same categories. Dow Jones/News Retrieval's 18 huge databases specialize in financial information. Mead Data Central, one of the newer specialty vendors, offers only full-text databases, including a vast law library and an impressive collection of articles from major newspapers, magazines, newsletters and news services.

Information utilities, like on-line vendors, offer access to a number of individual databases. To this they add a startling variety of personal services ranging from astrology readings to airline reservation systems. They allow you to exchange "electronic mail" with other users, bank, shop, or look for a job. The industry giants are The Source and CompuServe. Backed by *Reader's Digest,* the Source includes some 1,000 separate files, some of which are traditional databases (business news, commodities and stock quotations), others of which are personal information services (movie and restaurant reviews, electronic mail-order shopping services). CompuServe is an even more eclectic service with databases of interest to everyone from farmers to Wall Street analysts.

HOW DOES COMPUTERIZED
INFORMATION GATHERING WORK?

You're working in a newspaper, magazine, broadcast station, public relations firm or advertising agency office. On your desk is a computer. What do you need to begin using that machine as an information-gathering tool?

- *A modem.* These translating devices are available in two different speeds. The more costly, faster modem (1200 baud) can transmit and receive about 120 characters per second and is a good choice for those who plan to receive long documents from databases. The slower device (300 baud) is cheaper, but transmits and receives only about 30 characters per second. For relatively short messages—bibliographic citations rather than full-text documents, for example—a 300-baud modem is more than adequate.

- *A telephone.* The modem uses existing phone lines to call distant databases, and the phone company will charge you standard long-distance rates for the time your computer talks to the other computer. A less expensive option is to subscribe to one of several private services (Tymenet, Telenet, Uninet, Dialnet) that tie you into the database of your choice via a local number.

- *Special software.* Beyond the instructions your computer already has (internally or on a disk you insert) that allow you to write and edit, you will need special software that tells the computer how to use the modem and how to talk to distant databases.

- *An encyclopedic database service.* To gain access to a number of databases by calling only one number (and getting only one bill), you will probably want to subscribe to a service from a major vendor. The vendor will provide you with a catalog of its services and detailed instructional material.

The cost of going on-line varies greatly, depending on which databases you use, how quickly you can search and what time of the day you ask for the information. After the initial several-hundred-dollar outlay for the modem and software, regular search costs include phone rates, vendor charges, database charges and per item fees. Phone rates can be quite low ($6 per hour, for example) if you use one of the private services instead of your regular long-distance company. The phone charge per search is usually minimal, because most searches are completed in 10 minutes or less. Vendor charges are the fees the encyclopedic database companies or information utilities assess you for their services. Some cost nothing to join; others have annual subscription fees (from as low as $50 to as high as several thousand dollars) or minimum use charges. You also pay a database charge for using each information storehouse. These per hour costs range from $10 to almost $300. The per item charge (10 cents to more than $10) is assessed for every citation, abstract or full-text document you either see on the screen or print out.

The costs may sound daunting, but they shouldn't necessarily intimidate you. When all goes well, computer searching can be quick, making per hour prices low. And vendors frequently offer special rates, particularly if you use their services often or during off-hours. Surprisingly, old-fashioned legwork often costs more than high-tech searching.

What *is* intimidating is the thought of going on-line for the first time, plugging into an untried library system and being forced to communicate in an unfamiliar way. That's why vendors supply instructional manuals that take you through the search process step-by-step and include sample searches. But before you sign with a vendor and receive that material, you may want to read about the on-line world from an independent expert. Alfred Glossbrenner's *The Complete Handbook of Personal Computer Communications* is an excellent starting point.

Some media organizations and many individual freelancers may decide to let experts do the searching for them. Library schools now train their students in computer information gathering. A news organization could easily hire a trained searcher to take care of all requests, just as it now employs "librarians" to maintain morgue files. Freelancers may find it more cost effective to depend on searchers already employed by nearby libraries. But even if you have the luxury of using a specialist, you still need to know what databases are available and what you can expect from them.

SPECIALIZED DATABASES

You can read the entire text of Federal Communications Commission reports, check the progress of major Department of Defense programs, look up the breeding record of your favorite race horse or verify Brazilian coffee prices—all by punching a few keys. The on-line world grows more diverse every day as the information industry continues to boom. Today there are more than 1,300 publicly available databases. Many of them can provide journalists—from account executives to city hall reporters—with the quick, up-to-date information they need to do their jobs well.

Because the on-line information industry is so dynamic, keeping abreast of new databases and services is sometimes difficult. The following directories may be helpful: Owen Davies and Mike Edelhart's *Omni Online Database Directory* and DB Newsletter Associates' *Guide to Online Databases*. The industry also has its own trade group, the Information Industry Association, with headquarters in Washington, D.C.

To give you a sampling of the scope of information available via your desktop computer, we've selected the following 35 databases. Some are full-text sources that allow you to use the computer for the entire information-gathering process. Others are bibliographic databases that direct you to materials in the library or elsewhere. Keep in mind that our selection represents less than 3 percent of the on-line information world and only a small portion of the databases containing information relevant to journalists.

Business and economics

Disclosure II. This database provides easy access to current, accurate corporate information on 8,800 publicly owned companies. Drawn from annual and periodic reports filed with the Security and Exchange Commission (10-K, 10-Q, 8-K and other reports), the information includes complete balance sheets and income statements, the names of officers and directors, and subsidiaries. It is updated weekly. (Available through DIALOG, Dow Jones News/Retrieval Service and other services.)

Dow Jones News. This is the place to look for business and financial news stories from *The Wall Street Journal, Barron's* and the Dow Jones News Service. The database is continuously updated and dates back to 1979. (Available through Dow Jones News/Retrieval.)

Electronic Yellow Pages. An ingenious Connecticut company fed information from almost 5,000 telephone books and special guides into seven computerized directories: construction companies, manufacturers, professionals, financial institutions, retailers, service organizations and wholesalers. Updated every six months, these databases make it easy to locate businesses throughout the United States. (Available through DIALOG.)

Standard and Poor's General Information File. The standard source of information about U.S. corporations, Standard and Poor's has gone digital. This database contains financial profiles of 3,000 major U.S. corporations with publicly traded stock. Information includes net sales, income and earnings per share plus other corporate details. (Available through CompuServe.)

Trade and Industry Index. Including references to more than 1,500 business-related sources, abstracts of material appearing in some 300 trade and industry journals and the full text of 85 journals, this database offers broad coverage of industry topics. Updated monthly, it began in 1981. (The box on page 120 shows the kind of information you would get from the *Trade and Industry Index.*) (Available through DIALOG.)

Education

ERIC. An impressive catalog of educational materials gathered by 16 Educational Resources Information Centers throughout the United States, ERIC indexes and abstracts a broad range of information on subjects from teaching the handicapped to overcoming math anxiety. One main file identifies the most significant and timely educational research reports and projects. The other indexes more than 700 periodicals that cover education-related topics. Updated monthly, it dates to 1966. (Available through BRS, DIALOG and others.)

Energy and the environment

DOE Energy Data Base. The database of the U.S. Department of Energy, this is one of the world's largest sources of references on energy and related topics. Covering fossil, wind, tidal, solar, geothermal and nuclear energy plus conservation, pollution, energy policy and other subjects, it indexes and abstracts all unclassified information that flows into the Department of Energy. Material from journal articles, reports, conference papers, books, patents and dissertations update this resource bimonthly. (Available through DIALOG, Mead Data Central and others.)

ENERGYNET. An up-to-date directory of almost 3,000 organizations and 8,000 people in energy-related fields, this database includes information on profit and non-profit organizations, trade and professional associations, and government agencies and committees. Each listing contains the names, addresses and phone numbers of key energy contacts as well as descriptions of the organization, if appropriate. (Available through DIALOG and others.)

ENVIROLINE. A comprehensive index to the broad field of environmental studies, this database indexes and abstracts articles from more than 5,000 publications around the world. Interdisciplinary in nature, it covers a wide range of environmental issues from legal, political, technological, scientific and economic perspectives. (Available through DIALOG and others.)

Government documents

ASI. This is the computerized version of the *American Statistics Index*, the comprehensive index to statistical publications

Search 1

You're a print reporter in the recession-wracked Pacific Northwest assigned to write a story on the timber industry. For the background information you need to get started, you plug into Trade and Industry Index. You ask the computer to search for all articles pertaining to *forest, lumber, timber* or *wood* and combine these descriptors with *northwest.* Here's what you get:

```
               File148:Trade and Industry Index -
               81-85/Aug
               (Copr. 1985 IAC) * FMT 9 = $7.00
                       Set Items Description
                       --- ----- -----------
              ┌ ? ss forest? or lumber or timber or wood
Instructions: Find   1  2406 FOREST?
references to forest, 2  1256 LUMBER
lumber, timber or ─┤  3   389 TIMBER
wood in the          4  2423 WOOD
Northwest            5  5481  1 OR 2 OR 3 OR 4
              └ ? s northwest
                       6  1788 NORTHWEST
Computer's response: ┌ ? c 5 and 6
38 items include all ─┤ 7    38  5 AND 6
key words         └ 7/5/3
                  1257392   DATABASE:  MI  File  47 *Use
                  Format 9 for FULL TEXT*
Title ──────      Northwest's problems; imports, energy
                  costs hit lumber, aluminum.
Author ──────     Kuzela, Lad
Publication information ──── Industry Week  v225  p28(2)
                  April 15 1985
                    CODEN: IWEEA
Full text is available ──── AVAILABILITY:  FULL TEXT Online
                    LINE COUNT: 00055
                    SIC CODE: 3334; 2646
              ┌   DESCRIPTORS: aluminum industry and
Other words the   trade-economic conditions;  wood-pulp
database uses to ─┤ industry-economic conditions;  United
classify this story States. Bonneville Power Administration-
              └ rates
```

You can instruct the computer to give you (on-screen or as a printout) all 38 citations or to stop at any point. Some articles, like the *Industry Week* story listed in the first citation, are available on-line. That means the database includes the full text of the article and, with a few more keystrokes, you can read it in its entirety. If a number of helpful articles are available on-line, your information search may be both quick and productive.

```
                 7/5/4
                 1232359    DATABASE: TI File 148; ABD
Title ─────      Selling  social  change  to  sell  lumber;
                 the Northwest timber industry is trying to
                 sell    more    finished    products    to    the
                 Japanese  by  convincing  them  to  build
                 western  style  homes.
Author ─────      Hill,  Robert  L.
Publication information ─────  Oregon Business Magazine   p47(5)
                 March   1985
                     illustration; table Sources of Japanese
                 timber  imports  from  North  America  for  logs
                 and  finished  and  semi-finished  products.;
Illustrations and   graph    Land    prices    in    Japan.;    table
graphs           Estimated  Japanese  timber  demand  January-
                 June   1985   from   South   Sea   Areas,   North
                 America,  New  Zealand  and  Chile.
                     GEOGRAPHIC LOCATION: Oregon NNUSOOR
                     Northwestern  lumber  and  forest  products
                 industries   are   trying   to   expand   their
                 market  share  of  logs,  lumber,  and  finished
Summary of article ─────  products    in    Japan.    The    Western    Wood
                 Products    Association    pushes    2-by-4
                 construction,  while  Parr  International  of
                 Aloha  exports  lumber,  doors  and  windows
                 for  American-style  homes.
                     SIC  CODE:  2400;  5031;  1521;  1500
                     DESCRIPTORS:    lumber    trade--Oregon;
                 forest  products  industry--Oregon;  Western
                 Wood   Products   Association;   construction
                 industry--Oregon;  Parr  International  of
                 Aloha
```

Other articles, like the *Oregon Business* magazine story listed in the second citation, are not available in the database. But the citation tells you the issue and page number and gives you a summary of the story. Armed with this information, you may be able to locate the magazine in your library. If the summary suggests that the article would be particularly helpful but your library doesn't have a subscription, you can call the magazine and interview the author.

generated by all branches of the federal government (see Chapter 5). Citations and abstracts are available for a wide range of data including population and economic censuses, Consumer Price Index reports, unemployment, agriculture, education and international trade. It is updated monthly. (Available through SDC, DIALOG.)

CIS/Index. The on-line version of Congressional Information Services' *Index to Publications of the United States Congress,* it provides access to the working papers published by the nearly 300 House, Senate and Joint committees and subcommittees each year (see Chapter 5). One file indexes the reports, documents, hearings and papers; the other abstracts them. *CIS/ Index* is updated monthly, and material is available back through 1970. (Available through SDC, DIALOG.)

GPO Monthly Catalog. The machine-readable equivalent of the printed *Monthly Catalog of United States Government Publications,* this database is the federal government's official index to its publications (see Chapter 5). Updated monthly, it includes a wealth of information on a wide range of topics from health to hydraulic geometry. (Available through SDC, DIALOG.)

Health

Environmental Health News. This database offers the full text of news briefs on environmental and occupational health, including new laws, government guidelines and court decisions. The information dates back to late 1981 and comes chiefly from four federal government sources: the Occupational Safety and Health Administration, the National Institute of Occupational Safety and Health, the Environmental Protection Agency and the Toxic Control Substances Act. (Available through Occupational Health Services.)

MEDLINE. Probably the major source for biomedical literature, MEDLINE corresponds to three printed indexes: *Index Medicus, Index to Dental Literature* and *International Nursing Index*. This database is updated monthly and indexes and summarizes research on topics from AIDS to zinc that has been published in more than 3,000 international journals. (The box on page 124 shows the kind of information you would get from MEDLINE.) (Available through BRS, DIALOG and others.)

Mental Health Abstracts. An electronic bibliography of more than 450,000 citations and abstracts, this database includes a wide range of information related to mental health published in 1,200 journals, books and reports. Records date back to 1969. (Available through BRS, DIALOG and others.)

Law and legislation

LEXIS. A welcome replacement for tedious searches through law libraries, this vast database contains the full texts of court decisions, statutes, regulations and other legal materials. LEXIS includes decisions from the Supreme Court, the U.S. Court of Appeals, District Courts and the U.S. Court of Claims; IRS codes and rulings; Federal Communications Commission reports; state court decisions from 1821 on; National Labor Relations Board reports; and much more. Now considered a standard legal reference tool, LEXIS is available at most law schools and many major law firms. (Available through Mead Data Central.)

Public Affairs Information. The database for serious observers of Congress, PAI offers complete analysis of all legislation currently pending in Congress and in the state legislatures. The information includes the bill's legislative history, its supporters and opponents and the chances the bill will pass. House, Senate and committee schedules are also listed. (Available through Public Affairs Information.)

WESTLAW. Another massive legal research tool, this database offers the full text of Supreme Court and other federal court decisions, as well as rulings on military, maritime, bankruptcy, tax, labor and securities cases at various judicial levels. It includes a collection of concise, copyrighted case summaries that allow quick research. (Available through West Publishing.)

Search 2

You're a broadcast journalist who has just reported a major breaking story: A local woman has been diagnosed as having AIDS, and medical authorities have traced the illness back to a blood transfusion she received at an area hospital. You've covered the immediate news story, but you know your viewers deserve an in-depth look at the problem. Sources at the hospital are not talking. You know of no local experts who could fill you in on this complex issue. Where do you go? MEDLINE. You search the database for all references that include both *AIDS* and *transfusion*. Then you limit the search to the current year. Here's what you find:

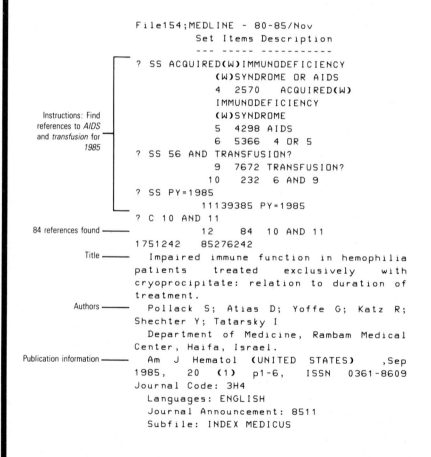

```
File154;MEDLINE - 80-85/Nov
        Set Items Description
        --- ----- -----------
? SS ACQUIRED(W)IMMUNODEFICIENCY
            (W)SYNDROME OR AIDS
        4   2570    ACQUIRED(W)
            IMMUNODEFICIENCY
            (W)SYNDROME
        5   4298  AIDS
        6   5366   4 OR 5
? SS 56 AND TRANSFUSION?
        9   7672 TRANSFUSION?
        10    232   6 AND 9
? SS PY=1985
        11139385 PY=1985
? C 10 AND 11
        12    84   10 AND 11
1751242   85276242
    Impaired  immune  function  in  hemophilia
patients      treated      exclusively      with
cryoprocipitate:  relation  to  duration  of
treatment.
    Pollack  S;  Atias  D;  Yoffe  G;  Katz  R;
Shechter  Y;  Tatarsky  I
    Department  of  Medicine,  Rambam  Medical
Center,  Haifa,  Israel.
    Am   J   Hematol   (UNITED   STATES)    ,Sep
1985,   20   (1)   p1-6,   ISSN   0361-8609
Journal Code: 3H4
    Languages: ENGLISH
    Journal Announcement: 8511
    Subfile: INDEX MEDICUS
```

Instructions: Find references to *AIDS* and *transfusion* for 1985

84 references found

Title

Authors

Publication information

The search reveals 84 sources. You can instruct the computer to give you the full reference, which includes a summary of the article (as in the first reference to the *American Journal of Hematology*), or an abbreviated reference (as in the second reference to *Transfusion*). This database does not include the full text of indexed articles.

Summary of article —

Recently, abnormalities of cell-mediated immunity were found in hemophiliac patients receiving factor VIII concentrate therapy. Contradictory results were reported concerning cellular immune functions in hemophiliacs treated only with cryoprecipitate or fresh frozen plasma. Therefore, we evaluated the immunological status of 15 Israeli patients with severe classic hemophilia-A who were treated only with cryoprecipitate and never exposed to factor VIII concentrate whether of commercial source or blood bank prepared. As a group, only mildly depressed cellular immune functions and slight reduction in the helper to suppressor cell ratio were found. However, when patients treated more than 15 years were analyzed separately, a significant reduction in proportion of T cells, T-helper cells, helper to suppressor ratio, and proliferative response to phytohemaslutinin and pokeweed mitogen were observed compared to patients treated for less than 15 years and normal controls. Proportion of T-suppressor cells, Con A-activated suppressor activity, and IgG and IgA levels were significantly elevated in patients treated for more than 15 years. These results may support the view that derangement of immune function in hemophiliacs results from infusion of foreign proteins or an ubiquitous virus rather than contracting AIDS infectious agent.

1748826   85273826

Title —   Anti-HTLV-III testing of blood donors: reproducibility and confirmability of commercial test kits.

Authors —   Holland PV; Richards CA; Teghtmeyer JR; Douville CM; Carlson JR; Hinrichs SH; Pedersen NC
Sacramento Medical Foundation Blood Center, CA.

Publication information —   Transfusion (UNITED STATES)   ,Jul-Aug 1985, 25 (4) p395-7, ISSN 0041 1132 Journal Code: WDN

With this information—which would have taken you hours to find using printed library indexes—you can do either of two things. If you are able to understand the language of medical journals, you can use the MEDLINE citations to quickly locate the articles in the library. If you don't have a science background, the citations can pinpoint experts (the authors of the articles) for you to call for interviews.

Market research

Arbitron TV. Program preferences from the Arbitron rating system are analyzed and presented geographically in this database, offering the quickest access to information needed for various advertising, marketing and programming decisions. Arbitron also measures the daily audience response to programs in 11 major U.S. cities. (Available through Interactive Market Systems and Telmar Media Systems.)

ADTRACK. Designed primarily for advertising agencies and magazine publishers, this database indexes all advertisements of one-quarter page or larger appearing in 148 major U.S. consumer magazines (accounting for more than 98 percent of major magazine advertising revenue). The information includes the product, company name, date and place of publication and ad size. Sometimes the designers and artists who created the ad are noted. Dating back to 1980, ADTRACK is growing at the rate of almost 5,000 items a month. (The box on page 127 shows the kind of information you would get from ADTRACK.) (Available through DIALOG.)

AMI. Easy to use and up-to-date, Advertising & Marketing Intelligence includes 125,000 abstracts of articles from more than 60 U.S. trade and professional magazines that cover the advertising, marketing and public relations fields. Information on new products and campaigns, account and executive changes, rates and research is all here. This database dates to 1979. (Available through Mead Data Central.)

FIND/SVP. An important market research tool, this database indexes and summarizes industry and market research reports, studies and surveys from more than 300 publishers. The full reports can be purchased from FIND/SVP. (Available through DIALOG.)

MRI. Detailed information on the media habits, buying patterns and demographics of U.S. consumers makes up this market research database. The information, which is based on questionnaires and interviews with more than 20,000 adults, includes newspaper and magazine reading habits and exposure to TV, cable and radio. (Available through Interactive Market Systems, Telmar Media Systems and others.)

Search 3

Your advertising agency just landed the account for a new premium brand yogurt. The brand's main competitor is Yoplait. To make careful, informed media buying decisions, you need to know where Yoplait advertises. ADTRACK can tell you. You log on and ask the computer to locate all Yoplait yogurt ads that have appeared in the past year and to limit its search to only full-color ads. Here's what you get:

```
              File43:ADTRACK 80-84/Sep
              Copr. Corporate Intelligence of Minn.
                    Set Items Description
                    --- ----- -----------
              ? ss yoplait or yogurt
                       1      28  YOPLAIT
                       2     137  YOGURT
                       3     137  1 OR 2
              ? ss ac=full color
                 4218094  AC=FULL COLOR
              ? c 1 and 4
                       5      28  1 AND 4
              ? type 5/5/1-3
              5/5/1
                354535
                YOPLAIT USA
                BREAKFAST YOGURT-CUSTARD STYLE YOGURT
                PEOPLE,     8311,   ISSN 0093-7673
                11/07/83    Page: 57    1 Page
                FULL COLOR
                MANY-UNSPECIFIED SPOKESPERSON
                YOGURT .(20264321)

              5/5/2
                348304
                YOPLAIT; SODIMA
                YOGURT
                WORKING WOMAN, 8309,    ISSN 0145-5761
                09/83    Page: 222    1 Page
                FULL COLOR
                MANY-SPECIFIED SPOKESPERSON
                CO-OP AD
                YOGURT .(20264321)
```

Labels (left margin):
- Instructions: Find all full-color *Yoplait yogurt ads*
- Computer's response: 28 full-color Yoplait ads
- Company
- Brand
- Publication
- Date, page, ad size
- Is a particular spokesperson used?

You ask the computer to print out the references to all 28 Yoplait ads. Now you know where and when your competition advertised its product. That information alone can help you make a media buying decision. If, however, you want to see the ads themselves to study the competition's tactics, you will need to go to the library and locate the individual magazines. ADTRACK does not include copies of the ads.

Nielsen Television Index. The most influential audience measurement company in the United States, Nielsen provides this on-line service for quick, easy accessibility. (Available through Interactive Market Systems, Telmar Media Systems and others.)

Print media guides

Magazine ASAP. This full-text database contains the entire contents of 50 popular general interest magazines from *National Review* to *Stereo Review.* (Available through DIALOG.)

Magazine Index. A large database that indexes articles from more than 400 general interest magazines, Magazine Index's on-line service corresponds to the microfilm version carried by most libraries. It carries publications dating back to 1977 and is currently being backdated to 1959. The listings are updated monthly. (Available through DIALOG.)

National newspaper index. This is an index to all major news stories and columns, plus features, obituaries, letters to the editor and cartoons published in *The Christian Science Monitor,* the Washington *Post,* the Los Angeles *Times,* the New York *Times* and *The Wall Street Journal.* Updated monthly, it dates from 1979. Libraries may carry a microform edition. (Available through DIALOG.)

Newsearch. The place to look for up-to-date information in the print media, this database references more than 400 magazines, 750 law journals and newspapers, 330 trade journals, a variety of business publications and five major newspapers (*The Christian Science Monitor,* the Washington *Post,* the New York *Times,* the Los Angeles *Times* and *The Wall Street Journal*). Updated daily, it retains information for one month before transferring it to other databases like the Magazine Index. (Available through DIALOG.)

NEXIS. Another full-text service, NEXIS offers articles from 11 major newspapers, 38 magazines, 50 newsletters, a variety of newswires (including the Associated Press world, national and business wires and Reuters General News), the *Federal Register,* the *Encyclopaedia Britannica* plus assorted other services. Most publications are fed into the system as soon as their next issue comes out. Some publications are available only from January 1981; others date to 1975. (Available through Mead Data Central.)

Science and technology

Conference Papers Index. A bibliographic guide to current research in science and technology, CPI provides access to more than 100,000 papers presented at some 1,000 major regional, national and international meetings each year. The information includes titles and the names and addresses of authors. Dating back to 1973, the database includes well over a million items. (Available through DIALOG.)

FEDRIP. The Federal Research in Progress database offers access to information about ongoing federally sponsored research projects in the physical and life sciences and in engineering. Records include the investigator's name, sponsoring organization and, in most cases, a description of the research. After the research is completed and a full report is published, references to the work appear in NTIS (see next entry). (Available through DIALOG.)

NTIS. This is the national computerized clearinghouse for unclassified technical research sponsored by the federal government. NASA, the departments of Energy, Commerce and Transportation and some 240 other federal agencies finance research and development projects that span both the social and physical sciences. The reports themselves are available for sale from these agencies. The guide to the reports is NTIS. Reports date from 1963, are updated biweekly, and number more than a million. (Available through BRS, SDC, DIALOG and others.)

SCISEARCH. With almost 6 million records, this massive multidisciplinary index claims to include 90 percent of "the world's most significant scientific and technical literature." Covering every area in the pure and applied sciences, SCISEARCH indexes articles, reports of meetings, letters, editorials and other items from about 2,600 major scientific and technical journals. The service is updated biweekly. (Available through DIALOG.)

Social sciences

PAIS International. This is a major reference source for information in all fields of social science including political science, sociology, international relations, economics and law. The database indexes more than 800 English-language journals and 6,000 newspapers, pamphlets, directories, reports and other documents. Monthly updates add about 1,800 records. (Available through BRS, DIALOG and other services.)

Social SCISEARCH. A multidisciplinary database with almost a million and a half items, Social SCISEARCH indexes significant material from the 1,500 most important social science journals in the world and selected items from 3,000 additional journals. All areas of the social and behavioral sciences are covered, including sociology, psychology, anthropology, political science, economics and urban planning. The index dates back to 1972 and is updated monthly. (Available through BRS, DIALOG and others.)

SNAKES IN EDEN

On-line information gathering does have its darker side. It takes practice, commitment—and a good instruction manual—to become familiar with search language and commands. Costs can skyrocket if you don't know the step-by-step procedures, can't think like an indexer, aren't specific enough in your information requests or choose the wrong database for your search.

Another problem is the lack of accessibility of some databases. While DIALOG and BRS offer a vast array of information relevant to the journalist, some potentially important databases are available only through specialty vendors. Other databases are part of much smaller information systems or are available only through their creators. That can mean scores of different phone numbers, log-on commands, search procedures—and bills.

But these problems are mundane compared with the deeper concerns facing a society rushing headlong into an information age. Consider three of these concerns and their implications for working communicators and their audiences.

- Computerization of information may mean that the information-rich get richer while the information-poor get poorer. More and more information is being fed directly into databases without being published in any universally accessible form like a printed document, report or article. That means those who have computers and can afford to use them as information-gathering tools have access to "public" information that the rest of the public does not. Mass communicators, corporate moguls, financiers and a handful of other professionals who use computers as information-gathering tools will become increasingly information-rich. They may choose to share their information—or to hoard it.

■ Lightning-quick, invisible censorship is possible in an age of computer-stored information. In the United States, censorship issues become public battles. A school district tries to purge *Huckleberry Finn* from the curriculum. Ronald Reagan muzzles the literary aspirations of FBI agents. The media report these events; the public discusses them. But in an age of digitalized information, censorship can be both swift and secret. It takes only one person, a few keystrokes and a split second to erase complete files. If those files exist only in computerized form, they may be lost forever. In a few moments or a few years, no one will remember that they ever existed. Imagine a zealous government official wiping out a sensitive but unclassified Department of Defense file. Imagine a harried bank employee erasing your entire credit history.

■ Computerization makes private information dangerously accessible. With patience, the right password and command language, and a moderate knowledge of computers, anyone can raid information from virtually any database around the world. The 12-year-old hackers who, for fun, penetrate complex computer systems have shown just how possible it is for outsiders to gain access to private information. And computers now house enormous amounts of personal information about almost all of us, from criminal records to consumer habits. This has obvious implications for every individual. It also presents new legal and ethical problems for journalistic information-gatherers. If it is possible—although not necessarily legal—to obtain private information about someone, how far will the enterprising, perhaps well-meaning, journalist go? Suppose quietly and unobtrusively breaking into a database means the difference between a significant investigative story or no story at all?

These are important issues to ponder and discuss, for computerization of information is more than just a new technology. The information revolution has far greater implications for our society than simply quickening the pace of communication and changing the workplace. It can change how we think, how we act, and what we value.

But regardless of the thorny issues created by computerization of information, electronic libraries are a boon to the working journalist. Their convenience and speed are unparalleled; their scope is constantly growing. Perhaps some day databases will entirely replace library collections—but that day is still in the distant future. Today's journalist needs to be proficient in using both computerized and traditional searching methods. They complement one another and can lead to faster, more efficient, more productive information gathering.

Institutional Knowledge

7

You're a newspaper reporter researching a story about the siting of a nuclear waste dump in your state. How exactly is spent nuclear fuel stored? Will it pose a hazard to people or the environment? You need to know.

You're a television journalist organizing a story on an outbreak of measles in the local schools. Why is it happening? Is it part of a national epidemic? You need to know.

You're a writer for a regional magazine gathering information for a story on the importance of defense industries to your area's economy. What companies have defense contracts? How much of the defense dollar is spent in your region compared with other areas? You need to know.

You're an advertising account executive assigned to a new client, a filbert growers association. What's the basic supply of and demand for filberts? Are there potential foreign markets? You need to know.

And, of course, you need to know fast. Where do you go? Via your telephone, you go to the most prodigious, most prolific source of information in the world—the U.S. federal government.

SAILING THROUGH BYZANTIUM

With its 62 independent agencies, boards, commissions and corporations, its 51 congressional committees, 13 departments and three branches, the federal government employs almost 3 million civilian workers. According to Washington, D.C., research expert Matthew Lesko, some 710,000 of them are information specialists. Imagine every man, woman and child in San Francisco working five days a week to collect, analyze and evaluate information, and you begin to get an idea of how vast a resource the federal government is. As a taxpayer you may shudder. But as an information-gatherer, you have to cheer.

Experts on everything—beekeeping, bilingual education, bankruptcy, birth defects—are just a phone call away. They have facts and figures. They know about trends and timetables. They are paid, by us, to think, write and talk about their specialties.

Skilled journalists—those who understand that good reporting depends on solid, accurate, timely information—appreciate and use the resources of the federal government. They know where to get a crash course in an unfamiliar subject, how to get information too new to be published, and who to contact for insightful comments. They know that the agencies of the federal government collect information about regional, state and even local concerns. They know that regional offices of federal agencies are prime information centers.

Unlike the lazy or ill-prepared journalist who may settle for a phone call to an "authorized" government spokesperson, these journalists know how to dig for information sources below the top layer of officialdom. Impressively titled bureaucrats may not be directly involved with the issues the journalist wants to know about. Because of their position, they may have a vested interest in communicating or suppressing certain facts. Because of their political or personal agendas, they may be less than forthright or accurate sources of information. One example brings this point home.

In the spring of 1984, Secretary of Health and Human Services Margaret Heckler—an impressively titled, official spokesperson—told reporters about a major medical breakthrough. Government researchers had identified the virus responsible for Acquired Immune Deficiency Syndrome (AIDS), she announced, and a diagnostic blood test would be "widely available within about six months." A preventive vaccine would be "ready for testing in approximately two years," she said.

A year later—with the AIDS epidemic escalating and no effective test or vaccine in sight—two reporters for *Mother Jones* magazine approached the story by going beyond interviews with top officials. They talked to the physicians and scientists directly involved in AIDS research. They talked to experts at the Centers for Disease Control, Office of Technology Assessment, National Cancer Institute and Office of Management and Budget. They talked to congressional committee aides and assistant secretaries.

The story that emerged ("At Risk," by David Talbot and Larry Bush, *Mother Jones,* April 1985) directly and forcefully contradicted

Heckler's official pronouncement, which one researcher called "just political nonsense." Because the two reporters understood Washington bureaucracy and were committed to meticulous research, they were able to gather authoritative, often provocative statements from expert sources.

What about the information-seekers introduced at the beginning of this chapter? They might begin their searches this way:

- The newspaper reporter on the nuclear waste dump story contacts an expert at the Office of Nuclear Waste Management in the Department of Energy.

- The TV journalist covering the measles outbreak talks to a physician at the Centers for Disease Control, an agency within the Department of Health and Human Services.

- The magazine writer looking for defense contract information phones the Department of Defense's Contract Audit Agency.

- The advertising executive with the filbert growers account picks the brains of an agricultural economist in the Department of Agriculture.

They don't become lost in the Byzantine bureaucracy. They aren't put on indefinite hold or transferred from one office to another until they're hoarse from explaining their mission. They know where to go. They already know what you're about to discover.

FINDING SOURCES

The federal government is an unparalleled source of information, but it can also be an unparalleled source of frustration to the journalist looking for fast answers. It's easy to see why. The bureaucracy is so vast and so tangled that few understand it. Cabinet-level departments are composed of divisions, which themselves contain offices that include agencies made up of bureaus that contain departments. Information offices and information experts exist at all levels. In a system so complex, workers may not know what others do in their own department. Information experts may not know of the existence of other specialists working in their field but not physically in their office. Agencies with overlapping expertise and information may be found in several different departments.

It is difficult for most people—including novice journalists—to know where to begin looking for information in the federal government. For example, they know there's a Department of Labor, but they don't know that within that department is a bureau, and within that bureau is an expert who can tell them all they want to know about union wage rates or the changing makeup of the family budget. A phone call to a general information number may never get them to that expert. But the expert's number is listed in an easily accessible directory. And who understands the government well enough to know that vital information on the environment can be found in five cabinet-level departments, a regulatory agency, a spate of congressional subcommittees and a number of advisory groups and task forces?

Mercifully, the government understands the problem and publishes guides to itself—from general directories to agency-by-agency phone books. A handful of independent publishers are also in the business of deciphering the bureaucratic maze. Some of these federal guidebooks can be found in the reference collections of newspapers, magazines and broadcast stations. Most or all, depending on the size of the library, can be found in the government documents section of public or university libraries.

By consulting these books, a researcher can start with little understanding of the federal government and end with an impressive list of experts' and specialists' phone numbers. The trick is knowing what to expect from each directory and how to use the directories in logical order. The search for federal government sources can be a multistep process, depending on the kind of information you're seeking.

Level 1: The basics

Journalistic researchers who aren't familiar with the structure of the federal government should first consult either of two basic guidebooks. The information in these books, like that in encyclopedias or almanacs, is broad but shallow. Both offer insight into how the federal government is organized and what department has responsibility for which body of information. But neither gives the rich detail necessary for the journalist who wants to go beyond agency flaks and official spokespersons. The back-of-the-book subject indexes are better and faster guides to these books than the tables of contents.

- *The United States Government Manual* is the official handbook of the federal government. It offers descriptive information on the agencies of the three branches of government, as well as independent and quasi-official agencies, boards, committees and commissions. Each listing includes a roster of the agency's top officials, a summary of the agency's purpose, a brief history, a description of its programs and activities and a section on sources of information.

■ Matthew Lesko's *Information USA* is one researcher's attempt to bridge the gap between information source and information user. The book is aimed at a general audience and, like the *Manual,* provides important, basic information. It describes the divisions, departments and committees within the three branches of government, as well as the independent agencies, boards, commissions, committees and government corporations. Each listing includes the address, phone number, estimated budget and number of employees in the department. The entries describe the department's internal structure and offer sections on data experts and major printed sources of information. Regional offices of federal agencies are also listed.

Level 2: Expanding

Now the journalist knows, in general terms, which agencies within the federal government are responsible for generating what information. The Level 2 reference books expand on that knowledge by offering a more detailed look at what these agencies do and who works for them. These guides help the journalist create a list of individual sources.

■ *Congressional Quarterly's Washington Information Directory* is a guide to 5,000 information sources in the legislative and executive branches and non-profit associations. Conveniently divided into 16 major subject areas (*science, defense, housing*), the book lists the key agencies, committees and people working in each area. Each chapter includes the names of relevant organizations, addresses, phone numbers, names and titles of directors or contacts for specific subjects and capsule descriptions of the work they do. A good source of information on congressional committees and subcommittees, this directory includes the names and phone numbers of committee members.

■ *Congressional Quarterly's Federal Regulatory Directory* includes extensive profiles of the 13 largest, most important regulatory agencies and abbreviated entries for 93 other agencies. Information hounds who know which agency they're looking for can use this detailed guide to help negotiate their way through the regulatory maze to a specific expert. The longer profiles include descriptions of the agency's history, powers, authority and internal organization. Also included are biographical sketches of each board member or commissioner, addresses and phone numbers of key contacts, and special sections listing printed sources of information. Journalists will find the lists of regional offices particularly helpful. The

93 abbreviated entries include summaries of agency responsibilities, lists of phone contacts, information sources and addresses of regional offices.

Level 3: Digging deeper

Level 3 reference guides open even more of the federal government to the inquiring journalist by listing tens of thousands of government sources from top decision makers to lowly, but often information-rich, underlings. Organized like phone books, these guides are extremely valuable—but only to those who already know what they're looking for. Because they contain far more information and are more likely to be in a nearby library, these directories are superior to individual agency or Washington, D.C., phone books.

- *The Congressional Staff Directory* is a comprehensive guide to the thousands of people who work in the House and Senate. All senators and their staffs—including such excellent, overlooked sources of information as research and legislative assistants—are listed with addresses and phone numbers. Representatives and the districts they serve are also included. Additionally, the book details the standing committees of the House and Senate and their respective subcommittees, joint congressional committees and key personnel in the executive branch and independent government agencies. In all there are 3,200 biographies of key staff members.

- *The Federal Staff Directory* lists 27,000 top decision makers in the executive branch, including key administrators and their staff assistants in the Office of the President, the cabinet-level departments and certain independent agencies. Each entry includes the person's job title, address and phone number. The directory also includes 1,500 biographies of top officials.

- *The Washington Monitor's Congressional Yellow Book* and *Federal Yellow Book* are constantly updated looseleaf directories of government officials and their staffs. The congressional directory includes the name, address, phone number, political affiliation, state/district and committee and subcommittee assignments of each senator and representative. The book also lists key staff members with their responsibilities and phone numbers. The federal directory lists the names, addresses and phone numbers of officials and their key staffers in the divisions, bureaus and offices of the federal government.

Level 4: Specializing

For the journalist looking for even more diverse, more specialized sources of information, Level 4 references provide access to experts not listed in other directories.

- *Encyclopedia of Governmental Advisory Agencies* is a directory of presidential, public and interagency advisory committees as well as government-related boards, panels, task forces and commissions. Organized by area (*agriculture, business, education*), the book describes the organization, its history and scope of authority, programs, membership and staff.
- *Government Research Centers Directory* is a guide to U.S. government research and development centers, labs, bureaus, test facilities, experiment stations, data collection and analysis centers, and grants and research coordinating offices in agriculture, art, business, education, energy, engineering, the environment, medicine, military science and basic and applied science.

FOLLOWING THE TRAIL

An editor beckons a reporter one morning. "I've been hearing a lot of talk about how bad it is to stare at a video display terminal all day," the editor says, glancing up from the glowing VDT screen. "Find out about the potential health hazards. Millions of people work in front of computers. I think there's a story here."

The reporter ambles across the newsroom, silently plotting a research trail: Check the newspaper's own files of past stories; drop by the library and go through a few periodical indexes; consider tapping into a database; call the medical school and find someone to talk to. Maybe a clerical or typesetters union official. Maybe someone at a computer store. Who else is likely to know about VDTs and health? The reporter's mind goes blank. Then, an inspiration: The federal government is the greatest single source of information in the world. Among the scores of departments, committees and commissions, among the hundreds of thousands of information experts, there must be someone who knows about VDTs and health. But who?

The four-level approach to deciphering the federal bureaucracy can help this reporter locate the sources needed to do a quality job. Let's follow the research trail.

Level 1

Experimenting with the index at the back of *Information USA,* the reporter looks up *occupational safety.* The book notes the Occupational Safety and Health Administration (OSHA) within the Department of Labor, the National Institute for Safety and Health (NIOSH) within the Department of Health and Human Services, and the Occupational Safety and Health Review Committee, an independent agency. According to the brief descriptions of the agencies, any one or all of them could have information on the potential health hazards of VDTs. The reporter will have to check them further on Level 2.

Examining another index listing, *environmental protection,* the reporter finds a reference to the Environmental Protection Agency (EPA). But the entry doesn't make it clear whether this agency would be involved with the VDT issue. A Level 2 source will need to be consulted. Reasoning that VDTs are consumer products, the reporter tries that heading in the index and finds the Consumer Product Safety Commission, another source to explore on Level 2.

Level 2

From the *Information USA* entries, the reporter knows that the EPA, OSHA and the Consumer Product Safety Commission are federal regulatory agencies. To find out more about them and to locate specific departments that may have pertinent information, the reporter consults *Congressional Quarterly's Federal Regulatory Directory.* Skimming the 30-page entry for OSHA, the reporter realizes that this agency will be a valuable source and scribbles down several phone numbers.

The 23-page EPA entry shows the reporter that this agency may also be a good source. Under the Office of Radiation Programs, the directory lists the names and phone numbers of a half dozen administrators. Under the Office of Health Research, the directory lists the names and numbers of several officials. After scanning the 15-page entry for the Consumer Product Safety Commission, the reporter notes the names and numbers of several administrators whose job titles sound promising.

Now it's time to consult *Congressional Quarterly's Washington Information Directory.* Using the subject headings in the table of contents, the reporter first looks under *Health and Consumer Affairs.* Under the likely subheading *health research,* the directory lists a source the reporter has not encountered before, the National Eye Institute. Because it conducts and funds research on the eye and because eyestrain is a potential VDT hazard, the reporter adds a few more telephone numbers to the growing list.

The only other promising subject heading in the table of contents is *Employment and Labor*. The OSHA and NIOSH entries show that these agencies will be good sources but don't offer enough detail. The reporter will have to go to Level 3 sources to see how to use them. Looking under the subheading *research and development,* the reporter finds that the Bureau of Labor Statistics within the Department of Labor gathers and analyzes occupational safety and health statistics. Telephone numbers are listed. The reporter is also excited to find listings for two congressional subcommittees that have jurisdiction over occupational health and safety matters. Telephone numbers of the subcommittee chairs are listed, but the reporter will need to check Level 3 sources for more detail.

Level 3

Knowing from Level 1 and 2 directories that OSHA is in the Department of Labor, the reporter looks up that department in the *Federal Staff Directory* phonebook. The book lists the names, job titles and phone numbers of more than 50 OSHA executives. Skimming the surrounding pages, the reporter sees information on the Labor Department's safety and health statistics office and records the numbers of several specialists. A check under NIOSH in the Department of Health and Human Services nets two full pages of names and numbers. Several look promising.

Following up the Level 2 discovery of two congressional committees involved in occupational health and safety matters, the reporter next consults the *Congressional Staff Directory.* The book yields the specific information the reporter needs: names and numbers of all committee members and staff members, including the research assistants.

Level 4

Although the list of potential sources is impressive, the reporter decides to consult two more directories. Under the *Business, Industry, Economics and Labor* subject heading, the *Encyclopedia of Government Advisory Organizations* lists 27 agencies that advise the president or some federal department on occupational safety and health concerns. From the descriptions of their authorities, the reporter notes at least five potential sources for the VDT story.

Using the *Government Research Center Directory,* the reporter tries the *occupational safety* and *occupational health* listings and finds descriptions of three NIOSH research facilities, one of which looks useful.

The reporter's source list

By consulting a few directories in a logical order, our reporter has deciphered enough of the federal bureaucracy to compile an impressive list of possible sources. Although the reporter may decide to interview an official spokesperson or two, the source list makes it possible to dig deeper, asking questions of people below the top layer of officialdom. It steers the reporter to those people directly involved in gathering information about, researching and analyzing aspects of the VDT issue. Just how many sources are contacted depends on how much time the reporter has to complete the story and what the phone budget is. Here are the potential sources:

- Several specialists, by name, at OSHA
- Several specialists, by name, at NIOSH
- Several specialists, by name, at the EPA
- Several specialists, by name, at the Consumer Products Safety Commission
- Researchers at the National Eye Institute
- Occupational health experts in the Bureau of Labor Statistics
- Researchers, staffers and members of two congressional subcommittees
- Members of five governmental advisory agencies
- Scientists at a NIOSH-funded research facility

Imagine the potential diversity, quantity and quality of information the journalist might extract from these sources. The reporter can learn and ask questions about legislative research, congressional hearings, agency reports and scientific studies. The reporter can delve into departmental findings and interdepartmental debates. The reporter can gather data, opinions and speculations, and hear evidence, arguments and rebuttals. The reporter can, in short, use the knowledge and expertise of government specialists to amass detailed, authoritative and timely information. With information like this, the reporter is well on the way to writing a solid story.

DISCOVERING IMPORTANT SOURCES

Inestimable information riches are buried within the federal bureaucracy, all accessible by following the research trail that starts with Level 1 directories. To show you just a fraction of what's available and to provide you with a handy reference directory, we've listed a number of institutional sources below. For research ease, they are grouped under subject headings that correspond to the issues journalists commonly cover. Where relevant, brief descriptions are included. Telephone numbers and addresses are omitted because they sometimes change. Remember that many federal agencies maintain regional offices throughout the country. The experts at these offices gather and interpret data that may be of particular relevance to your area.

Business and economics

Bureau of the Census, Department of Commerce. Statistical information on retail, wholesale and service industries. Scores of data experts in individual fields—for example, minority employment and housing construction.

Bureau of Industrial Economics, Department of Commerce. The agency has 100 analysts who monitor specific industries from footware to fertilizers.

Bureau of Economic Analysis, Department of Commerce. Large staff of economists who monitor various aspects of the national, regional and state economies, such as corporate profits, capital investment and personal income.

Federal Deposit Insurance Corporation. Detailed financial reports from all member banks. Trends and statistics are available from experts in the Division of Research.

Securities and Exchange Commission. Detailed quarterly and annual reports submitted by most publicly held companies.

Federal Trade Commission. Specialists in individual industries, trade practices, advertising, franchising, credit.

Antitrust division, Department of Justice. Legal experts on antitrust actions.

Senate Subcommittee on Securities, Committee on Banking, Housing and Urban Affairs; House Subcommittee on Telecommunications, Consumer Protection and Finance, Committee on Energy and Commerce. Information sources on stocks, bonds and securities.

Consumer affairs

Office of the Special Assistant to the President for Consumer Affairs, White House. Governmentwide coordinator of programs.

Consumer Product Safety Commission. Experts on the causes, severity and prevention of consumer product-related deaths, illnesses and injuries.

Federal Drug Administration. Experts on the purity and safety of foods, drugs, radiological and biological products, medical devices and cosmetics.

Food Safety and Quality Service, Marketing and Inspection Service, Department of Agriculture. Experts on the quality and nutritional value of meats, poultry, fruits and vegetables.

Federal Trade Commission. Legal specialists on false and deceptive advertising.

Senate Subcommittee on Consumer Affairs of the Committee on Banking and Urban Affairs. Information sources on consumer credit.

House Subcommittee on Health and Environment of the Committee on Energy and Commerce. Information sources on labeling, packaging and product safety.

Crime

Bureau of the Census, Department of Commerce. Data experts on crime statistics.

Uniform Crime Reporting Section, FBI, Department of Justice. Data experts on crime trends.

National Institute of Justice, Department of Justice. Specialists on violent crime, career criminals, treatment of criminals and rehabilitation.

National Institute of Corrections, Department of Justice. Information on prisons and jails, treatment of offenders, new techniques.

Drug Enforcement Administration, Department of Justice. Legal experts on narcotics and dangerous drugs.

National Center on Child Abuse and Neglect, Department of Health and Human Services (HHS). Information sources on identification, prevention and treatment of child abuse and neglect.

National Center for the Prevention and Control of Rape, National Institute of Mental Health, HHS. Information sources on prevention and control of rape.

Fraud Section, Criminal Division, Department of Justice. Legal experts on white-collar crime.

Organized Crime and Racketeering, Criminal Division, Department of Justice. Legal experts on organized crime, including narcotics, vice and loan sharking.

Education

Bureau of the Census, Department of Commerce. Data experts on education levels, school enrollment and similar topics.

National Center for Education Statistics, Department of Education. Information sources on a wide variety of education-related measurements, including enrollment, teacher population, school libraries, higher education finances.

Education Reference and Information Center (ERIC). Network of information clearinghouses at various universities. Includes experts on a wide variety of education topics such as the educational development of children and teacher training.

Bureau of Elementary and Secondary Education, Bureau of Higher and Continuing Education, Department of Education. Specialists on issues and concerns in all levels of education.

Bureau of Education for the Handicapped, Division of Education for the Disadvantaged, Department of Education. Information sources on issues affecting the education of physically or emotionally handicapped children and educationally deprived children.

House subcommittees on Elementary, Secondary and Vocational Education; Postsecondary Education; and Select Education of the Committee on Education and Labor.

Senate subcommittees on Education, Arts and Humanities, and on the Handicapped of the Committee on Labor and Human Resources.

Energy

National Energy Information Center, Department of Energy. Central clearinghouse for energy information sources in the government.

Energy Information Administration, Department of Energy. Data experts on energy production, demand, consumption, reserves.

Short-term, Mid-term and Long-term Analysis divisions, Department of Energy. Specialists on the future of energy production, supply, consumption, prices, imports and alternative sources.

Conservation and Solar Energy, Department of Energy. Experts on research and development of advanced technologies.

Office of Resource Management, Acquisition and Administration, Department of Energy. Experts on nuclear energy research including nuclear waste management (also in the Office of Nuclear Waste Management).

Nuclear Regulatory Agency. Information sources on construction and operation of nuclear reactors and other facilities, and on the handling, transportation and disposal of nuclear material.

Senate Subcommittee on Energy and Water of the Committee on Appropriations; Senate Committee on Energy and Natural Resources.

House Subcommittee on Energy and Water of the Committee on Appropriations; House subcommittees on Energy, Conservation and Power, and on Synthetic Fuels of the Committee on Energy and Commerce.

The environment and natural resources

Environmental Data and Information Service, National Oceanic and Atmospheric Administration (NOAA), Department of Commerce. Information specialists in oceanography, meteorology, geology, pollution.

National Marine Fisheries Service, NOAA. Experts on fish and commercial fishing.

U.S. Fish and Wildlife Service, Department of Interior. Information sources on endangered and threatened species, migratory and game birds, fish and wildlife.

U. S. Forest Service, Department of Agriculture. Information specialists on forest ecology and economy, forest diseases and fires.

Soil Conservation Service, Department of Agriculture. Experts on soil and water conservation, pollution control and environmental improvement.

Bureau of Mines, Department of the Interior. Experts in minerals from antimony to zirconium.

Bureau of Land Management, Department of the Interior. Specialists in natural resources and environmental concerns about public land.

Environmental Protection Agency, Department of the Interior. Experts in air, water and noise pollution, and hazardous chemicals and wastes.

House Subcommittee on Natural Resources, Agriculture Research and Environment of the Committee on Science and Technology; House Subcommittee on Health and the Environment of the Committee on Energy and Commerce.

Senate Subcommittees on Environmental Pollution, Nuclear Regulation, Water Resources, Toxic Substances of the Committee on Environment and Public Works.

Health

Health Information Clearinghouse, Department of Health and Human Services. Referral service for almost any question on health and disease.

National Center for Health Statistics, HHS. Information sources on health, health needs and resources.

National Center for Toxicological Research, Food and Drug Administration, HHS. Experts on carcinogenic, mutagenic and teratogenic substances.

Alcohol, Drug Abuse and Mental Health Administration, HHS. Information sources on biological, psychological and behavioral aspects of alcoholism and drug abuse.

National Institutes of Health, HHS. Hundreds of researchers and experts divided among 11 institutes that deal with major health issues like cancer, arthritis, allergies, strokes and aging.

Centers for Disease Control, HHS. Wide variety of physicians and researchers with expert information on diseases, birth defects, environmental health problems, smoking.

Occupational Health and Safety Administration, Department of Labor. Information sources on workplace safety and health standards, and job-related injuries and illnesses.

House Subcommittee on Health and the Environment of the Committee on Energy and Commerce; House Subcommittee on Health and Safety of the Committee on Education and Labor.

Labor and employment

Bureau of Labor Statistics, Department of Labor. Hundreds of researchers, analysts and experts divided among a variety of offices and divisions, each specializing in an employment-related area (such as current employment analysis, employment structure and trends, labor–management relations, and occupational health and safety).

Office of Policy Evaluation and Research, Employment and Training Administration, Department of Labor. Information sources on labor market processes, factors contributing to unemployment, transition from school to work, retirement.

Employment Standards Division, Department of Labor. Specialists in workers' compensation, minimum wage, affirmative action hiring.

Immigration and Naturalization Service, Department of Justice. Legal experts on immigrants and illegal aliens.

Labor-Management Services Administration, Department of Labor. Information sources on the structure, financial condition and activities of labor unions.

National Labor Relations Board. Specialists in private-sector employer–union relations.

Women and minorities

Bureau of the Census, Department of Labor. Several experts in race and ethnic statistics, including those concerned with American Indians, Asian-Americans, Blacks and Hispanics.

Commission on Civil Rights. National clearinghouse for civil rights information.

Equal Employment and Opportunity Commission. Information sources on all federal equal employment programs.

Office of Civil Rights, Department of Education. Information sources on discrimination in education because of sex, race or handicap.

Commission on Status of Women, Women's Bureau, Department of Labor. Information specialists on the status of women.

Bureau of Indian Affairs, Department of Interior. Specialists on federal services and programs affecting American Indian tribes.

Civil Rights Division, Department of Justice. Legal experts on enforcement of anti-discrimination legislation.

Issues and Answers

8

L ike an inquisitive Bambi who encounters the dreaded Godzilla, the fresh, wide-eyed journalist soon discovers that government isn't the biggest creature in the forest—it *is* the forest.

That terrifying revelation should be warning enough to immerse oneself in civics, or else become hopelessly lost in an unceasing maze of councils, districts, agencies, commissions and boards. Several examples should illustrate the need to understand how active and complex government is below the federal level.

In 1981, followers of an Indian guru named Bhagwan Shree Rajneesh purchased the 68,000-acre Big Muddy Ranch in central Oregon. Several months later, county officials approved a Rajneeshee petition to incorporate 2,000 acres of the ranch into a new city to be called Rajneeshpuram.

That petition set off fireworks that kept journalists hopping until late in 1985, when the commune leader (1) was arrested and pleaded guilty to immigration fraud charges, (2) left the United States (for good, he said), and (3) ordered his followers to abandon the commune that once had a population of 3,500.

During the four years in which this story was "active," reporters had the opportunity for a thorough schooling in state and local government issues. To deal with such a complex, often volatile, story, they needed a firm foundation in civics. Here are some of the issues they dealt with:

- *Land use.* Could a large tract of land, designated by the county and state for agricultural use, become an urban area? What agencies and laws affected such issues as annexation, zoning changes and requests for building permits?

■ *The law.* Was the commune's takeover of the nearby town of Antelope and its school district legal? Were proper procedures followed in voter registration? Did Oregon's secretary of state improperly intervene in voter registration challenges?

■ *Education.* The commune set up its own schools and also directed the operation of schools in the local district. Did it maintain proper educational standards? Was it legal for the state superintendent of public instruction to withhold aid traditionally given to this district? What was the role of the Teachers' Standards and Practices Commission in this matter?

■ *Public safety.* When commune members started a police force to patrol Rajneeshpuram and surrounding areas, what controls and reviews were in place? What was the role of the state's Board of Police Standards and Training? What was the relationship between this new police force and area prosecutors and judges?

■ *Economics.* What was the corporate organization of the "Rajneesh Neo-Sannyas International Commune"? Who or what owned all its property, and what was its tax status? What information was available from the state's corporation commissioner?

These were just a few of the questions that reporters faced in covering this complicated story. As new issues arose, reporters had to dig deeper into the government institutions they had been covering for years—institutions they had *thought* they knew well. The executive, legislative and judicial branches of government were regularly contacted. Records and documents were searched. Information from agencies and associations working with government was an information lifeline.

In 1986, when the Rajneesh story had slowed to a trickle of second- or third-section stories, local reporters recalling the "four-year seige" remarked how little they had previously understood about government organization and activities. They were glad for the education.

A colorful and complicated story like Rajneeshpuram is not a frequent visitor to a reporter's notebook. Even though many stories may *seem* straightforward and ordinary, effectively reporting them may depend on a wide range of sources that must be quickly found. Consider this local incident from the police blotter.

A man burns a convenience store clerk with an electric cattle prod and takes more than $150 from the store till. He also steals the clerk's van. Less than two blocks away, he crashes into a utility pole and a fire hydrant. Police responding to the store alarm find the robber wedged in the van and cursing everyone in sight. Firefighters arrive; they pry open the van's door with a hydraulic Jaws of Life. They also hose down spilled gasoline from the van. The city-owned utility sends a crew to inspect the power pole. As police remove the increasingly agitated man, he bites one of the officers, who is sent to a hospital emergency room. There he meets the store clerk, who is being treated for burns. The suspect is arrested, booked into the city/county jail and is scheduled for a court appearance (arraignment) in the morning.

Reporters uncovering this story will get information from the logs of the police and fire departments, the jail, the court clerk and the hospital. They most likely will also deal with public information officers from the city, hospital and electric utility. These reporters know that the key to successful information gathering in stories such as these is understanding government organization and knowing contacts within government who help control the flow of information.

A cautionary note: It is not enough for journalists to approach public affairs with institutional know-how. Simply focusing on how the bureaucracy works could create an unwanted dependence on government officials for news. Rather, understanding government operations gives the reporter another tool to use in uncovering the news. In any story, journalists must look at the component issues and then search for the broadest sources possible to help explain what happened.

With that in mind, let's examine the information-gathering process by first looking at local and state governments and then reviewing issues and stories that require information from them.

UNDERSTANDING GOVERNMENT ORGANIZATION

Non-federal government units generally fall into one of these categories: state, county, city or special district. Some functions overlap, depending on constitutions, charters and method of financing. In some jurisdictions, for example, a district attorney (or prosecutor) may be part of a county organization but may receive some compensation (and regulation) from the state. In other areas, the "county" prosecutor may be called a *state's attorney* and is paid by the state. Learning these layers of government and how they operate is indispensable. Information from the office of the secretary of state, for example, will help give you an outline of state operations; similarly, contacting your state association of counties, your state league of cities and your state association of school boards will give you valuable background. But these checks are just a start.

Being aware of how government organizations interact is also important. This is where the reporter benefits from pursuing an issue rather than trailing a single bureaucracy. For example, if you were researching a story on a threatened teachers strike in a local school district, you might want to look at the issue from the viewpoints of *education, labor, justice* and *public safety.*

Under *education,* you would contact schoolboard members, administrators and key representatives for the teachers. Has the school board drafted a contingency plan to keep schools open in the event of a walkout? Is the district working with state education officials to ensure that teacher replacements are properly certified—thereby preventing a challenge to the district's number of official school days and preserving state contributions to local school financing?

Under *labor,* you need to examine applicable laws on public employee strikes. Has the collective bargaining process (if any) been abandoned or exhausted? What have the teachers' union and the board's management association said and done? Has the state taken a position on unemployment benefits for the strikers?

Under *justice,* has any court action been threatened? Have parents sued to keep the schools open? Have teachers active in the union or association been threatened, penalized or suspended? Has binding arbitration been ordered?

Under *public safety,* if a strike is authorized and the district seeks strike replacements, what plans have been made to ensure the safety of these replacements, as well as of administrators and students?

A story like this may not demand immediate investigation of all these aspects. But all of the above issues are related. By outlining how a story might go and in finding the information as the story develops, the reporter can ensure production of a complete and accurate story.

Most government units have legislative, executive and judicial components. At the state level, the legislative function is well-publicized, but city councils, county commissions and some special service districts can pass laws, too. Noting these similarities will help you understand the interrelationships of government.

Cities

Whether a city (or village) is governed by an elected mayor and council, an elected council with an appointed professional manager or a town meeting with an elected chair, the departments that these bodies control are essentially the same. In most urban organizations, the components will be public safety, public works, human resources, justice and finance.

A city, like most government units, offers services to its citizens. In exchange for providing police and fire protection, road improvements, a range of social services and court-administered justice, it imposes various charges. These can be taxes, which most often come from a levy based on the value of real and commercial property. They can also be user fees (such as a special charge to inspect a completed building to see if it meets all codes) or a special tax levy to pay off bonds for voter-approved projects such as a sewage treatment plant.

Decisions on services, policies and budgets are made by the elected council, with administrative support coming from a professional staff and with special perspectives coming from citizen advisory committees.

Counties

County organizations provide essentially the same services as cities but to a more widespread population. A county's legislative body is usually a commission or a council and executive. In some jurisdictions, the county commissioners, who are paid as full-time elected officials, serve as department heads; others exclusively use professional administrators who report to the policy-making commissioners.

Regardless of its administration, county government usually provides services for unincorporated (non-city) areas. However, it may also provide jail, court and assessment/taxation services for cities within the county. Fees for these services usually come from property taxes, special fees, state funds and federal grants.

Schools and other special districts

School districts and other special public-service providers, such as mass transit, fire protection and mosquito abatement districts, may not match city or county boundaries. They are carved-out jurisdictions intended to serve special populations and areas. Buffalo, New York, for example, receives bus and subway service through the Niagara Frontier Transit Authority, which also serves a neighboring county.

All of these districts impose another layer of fees (taxes) to pay for these services. Some state or federal funds may go to these districts (depending on the political climate). Most of these districts have an appointed executive—for example, a school superintendent or a rural fire chief, and an elected board.

The state

State organization is the most complicated and far-reaching, but its services have a common framework. Its major sections are executive (governor and agency heads), legislative (usually a house and senate) and judicial (various levels of courts). State laws often have an impact on the operations of cities, counties and special districts. Funds raised by the state through sales, income and corporate taxes are often passed on to other levels of government, making some type of accounting to the state necessary.

Here is an example of the relationships between the state and local governments:* A school district covering possibly one-half of a city and only one-eighth of the county may levy property taxes to finance its operations. It also may depend on state money (perhaps special disbursements from the legislature or a portion of the state income tax or lottery receipts). Most of its local levies must be approved by voters; applicable election laws are passed by the state legislature, and the elections may be conducted by the county. The county may also handle property assessment and tax billing and collection; it will disburse the school district's share. Teachers hired must not only meet standards set by local school boards (who may be influenced by existing labor-management agreements) but also by the state department in charge of teacher certification.

Because of all these possible interrelationships, it is helpful to look at information sources from a topical standpoint rather than from an organizational view. Therefore, we'll next examine these topics as part of the strategy for information gathering: public safety, justice and corrections, education, social services, public works, labor, economics and finance, and the environment.

Public safety

Police and firefighting services are the key segments of public safety. Although police work is one area of law enforcement (justice and corrections will be examined in a succeeding topic), there are many other components of police services, including jails, animal control, search/rescue and special teams. We'll look at police organization first.

Police. Covering police matters requires understanding police organization and procedures. Whether the information you seek comes

---

*Because local governments vary widely in organization, it is not possible to make these examples applicable to all areas.

from a city police department, a county sheriff's office or the state police or highway patrol, the information trail is the same.

The first step in developing an information base is to learn how the force or department operates by reading the department's administrative manuals. They detail areas of responsibility, the chain of command and departmental procedures. They will tell you when, how and where reports are filed and who is the appropriate resource for releasing and amplifying that information.

Like most agencies of government, a police force is inundated with paperwork. Most of that information is stored in a computer system, which is indeed a compelling reason to develop strong, trustworthy relationships with department sources. Such computer storage can add another layer of difficulty to an information search because the searcher now needs access to the machine as well as to personnel. Of course, good relationships have always been a prerequisite for speedy, dependable help.

As you become familiar with police department organization, your search for documents and resources will become easier. Your main reference will be a summary of activity, still referred to in some areas as a *police log* or *police blotter*. This is a list of carefully edited items, revealing usually just the type of complaint or crime, the time of the report, the case number and the name of the reporting officer.

In most cases, you will be able to request more information on an incident from the records clerk or the watch supervisor. This second level of information may come in several forms:

- *An incident report.* This will list the type of incident (burglary, assault and so on), the name of the victim or complainant, the name of or identifying information about the suspect, the damage done, missing items and additional offered information. Most important is the officer's narrative at the end of the report. It can provide material for further questions.

- *A custody report.* When a person is arrested, the incident and case number are also listed in this report. It will list the charges and describe the suspect, as well as any recovered property. Sensitive information, such as the names of juveniles arrested and the physical/mental state of a suspect may be listed. For example, recorded blood alcohol levels and evidence of drug ingestion may be noted. Because some of this information may be used as evidence, police and prosecutors are concerned about its premature (pretrial) release. Other reports relating to custody, such as booking statements and bail applications, may be filed at the jail.

- *An investigation report.* When a crime is committed but no arrest has been made, detectives investigate the case, gather evidence and attempt to find a suspect. In the process of this information gathering, much of the data may be used by the district attorney to bring before a grand jury, which is a secret, one-sided proceeding. If a public trial is held on the basis of the grand jury report (indictment), the media and the jury will learn of the evidence at the same time.

Because of the potential harm of early release of trial information, many police and media organizations have agreed to guidelines on reporting criminal proceedings. These stem from the 1968 Reardon Report, issued by the Advisory Committee on Fair Trial and Free Press of the American Bar Association. (See Chapter 3, pages 50–51.)

Concerned about the complex and volatile nature of police information, many police agencies have turned to public information or community relations officers to regulate the information flow within their departments. These personnel can help the media because they deal with newsgathering organizations regularly and seem to understand and appreciate the pressures on the media. The public information officer (PIO), then, becomes a third level of information for the reporter, who has by now scanned summaries and activity reports.

Because many police reports are now entered on secure computer networks, the PIO can be helpful in tracking particular cases and referring the reporter to appropriate police personnel for more detail. In many cases, the PIO may refer the reporter to the watch commander (usually a lieutenant or sergeant in charge of a shift), the patrol commander, the detective commander—or even the chief. In larger and more complicated organizations, the PIO can be a godsend. But it is important to remember that the PIO is not about to put his or her department in an unfavorable light.

In smaller departments, a reporter's strongest leads can come from the police dispatcher—the employee (possibly not even a sworn officer) who first receives a call for assistance and then contacts an officer to handle the case. That information becomes part of the police log, which is the beginning of the information trail.

One fact of life about police reporting is that news of ongoing investigations is more difficult to obtain. While it is not the media's business to interfere with the law enforcement process, the media need to be assured that police business is being conducted in a proper manner. But because reports may contain "creative writing and routing" (in the words of a veteran detective), the reporter needs to cultivate the proper sources and to create an atmosphere of trust if police reporting is to be fair and effective. And—short of obtaining a court order forcing release of what should be public information—there is nothing to ensure speedy disclosure if sources are not cultivated.

Keeping in mind police organization and media relationships, let's examine how a reporter might track a story that begins with a case number and title on a computer summary of activity: #2203—Apparent Homicide.

A 28-year-old woman is found dead in her hotel room. A maid reports this information to the police, who investigate, confirm the death, notify the next of kin and write a preliminary report. That information is turned over to detectives, who act on the premise that the death has been caused by strangulation. A day later, that premise is verified by the county coroner.

Once next of kin are notified, the reporter can learn the name, age, address and occupation of the victim. The PIO can direct the reporter to the detectives, who will be reluctant to release much information about the investigation at this point. Interviews with hotel employees and co-workers of the victim will yield background information but mostly conjecture about the death.

The medical examiner or coroner (usually employed by the county) reports that the victim was raped, put up a struggle and was strangled. Little other information will be released at this point because certain evidence may help detectives in their search for a suspect.

At this point, the reporter will be able to learn the approximate time and method of death, with enough details to confirm that a murder has been committed. Now the reporter will be seeking regular reports from detectives—perhaps through the PIO—on the progress of the investigation. In addition, the reporter will stay in touch with the office of the district attorney and its investigative arm for another view of the case's progress.

After several weeks' investigation, the woman's husband is arrested for murder, and two other people are arrested on conspiracy charges. The suspects are taken to jail and processed (booked) after a brief hearing in a circuit court denies them bail.

Interviews with the district attorney, detectives, court bailiff and jail booking officer should yield interesting information at this point. Many documents should also be available for review; however, remember that the district attorney needs to preserve the integrity of much of the evidence by not revealing it before the trial.

The trial begins. All admissible evidence is presented. Testimony may be freely quoted. Reporters see the background value of relevant documents and prior interviews when following this testimony. If a conviction is made, a presentence investigation will assist the judge in passing sentence.

Reporters should also use the considerable body of statistics compiled by police. These statistics provide much material for analysis of local, state and national crime. For example, examining city patrol activity and relating that to crimes in particular areas could produce an interesting story. Perhaps mounting public concern about robberies and assaults on a park jogging path has forced police to increase patrols in that area. Checking statistics for other areas could show that *before* the patrol change, there were actually 15 times as many robberies and assaults in an area filled with apartment complexes as in the park. These statistics, which are readily available, can temper emotion with facts and help the public to use police resources wisely.

The lesson should be clear: Learn department organization and procedures; appreciate the role and pressures of police work; cultivate good sources; and don't expect officers to give you a lesson in civics every time a new "situation" comes along. Be tough-minded, but do your homework!

Fire departments. Although the organization and activities of a fire department are not as complex as those of police agencies, its work is so intense and fast-breaking that good department-media relations are essential if a reporter is to obtain timely, accurate information.

Fire departments, which are involved with fire suppression, fire prevention and investigations, are generally part of a city organization, a city/county operation or a metropolitan service district. In unincorporated areas or in very small cities, a volunteer fire district with taxing powers may exist. Regardless of organization, however, uniform reporting standards are coordinated by the state fire marshal.

In medium-sized and large cities (50,000 people or more), your best contact is the department's public information officer, who will organize information received from firefighters at the scene, including battalion and department chiefs. In smaller departments and in volunteer districts, your best contact will be the fire chief. In both these situations, your initial information will come from the fire dispatcher, who takes the call, logs in the alarm and response times and receives radio updates. A caution—dispatchers can be helpful for brief pieces of information and for updates, but they cannot stay on the phone long. They are the department's main contact with both the public and with the firefighters.

In many jurisdictions, a dispatcher may handle calls for several fire districts even though he or she is employed by only one department. In uniform reporting systems like the 911 emergency number system, a central dispatcher coordinates many different fire and rescue calls. For the reporter, such a system provides a quick, comprehensive view of fire and rescue activity across a wide area.

Although fire stories may seem direct and uncomplicated, much information needs to be discovered, such as:

- *Who and what was involved.* Injuries and deaths. Escapes and rescues. Drama or irony about the occurrence. Prominence of victims.

- *Property damage.* The amount of loss and type of property. History of fires in the area. The existence and extent of insurance coverage. Damage or threats to adjacent property. Defects in sprinklers, alarms or hydrants.

- *Description of the fire and of rescues.* Heroism. Obstacles to successful firefighting.

- *Cause.* Statements of the fire marshal (the prime investigator) and firefighters. How the fire was discovered. Materials found at the scene. Suspicions. Related police reports of activity.

This information, found in a basic fire report, is available from the PIO or battalion chief. This public record tells you:

- The alarm time, arrival time and time that the responding units were back in service

- The address of the fire or rescue, the size and type of structure, the occupant/owner of the property, use of the property (lumber storage, private residence and so forth), the value of the structure and the actual loss

- The cause and area of fire origin, the form of heat or ignition, the area and extent of damage and fire confinement, the method of extinguishment and control

- The number of engines (water pumpers), trucks (hook and ladders), tankers and rescue vehicles

- The number of firefighters involved and the amount of aid from other fire districts

- The number of casualties

In most cases, a reporter should be able to obtain this information toward the end of a fire or shortly after units have returned to their stations. If the fire is "working" (a large, involved one), the reporter should go to the fire scene. Observing safety precautions and the orders of firefighters, the reporter should go to the command post where the PIO and battalion chief are stationed. A fire reported solely on the basis of documents will lack important description and narrative, not to mention possible sidebar features.

Of all the information available to reporters about a fire or rescue, the two most difficult areas are arson investigations and the conditions of people receiving emergency medical assistance.

For information about an arson probe, the reporter may be referred to the district attorney, who may be reluctant to reveal evidence that may jeopardize an arrest or trial. However, once the arrest is made, some information (including a request for a search warrant, for example) should be on file in the office of the court clerk.

Medical information can also be difficult to obtain because much of it is considered private and part of the doctor-patient relationship. However, a reporter listening to radio traffic between a hospital and emergency medical technicians (EMTs) might learn some interesting information. Because publication of that information may violate the Communications Act of 1934, you should use the material as background only and to try to verify it with another source.

To ensure reliable contacts with hospitals, reporters should cultivate relations with public information officers, emergency room personnel and floor supervisors. Most of these people are aware of the needs of the media. Codes of cooperation, which agree on material suitable for release, have been adopted nationwide in various forms; check on their existence in your area.

Fire marshals and insurance companies are valuable sources of interesting statistics. A reporter can discover the number and type of alarms per station and compare that with station staffing, types of emergency calls, false alarms by area and time, and smoke detector and sprinkler failures. Local statistics can be compared with those gathered by the state fire marshal.

Justice and corrections

Coverage of court activities generally is a straightforward, well-defined process. However, reporters also know the value of frequent contact with the clerk of court—a surprisingly mighty figure—in order to stay in touch with the flow of paperwork at all stages of a hearing or trial. Reporters also know that coverage of corrections issues is much more difficult because material is less accessible.

Let's examine court activities first by reviewing court organization, procedures in criminal and civil trials, useful contacts and resources, and issues in court reporting.

Court organization. Courts are organized by jurisdiction, which may involve both geography and types of cases. A justice of the peace court may serve a small region such as a village and may hear misdemeanor traffic and nuisance cases involving village ordinances. A circuit court, however, may be countywide and hear civil cases involving large sums of money and criminal cases dealing with all felonies, including murder.

Specialty courts such as small claims, probate and tax appeals courts may exist on several levels.*

From the lowest level to the highest, here is a possible alignment of courts:

- Justice of the peace courts have very limited jurisdiction and deal mostly with small civil cases and minor misdemeanors. The justice may possibly be neither a lawyer nor an experienced judge; he or she could be a village mayor.

- Municipal courts rule on violations of various city ordinances and may deal with minor misdemeanors for which no jail term is required.

- District courts rule on civil and criminal issues. Is a court of limited jurisdiction, in that it has a monetary limit on civil cases and sentence/fine limit on criminal matters. For example, it may rule on all misdemeanors but only minor felonies.

- Circuit courts handle all civil and criminal (non-federal) issues out of the jurisdiction of the lower courts.

- The state court of appeals is the first level in the judicial appeal process.

- The state supreme court is the second level of appeal. It sets precedents on state constitutional matters. The chief justice may also administer lower courts in the state.

- U.S. District Courts have original jurisdiction for all matters of federal law. Organized by region.

- The U.S. Court of Appeals is first level in the federal appeals process.

- The U.S. Supreme Court is highest court of appeal.

It is important to know the court alignment of your state, including the courts' jurisdictions and whether the judges are appointed or elected. Besides getting to know the judges, you should also know the clerk of court, who maintains trial records, and the process preceding and following the trial itself. For example, you could find applications for search warrants, background on subpoenas (orders to appear in court or to produce material), memoranda from judges and schedules of future cases. Other key personnel are the bailiff or marshal, who helps keep order and has frequent contact with defendants in criminal cases, and the court reporter, a stenographer who maintains the official public transcript of all court proceedings.

---

*An excellent resource on court organization is the annual edition of *Want's Federal-State Court Directory,* Want Publishing Co., 1511 K Street NW, Washington, D.C. 20005.

Court procedures. Attorneys and judges have studied law for at least three years after getting their undergraduate degrees. Their specialized discipline has a language that puts the layperson outside many discussions. Reporters must break down both language and process to help the audience understand how the law works.*

Whether the case is *civil* (personal or business) or *criminal* (a public offense against person or property), court proceedings have a predictable order:

1. *Someone files a complaint before the court.* In a civil matter, an individual or corporation files a lawsuit that seeks relief (translation: usually money) for certain allegations it must prove in court. In a criminal matter, the public's agent (the prosecutor or district attorney) files the complaint. This may be done through information gained in an arrest, an indictment by a grand jury or through an arrest warrant issued by a judge. At this stage, a substantial number of documents and reports are already available to the media.

2. *The person charged responds to the complaint.* In a civil matter, that usually is a denial of the *cause of action,* followed by a request for dismissal. In a criminal case, a judge may hold a preliminary hearing to hear such motions as dismissal on the grounds of insufficient evidence.

3. *The case is heard before either a judge, a panel of judges or a jury.* If the trial is by jury, the selection of jurors can become a fascinating process. How jurors are selected or rejected often sets the stage for an interesting trial.

4. *A decision on the case is made.* The decision comes after a generally long presentation of evidence and examination of witnesses. Lawyers sum up arguments, the judge gives instructions on matters of law to a jury, which may then deliberate for several days.

5. *The award is announced or sentence is passed.* An award is made in a civil case; the judge passes sentence in accordance with the jury's finding in a criminal case.

These findings are subject to appeal, which can tie up a case for several years. A lower court may find itself rehearing a case because an appeals court ruled that an error in law was made during the trial.

Because so much unfamiliar terminology is associated with court procedures, reporters need to explain certain terms to their audience. For example, an *affidavit* is a sworn statement taken outside of court

---

*An excellent, very readable source on court procedures is the handbook *Law and the Courts,* published by the American Bar Association.

without the opportunity for both sides of a case to examine the person making the statement. A *deposition* is actual testimony, under courtlike conditions and rules, taken outside of court. A lawyer may remove a potential juror with a *peremptory challenge* (for which he or she need not give a cause), but in most cases will have to state persuasive reasons to have the juror removed *for cause*.

A good aid in deciphering this language is *Black's Law Dictionary,* the "old faithful" of law libraries. A law clerk or court clerk can amplify most definitions and relate them to the case at hand.

Contacts and resources. The clerk of court can be the most helpful source in sorting out information about civil and criminal matters. By obtaining the *case files* from the clerk, you can follow the chronology of activity. For example, the following would be contained in a civil case file: the complaint, any answer or denial, special motions (such as to narrow the scope of the case or to remove certain parties), placement on the court calendar (docket), affidavits, depositions, subpoenas to appear or produce evidence, the trial transcript, jury instructions, and the verdict and judgment. This information can be helpful in your research in other cases—for example, trying to show a pattern of fraud complaints and convictions against several different corporations, all with the same principals (owners).

A criminal case file follows the same pattern, but it also contains such items as a jail booking report, an application for bail and its disposition, a list of evidence and exhibits, and bail information. The district attorney's office can be helpful in providing additional background information, but it will want to ensure that certain evidence not be revealed prematurely.

Attorneys for both sides may wish to be interviewed about a case, but the judge may sometimes stop them from discussing it because of its sensitive nature. While it is unconstitutional to prevent the press from reporting on these cases, it is an accepted practice of judges to hold *officers of the court* (lawyers) in contempt for violating their rules.

Reporters sometimes need to talk to a witness or a person who has been subpoenaed even though the district attorney's office is withholding the person's name. In this case, a reporter can go to the clerk of court or to the county department of finance. Every time a witness is ordered to appear or a person is ordered to bring certain evidence to a hearing, he or she will be reimbursed with a special, although small, fee and payment for mileage. In requesting reimbursement, that person lists a name, address and phone number so a check can be sent. These reimbursement requests are public records because the public wants to know how its tax money is spent. Checking these forms is also a good way to learn who has been ordered to appear in secret grand jury hearings.

Many agencies, associations and commissions also deal with justice and corrections, and they issue many documents on the subject. State bar associations, judicial fitness commissions and citizen advisory groups all monitor court performance and deal with complaints against attorneys and judges. The chief justice of the state supreme court often serves as chief administrative officer for county and state courts; he or she will issue reports about staffing, caseloads and financing. A reporter should monitor these reports to discover potential problems or irregularities. Contact your local prosecutor, public defender or county administrative officer to learn what official reports and oversight groups can give you more information about the justice system.

Issues in court reporting. There is more to court reporting than a recitation of trial proceedings. Reporters should also be concerned about delays in getting cases on the court calendar, extreme variation in awards and sentences, investigations of and complaints about lawyers and judges, the amount of plea bargaining (allowing defendants to plead guilty to a lesser charge to avoid a trial), possible abuse of the grand jury system and the ease with which some judges issue search warrants. Once you cultivate your sources and learn the "paper trail," you will find that your story supply seems never-ending.

Corrections systems. Correctional institutions, whether a local "holding tank" or a large state penitentiary, are often volatile story subjects. Social and economic costs, overcrowding, inmate assaults, revolts and the complicated, emotional issue of parole are subjects requiring focus, research and corroboration.

Several checkpoints for the reporter include the jail director (often a sworn police officer), the mayor or commissioner with responsibility for corrections, the state director of corrections, penitentiary and institution wardens, and parole board members. You will find that institution records are much more difficult to obtain; many states, for example, consider parole hearings confidential. Other issues may be raised through inmate organizations and through their newspapers at state and federal prisons.

Education

Many reporters will tell you that no aspect of government attracts as much public interest and controversy as education. Consider the breadth of these topics: the banning of *Huckleberry Finn* from a school library, the firing of a popular basketball coach in a school board "personnel session" closed to the media, a collective bargaining dispute between a teachers union and the administration, a recall election involving two school board members, the hiring of a new superintendent of schools, the arrest of a kindergarten teacher on child molestation charges, new graduation requirements, federal funding cuts for the training of mentally handicapped students and annual budget elections in some states.

To gather information and effectively report on issues involving such a diverse, complex system, you must understand several things about the schools.

How schools are organized. Schools exist in districts, which may not always match the boundaries of cities and counties. Except for state universities, their government is based on the *board,* composed of members elected either at large or by geographical zone. This system includes community college and educational service districts. Board members are responsible for adopting policies and budgets, setting elections on school matters, and implementing state and federal regulations applying to their districts.

The board members, who are generally unpaid, set policy direction for an administrative staff headed by a superintendent, with midmanagement composed of principals or department heads. Both the board chair and the superintendent are excellent contacts, but also consider program administrators, the board clerk (who may also be the budget and finance officer) and the district's public information officer. Familiarize yourself with the district and its schools by acquiring a staff directory and a district administrative manual.

In a state university system, boards of trustees or regents are usually appointed by the governor. Such a system may direct one major university or a group of related universities.

How schools are financed. Schools obtain revenue for their annual budgets through local property taxes (which may include special levies to retire debts for projects such as new buildings), from portions of state revenues (including income taxes, sales taxes and lottery receipts) and from federal grants. Important stories requiring detailed investigation include how budgets are formed (from committee formation to public election), the impact of collective bargaining on a district's resources, and a district's dependence on federal money for important programs such as special education. This chapter's sections on economics and labor include more on these matters.

Who are the pressure groups? Be sure to count parents among the "interested parties" on the education beat. They are joined by teachers and their unions (most likely an affiliate of the National Education Association or American Federation of Teachers), administrators, board members (aided by state and national school board associations), legislators, bureaucrats in state departments of education and by commissions on teaching standards.

Include on your list special interest and ad hoc groups such as an athletic booster club, a committee for fair school taxation or a group against sexist books. Learn the participants in every school story—you may be surprised at the size of the cast!

Schools and their constituent groups provide a large supply of information, opinions, reports and documents for the reporter. Here is a sample:

- School board minutes and memorandums
- Attendance reports
- Reports on curriculum reviews and changes
- Results of local, state and national testing of students
- Purchase orders and bid specifications
- Collective bargaining contracts and grievance reports
- Advisory reports of parent-teacher groups
- Budget worksheets of citizen committees
- Budget documents
- Reports of educational accrediting agencies
- Audits of the school's financial condition
- School rating reports from outside agencies

Social Services

The complexity of educational news coverage pales in comparison with that of the plodding giant of social service issues. Professor Robert Agranoff of Indiana University sees social service programs operating in communities through the following agencies:

1. Several units of local general-purpose government (cities, towns, townships)
2. Special-purpose local governments (school districts, recreation districts, library districts, mental health services districts, transportation districts, special education districts, sanitary districts, water districts)

3. Direct federal program operations (Social Security Administration offices, Veterans Administration offices)

4. Direct state program operations (substate units of state public assistance, rehabilitation, employment security, mental health and other agencies)

5. Regional units of state umbrella human services departments where substate functions are combined

6. Regional quasi-governments—special-purpose planning/program agencies (area agencies on aging, health planning agencies, employment and training consortia, regional housing authorities)

7. Regional general-purpose agencies (councils of governments, regional planning agencies, regional development districts)

8. Voluntary service delivery agencies (family service associations, the Salvation Army, Catholic Charities, mental health associations, homes for the aged, nutrition programs, senior centers)

9. Proprietary agencies (nursing homes, home health care agencies, group and sheltered homes)

10. Solo practitioners or group professional practices (medical, nursing, social work, psychology)*

Discover which of these structures or service categories operates in your community. Then you should learn who directs and funds them. Chances are that the federal government has a mighty role in the delivery of these services. A review of *The Catalogue of Federal Domestic Assistance* reveals this partial list of agencies and groups that filter aid and information down to local communities:

- Department of Agriculture: Human Nutrition Information Service; Extension Service
- Department of Health and Human Services: Public Health Service; Food and Drug Administration; Alcohol, Drug Abuse and Mental Health Administration; Administration on Aging; Social Security Administration
- Department of Housing and Urban Development: Community Planning and Development; Office of Fair Housing and Equal Opportunity
- Department of Labor: Employment and Training Administration (unemployment insurance)

---

*Robert Agranoff, ed., *Human Services on a Limited Budget* (Washington, D.C.: International City Management Association, 1983), 6–7.

- Veterans Administration: Veterans Benefits; Department of Medicine and Surgery

Federal dollars from these agencies trickle down to state and local levels to fund government and private, non-profit groups for programs dealing with such areas as child abuse, architectural barriers for the handicapped, day care for preschoolers, birth control, mental health counseling, nutrition for the elderly, foster homes, child support, venereal disease control and investigation, pest control, sanitation, food stamps and medical care for indigents.

This list only scratches the surface. To discover what services are offered in your community and state, look to special directories of human and social services published at several levels. A state department of human resources, for example, will have a large inventory of state and local programs. Most telephone directories today have special lists of social service and volunteer agencies. As you discover what agencies exist and who directs them, you will become aware of other directories and contacts. It can be an immense network.

Because most of these programs are tied to government funds, extensive reporting and evaluation procedures exist. These audits are public records. Some social service programs also require licensing; nursing home care is an example. States are supposed to inspect and regulate nursing homes carefully, and the federal government evaluates them as Medicare providers. These reports are public. If you had heard about complaints against a nursing home from a source who wanted anonymity, you could go to the appropriate state agency, such as the state health division, and search for records. There you would find the trail of complaints and their disposition. Records of violations of health and sanitation codes for restaurants are also available for your inspection.

Good reporting on these issues doesn't need to contain a tinge of scandal. Stories on a vital matter like the increasing transient populations in urban centers could take you from contacts in the federal Department of Health and Human Services to state offices of human resources or adult and family services, to city offices providing emergency shelter assistance, to the United Way and Salvation Army and to private and church-sponsored food and shelter programs. In a complex society that can't solve all the problems of maldistribution of wealth and services, no one group has a monopoly on aid.

Of all the human service programs in existence, none causes as much consternation, argument and investigation as health care. Every year, Congress wrestles with national health insurance, hospital cost control, Medicare and Medicaid benefits, drug rehabilitation programs, and assistance to prepaid medical insurance programs called health maintenance organizations (HMOs). It is estimated that federal expenditures for health care will exceed $700 billion by the end of this century, an almost 400 percent increase in 30 years.

The cost of health care is an ongoing story. Medical service organizations such as the American Medical Association and county medical societies, private and public hospitals, health systems agencies and hospital siting councils, and federally funded groups that monitor health care costs and distribution of services are all involved. These groups and their myriad reports provide strong source material for your reporting.

Because the topic of social services is so broad and complex, it is best to devise a general set of questions to help guide your information search. These include:

- Who funds the service?
- What is its scope?
- What are the reporting requirements?
- What evaluation/review procedures exist?
- What laws apply to this service?
- Who directs the service?
- Who appoints the administration and boards?
- How is this service linked to other services?
- How effective is it?

Public Works

A government does more than provide public safety, education and social services. It is also a contractor of massive proportions, doling out public funds for construction of roads, bridges, airports and water, sewer and mass transit systems. This package of government services is called public works. In late 19th century American government, public works was synonymous with the "pork barrel"—a scornful characterization of how politicians used tax money to finance favorite projects that would provide patronage to their districts and possibly some financial kickbacks as well. Although many public works projects are necessary and worthwhile, the potential for fraud and waste is great. A reporter needs to follow the dollar to discover (1) how projects are given their priority, (2) how contracts are awarded, and (3) what quality control and review measures for the projects are in place.

Following this trail is difficult. Many of the billions spent annually on these projects originate with the federal government. Drive by any municipal project under construction today, and you will see a billboard describing the project, its contractor, estimated date of completion and method of financing. For a wastewater treatment project, you will see the name of the Environmental Protection Agency prominently displayed as the sole or main financier.

While their activity is monitored by the affected agency and by the Government Accounting Office (GAO), the recipient government controls most design work, contracting and awarding of bids. Once again, a knowledge of state and local government and the roles of its many agencies becomes important. To adequately monitor a public works project, you should:

1. Obtain the grant application from the recipient government and read a description of the project. Ask to see correspondence about the application and its acceptance.

2. Contact the appropriate department head (for example, county roads director) and discuss the project. Get introduced to the project officer.

3. Check with the finance director of the affected agency to discuss project specifications and project bidding and award procedures. This is a good contact in case of cost overruns and unwelcome "discoveries" during an audit.

4. Examine the revenue sources of all local government expenditures for this project (for example, supplying administrative help or providing equipment).

5. Talk with local contractors and union representatives for their views on the project and the bidding and award process. Their statements may be jaundiced, but if there is a pattern in their complaints or observations, you may be on an interesting trail.

6. Check the disbursements from the government unit's finance department and compare them with reports filed with the federal agency that gave the grant.

Special commissions may also be key actors in public works projects. Such appointed bodies as airport, highway and metropolitan wastewater commissions exercise great influence in project, site and contract selection. These commissions keep minutes of their meetings, which are usually public. Their reports make their way to city councils and county commissions, which consider that information before voting on relevant project and money matters. Be watchful of how these appointed groups intend to finance their projects; in addition to federal money, they may also depend on local property taxes, user fees (such as landing and hangar fees to finance an airport runway extension), and the issuance of special tax-exempt bonds, to be retired later by taxpayers.

Labor

While labor union membership in the private sector has been declining in recent years, unionization of public employees has risen dramatically. Terms like *arbitration, mediation* and *picket line* are today familiar ones to many police officers, firefighters, teachers and public health nurses. These groups have strong representation, supported by such unions as the American Federation of Teachers, the International Association of Fire Fighters and the American Federation of State, County and Municipal Employees.

Bringing collective bargaining into the government arena has had two significant effects. First, governments do not want citizens to suffer a curtailment or disruption of essential public services. While some states prohibit strikes by public safety personnel, all other public employee strikes may be legal once a labor contract expires. In an attempt to prevent strikes, many local governments have established binding arbitration, which means that both sides turn to a disinterested third party for a decision. Check your jurisdiction for applicable labor laws; they may be part of a city charter or state statute. Second, acceptance of a negotiated contract can put a strain on local governments, which must find ways of financing the pact.

A reporter soon discovers it is easier to report the outcome of labor issues than the process. Because so much of the process revolves around personnel questions, meetings dealing with such issues as collective bargaining and arbitration of disputes are not open to the public. However, all outcomes must be approved by the governing body, which must meet in public to vote on proposed agreements.

Some obvious sources for information on public employee labor questions include the personnel officer for the government unit; the local union or federation president (or business agent); and the director of the state's agency for public employee labor issues, sometimes called a public employee relations board. To work with these people and understand the issues, here are some suggestions:

1. Become familiar with the labor-management history of the government unit. Don't be surprised if the public employee unions are relatively new organizations.
2. Obtain relevant collective bargaining contracts. They show which jobs are covered by the agreement, the pay ranges, and the issues subject to grievance procedures. They may also reflect negotiation trends.

3. Get on the mailing lists of relevant labor unions and management groups. You will want to know the agenda of such groups as the International Association of Fire Fighters and state and national League of Cities association, as well as that of regional associations of management groups that advise on collective bargaining matters. A brief talk with union and management leaders will reveal these valuable sources.

4. Become familiar with the work and publications of your state's labor commissioner and of the National Labor Relations Board, which deals with private sector employees and their right to organize and bargain collectively. A key publication is the Bureau of National Affair's *Government Employee Relations Report,* which gives a weekly look at legislative, judicial and administrative actions affecting public employees.

5. Investigate political activity of the public employee unions in your region. Many form PACs—political action committees—to lobby for legislation and to finance campaigns of favored candidates. In the public arena, teachers represented by NEA and AFT have well-financed PACs. All PACs must submit statements of organization and accounts of receipts and expenditures. These forms are usually filed with the secretary of state. However, your local elections clerk should also have information on these PACs.

Reporters covering the labor beat should be familiar with collective bargaining, especially with the public posturing that surrounds a private process. However, they should look beyond unionization matters. They should also study economic and workplace factors such as cost-of-living increases, retirement/pension plans, vacation time, health insurance, staffing levels, worker safety and the right to strike and grieve. Both statistics and narrative accounts concerning these issues are available from personnel officers of government unions, from the state department of labor and/or employment, and from the U.S. Department of Labor's Bureau of Labor Statistics.

A sensitive and complicated labor issue today is comparable worth, a theory of job comparison that studies education and work requirements in order to identify similar jobs. It is an attempt to challenge higher premiums placed on jobs traditionally held by men and to upgrade jobs of similar skills and training traditionally held by women. Proponents of comparable worth would say, for example, that the job specifications and training for a plumber and a nurse are similar; they want to know why plumbers, who are mostly male, are much higher paid than nurses, who are mostly women. Comparable worth is already an issue in the public sector, and reporters must be prepared to explain it.

Other important issues include discrimination in hiring and promotion, occupational safety and health, the flexible work schedule and workplace, and wage renegotiation to save the jobs of fellow workers.

Economics and finance

The speed of the government vehicle may be sluggish, but it drives with amazing constancy, thanks to a never-ending flow of fuel—your tax money. How government appropriates, budgets and spends this money is of great importance to reporters and their audience.

Examining budgets and asking questions about resources and expenditures are central to understanding the circular flow of public money and services. On the city/county level, three important sources of information are the assessor, the director of finance and the chief budget officer. They can provide the documentation you need. The explanations may take longer, because you may have to interview many department heads. On the state level, the staff budget officer for the legislature, the legislature's research staff and the state treasurer are key sources.

Let's look at two important areas to master: the budgeting process and assessment/taxation.

Learning about budgets. Most government budgets, whether for the state, a school board or a special sewer district, wind their way through a process of department proposals, administrative presentations, citizen committee review and approval by elected officials. In many cases, the approved budget may face a public vote.

Before you can adequately explain the budget process, you need to know:

1. Whether the budget item represents an increase or decrease from previous fiscal years, and why.

2. The background for new budget items and for substantial changes in existing ones; for example, a large increase in the fire department budget may reflect a need to increase staffing at a station. That change may have resulted from a study of alarms and responses and from demands made in collective bargaining sessions.

3. How these budget items will be paid for. Property taxes do not cover the major share of expenses in many cities and counties. Local payroll taxes, shares of state liquor and gas taxes, hotel and rental car taxes, amusement license revenue, parking and court fines, money from special fees and permits, and state and federal revenue sharing all contribute to the public treasury. There may even be a special employer tax to finance mass transit.

The public wants to know the costs of these services and the reasons for them. The reporter generally will find officials eager to explain budgets because government may be looking for new revenue sources or may face an election to approve a special levy. With a little research, the reporter soon finds that the document that appeared to be burdensome babble is actually an eye-opening chart of a government's goals for a community.

Assessment and taxation. Taxes assessed against personal and business property may not provide the largest share of government revenue, but they do cause giant-sized headaches and complaints. When Californians passed Proposition 13, they effectively rebelled against high assessments and escalating property taxes. They forced government to cut services or look elsewhere for revenue. This rebellion has not been carried to many other states, so it's safe to assume that property taxes will be an important revenue source for a long time. Let's examine the process.

Your property, whether it is a four-bedroom house on a quarter-acre lot or a 90,000 square-foot factory, is listed on tax rolls. The value of the property must be estimated to levy taxes to be paid to various taxing districts serving that property. This task is generally handled by the county assessor's office, which handles all paperwork and collections for all taxing districts. Property is usually valued every year, either by computer or by physical inspection. An assessor determines the *true cash value* (TCV) at today's market rates.* Let's assume the assessor values a four-bedroom house at $100,000. Here is a possible property tax bill, depending on what percentage of the TCV is used as the basis for the levy:

Government Unit	Levy per $1,000 TCV	Cost at 100% TCV	Cost at 30% TCV
School district	$12	$1,200	$360
City	3	300	90
County	2	200	60
Community college	1	100	30
Sewer	50¢	50	15
Total tax bill		$1,850	$555

*Not many states tax at the full cash value of property. Michigan, for example, assesses at 50 percent TCV; Colorado, at around 22 percent. Check your state laws on assessment procedures.

Property owners can appeal their assessments to a review board and even through the courts. This can be a costly process, which is why only large property owners usually follow through on appeals. Because large amounts of money are at stake, the reporter should examine the appeals process, who sits on the review board and what conflicts of interest might exist in certain cases.

If the assessment stands, the taxes are not automatic. In many cases, voters have the right to approve or reject annual operating levies.

This process also applies to business property. However, in many cases, business inventories may also be taxed.

There are several things to look for when covering assessment and taxation matters. For example:

1. How often is property physically inspected? Is the assessment staff large enough to cover the taxing district and capable enough to determine current market values?

2. What is the process for foreclosure of property for non-payment of taxes? Are the penalty interest rates on delinquent accounts so low that some property owners withhold payments temporarily to take advantage of higher interest rates in financial markets?

3. How much of the operating budget is covered by the property tax levy?

4. What are the various ways of raising assessments and taxation in the district?

5. Are legal descriptions of property, a property address index and a property owner index readily available for public inspection? If not, why?

6. Is there much discrepancy between assessment records and mortgage records showing the actual recent selling price of that property?

A wealth of information of this type can be found at the assessor's or county clerk's office. Deeds, surveys, mortgage records, payment records and ownership files are waiting for your inspection. Use them!

A final note on this topic: Play the role of auditor and examine complete budget documents. Better yet, make the official annual auditor's report required reading. If discrepancies exist in the handling of funds, the auditors will mention them—subtly perhaps, but their exceptions to a "a clean bill of health" for the organization will be there. As you examine budgets and audits, you will soon find that government is big, complicated business. For example, the Seattle Mariners baseball team leases stadium space from King County. The county also takes a big percentage of the team's ticket sales and concessions and parking income. Some counties are in the logging business.

Other government units, like one state university system, own valuable real estate that brings in lease and rental revenue. Keep poring over those budgets—you'll soon learn what makes government run.

The environment

Toxic wastes, radiation leaks, air pollution, solid waste disposal, bacterial contamination, noise: These are a few of the important issues that make environmental reporting a challenging but frustrating job. Reporters must be familiar with environmental concerns and protections in their areas and knowledgeable about the agencies that monitor these issues.

Every level of government is concerned about environmental issues. Politicians rail about them. Business executives express concern for the environment but urge adoption of cost-effective measures that protect the environment while saving the economy. Citizen lobbies for environmental protection make their presence felt. Clearly, the reporter covering the environment has many constituencies to monitor.

On the municipal level, city health and sanitation departments monitor the quality of water and sewage treatment. On the county level, the public health department and the county sanitarian examine control standards for septic-type sewer systems and monitor their effects on soil and water. Officials of sewer districts are watchful for the dumping of hazardous or flammable wastes into sewer systems. On a state and regional basis, departments of environmental quality and natural resources monitor air quality and set water quality and sewage treatment standards. All these government levels are affected by the rulings—and the considerable financial clout—of the federal Environmental Protection Agency and the Public Health Service.

So much government involvement means paperwork. Mountains of reports and required filings make interesting reading if a reporter is compiling a case against a chemical manufacturer suspected of violating the terms of a wastewater discharge permit. By talking with local and state inspectors, reviewing reports of contamination of nearby water tables, tabulating past violations and finding employees angry enough to talk about these violations, a reporter can find the information to present a compelling, well-documented story.

An environmental agency may show one face to the public but present an entirely different one to other government agencies. Remember that a city agency may report to the state and the state, to the federal government. Obtain these reports to see what kind of job is being done in your area. Check local agencies to see what citizen complaints have been filed and review the agency telephone logs used to record suspected violations.

A large amount of environmental information comes from other agencies, such as fire departments, the U.S. Forest Service, the Soil and Reclamation Service, the Fish and Wildlife Service—even the Coast Guard and the Army Corps of Engineers.

To help translate the more complex nature of environmental issues, it is helpful to read such publications as *Environmental Action* and the Sierra Club's newsletter. You can get help from nearby universities by contacting their news bureaus to see if there is a faculty expert on your subject. Also use the public information offices of the state and federal environmental protection agencies. Finally, the Media Resources Service of the Scientist's Institute for Public Information, a 24-hour service, can find experts to answer questions about any scientific matter. The New York-based service has a toll-free number: 800–223–1730.

KEEP WATCHING AND LEARNING

The issues raised in this chapter should persuade you as a reporter to learn about government—and to carefully follow the paper trail it leaves as it goes through its bureaucratic paces. Ask again and again:

- How is the program funded?
- Who administers and reviews it?
- Who benefits from it? Who doesn't?
- What laws affect it?
- What public records does it provide?

Not all your searching will reveal waste, inefficiency and fraud. Your function is to inform—to explain, to analyze, to predict.

Learn government organization and services first. Be sure to corroborate your information. More often than not, people working within the government (but not necessarily at its political levels) will be your strongest sources.

The media are watchdogs of the government. Watch intently. Watch for a long time. Then pick your time to bark. When you hear the howling inside government's chambers, you'll know your readers and viewers have decided to bite.

Beyond the Press Release

9

Is the American business world a closed society?

It's a common but flawed image. It's a picture of the business-industrial complex as a secure fortress, guarded by public relations agents who release carefully screened information to the unsuspecting media. Requests for further information echo off stone parapets—or are answered slowly and cryptically by wary executives.

But the days of tight-lipped robber barons and their lieutenants are over, for the most part. Today, one in five Americans owns stock in American business. These shareholders (almost 50 million) want to know what's going on. So do the media. Fortunately, most corporations today have little control over the stockpile of information to which the journalist has access. Because of media attention, government regulation and citizen watchdog activities, American business—and its effect on virtually every segment of American life—is under intense scrutiny. People want to know about business affairs and the economic machinery that drives their lives.

This attention is responsible for the new, higher profile of American corporate life. It also explains why reporters on *all* beats need to understand American business. With that understanding and the aid of careful, deliberate information-gathering techniques, the reporter can monitor business activities and explain their effects.

This chapter examines strategies, sources and processes of business and economic reporting, with special emphasis on the influence of business on science, the environment, health and consumer affairs reporting. Our analysis includes foundations and other not-for-profit firms. The chapter also looks at the influence of the public relations practitioner in the information-gathering process.

WHY BUSINESS NEEDS A WATCHDOG

The impact of business on society is obvious: Unregulated, unwatched commerce can have drastic effects on the physical and economic welfare of citizens. However, government regulation is not enough. A responsible, thorough and sensitive media watchdog is necessary. Consider these incidents:

- In 1962, a speaker at the American College of Physicians Conference decried the use of a sedative in Europe called thalidomide, which, she said, was responsible for thousands of births of deformed children. This revelation received widespread media attention. However, what had not been reported before this revelation was how dangerously close the U.S. Food and Drug Administration had been to approving use of the William S. Merrel Company's version of the drug, Kevadon. The public later learned that an FDA researcher, Dr. Frances Kelsey, had withstood tremendous pressure from the company to authorize the use of Kevadon. When questioned later about the drug, the company blithely said there was no problem because it had not been released. *Question:* Where were the watchdog media in the several years before a physician had to make a public plea at a convention about this drug?

- In 1971, the weekly *Sun* newspaper in Omaha, Nebraska, examined fund-raising activities of the famed Boys Town complex, which for more than 30 years had pleaded that "there will be no joyous Christmas season this year" for its deprived children. Using public records and interviewing fund-raising experts, this small newspaper staff discovered that Boys Town had a net worth of almost $200 million, with projected annual revenues of more than $25 million— for a home that housed only 665 boys! This report, picked up by the major media, resulted in massive changes at Boys Town and in its fund-raising campaigns—and won the newspaper the Pulitzer Prize for Public Service.

- Since 1972, almost 15,000 lawsuits have been filed by women who claimed that the A. H. Robins Co.'s Dalkon Shield—an intrauterine device for birth control—caused pelvic inflammations, sterility, spontaneous abortions and death. Generally, only silence came from the company in response to media questions. After years of court battles, the company began a $4-million public relations campaign in 1984 to inform women who might still be using the shield that it poses a serious health hazard. In trying to catch up with this story, reporters used court records, interviews with doctors, trade press reports (for example, in pharmaceutical and financial journals) and opinions of industry analysts for their research. In 1985, the company filed for relief from multimillion dollar court judgments by seeking reorganization under federal bankruptcy laws. This action has raised an important issue for media examination—the ability of corporations to use bankruptcy laws to avoid financial and legal liabilities.

- During 1980–85, at least 138 people were killed in accidents involving Ford Motor Company cars, allegedly caused when the vehicles slipped from *park* to *reverse* gear while the engine was running. The General Accounting Office, an effective and generally unrestrained federal watchdog agency, compiled this information. Although the National Highway Traffic Safety administrator recommended a recall of certain Ford cars, she was overruled by the secretary of transportation. *Question:* Wouldn't even a few deaths that resulted in public court cases have been enough to alert the media? Why did it take so long for this story to appear? Certainly the information was there. Research into congressional hearings, trade press reports, audits by consumer groups, lawsuit transcripts and persistent inquiries to the company could—and eventually did—yield important results.

- In 1984, 2,000 people died in Bhopal, India, when methyl isocyanate gas leaked from a Union Carbide chemical plant there. The U.S.-based corporation said that no such leakage was possible at its Institute, West Virginia, plant. But in August, 1985, the toxic chemicals aldicarb oxime and methylene chloride leaked at the Institute plant, injuring more than 100 people. In response to inquiries, the company stonewalled both the press and public. Several days after the incident, government investigators started to piece together a pattern of improper procedures at the plant—and a few days later the Union Carbide chairman issued a public apology to the town.

These examples are not intended to show all American businesses as unethical or uncaring. Nor are they meant to imply that a reporter's focus should always be on wrongdoing. They should show, however, why the media must routinely and carefully gather as much information as possible about business and economic matters.

LEARNING THE BUSINESS OF BUSINESS

To effectively monitor the business world, you must learn how it operates. You need not become an expert, but you must know where to go to find the information you need. To begin, you must learn business terms and definitions. You must grasp principles of economics and law. You should know when to seek an expert (see Chapter 10), especially when matters become complex and technical.

The business beat

All areas of reporting deal with business in some way. Regardless of how and why business is covered, however, the reporter finds that "business" stories inevitably fall into one of three categories: *performance, competition* or *impact*. Many stories will include all these elements. *Performance* is important because it tells the tale of success, failure and corporate conduct. *Competition,* an integral aspect of a capitalist society, gives clues to possible strategies, innovations or perhaps problems. *Impact* focuses on the results of corporate activity as they affect consumers, shareholders and institutions.

Examine these elements in the following story topics:

- *Profits and losses.* How has the company acquired its market share? Has the company rebounded from adversity to become profitable again? Has the company actually lost money or just suffered a drop in earnings? If the company has losses, what is its explanation? How do financial analysts explain the company's performance and its prospects? What social costs (such as impacts on health, welfare, employment, or the environment) are involved in the operation and profitability of the firm?

- *Product performance.* What new products and markets have been created? Who are the innovators and entrepreneurs behind them? What is the safety record of the product? Has competition led to complaints of false advertising claims or patent infringement?

- *Employment and labor.* What is the impact of the corporation on the economic and social life of the community? What is its labor record? Are there occupational safety and health concerns?

- *Shareholder concerns.* Is the earnings record of the corporation satisfactory? How has company responded to criticism or proxy fights? Are there problems with mergers, takeovers or elections of directors?

- *Lobbying and PR efforts of business.* To what political campaigns does the corporation contribute? Is it a member of a political action committee? What is its lobbying and public relations record?

- *Government concerns and responses.* What is the corporate record in areas such as antitrust, consumer fraud, safety and equal employment? What is the role of business in such matters as foreign trade, balance of payments and cost of living?

As you can see, covering the world of business is more than a matter of picking up a company's news release, lightly editing it and then "announcing" that the firm has increased its dividend by 15 cents or that its profits have dropped because of "pesky" consumer lawsuits. Your audience wants to know *why.* It wants background, and it also needs forecasting. To provide comprehensive coverage, you must prepare yourself with the proper background.

Schooling yourself about business

You don't need a master's degree in business administration or a law degree to be a solid business reporter or to deal with important business components in all types of stories, but it could help. Many publications and broadcast stations today are, in fact, turning to people with these backgrounds to report on business affairs. Student journalists, however, can add to their qualifications by taking courses in economics (basic macro- and micro-economics as well as work in economic analysis, public policy, labor and banking), political science (the theory of government administrative organization and regulation), business and marketing (accounting, taxation, corporate structure and policy, market organization), and law (torts, contracts, administrative law). Fortunately, most accredited schools of journalism are located in universities where such coursework is available.

Beyond this preparation, student journalists and beginning professionals must keep their eyes on matters of business interest. Staying current with the trade press (see page 194) and making contact with industry experts (page 197) are two good methods of continuing your education.

Here are a few sources that may be of help:

Donald Kirsch. *Financial and Economic Journalism.* New York: New York University Press, 1978. A good introductory book that explores the most common business stories, this work explains financial processes by using a long case study of a private firm going public.

Lorna M. Daniells. *Business Information Sources*. Rev. ed. Berkeley: University of California Press, 1985. Daniells' book is a marvelous compendium of reference works, directories and associations. The entire volume is worth reviewing to get an idea of the breadth of resources available.

Mark Nadel. *Corporations and Political Accountability*. Lexington, Mass: D. C. Heath & Co., 1976. This work is a bit dated but contains an excellent analysis of corporate life and public policy.

Before moving on to a discussion of sources, let's examine the three principal types of business organizations: the privately held, for-profit corporation; the publicly traded, for-profit corporation; and the not-for-profit corporation, a category that includes various philanthropic and public service foundations.

The privately held corporation

A private, for-profit corporation is a business that does not issue stock to the public. Such firms are generally owned by family members or by a limited circle of investors. As a result, very little of this corporation's life comes under government scrutiny. The Securities and Exchange Commission cannot require annual public reports from this corporation because the public is not involved in the trading of its stock. However, the government and public are interested in the private corporation's impact on society.

The government, through enforcement of laws and regulations regarding monopolies, price discrimination, safety, fair employment practices and labor organization, can investigate and report on the activities of private corporations. In addition, whenever a private firm initiates or responds to a lawsuit, most of the information brought before the court is a public record.

An example of the private corporation would be the Newhouse holdings, also known as Advance Publications, a newspaper, magazine and broadcast conglomerate founded by the late S. I. Newhouse and willed to his sons in 1979. You won't find much about this publicity-shy firm in Dun & Bradstreet or the trade press, but that didn't deter journalist Richard Meeker from researching the press baron and writing his biography. His use of court records, personal interviews, government documents and painstakingly sought accounts in the trade press over 30 years allowed him to present a more public picture of a very quiet and fantastically profitable company.*

Another example is the family-held Adolph Coors Brewing Company of Golden, Colorado. With no public stockholders to account to, Coors is operated by a close-knit family; it reluctantly reveals small aspects of its operation to the public during a labor dispute or a lobbying effort at a state legislature.

The Nike corporation began as a small, privately held firm, but with the fitness boom and the resulting demand for running shoes and apparel, the company's rapid growth forced it to seek new capital from public shareholders—thus opening the company to public trading and scrutiny.

The publicly traded corporation

A treasure of information is available for this type of corporation, the most common in the United States. Such corporations raise capital by selling shares to the public. The government wants to ensure that these shareholders are treated fairly and that they receive sufficient information about the firm's activities. This includes a detailed annual report with information on assets, expenditures, debts, profits, dividends and prospects for future earnings. A publicly traded firm also must notify shareholders and the government about management changes, pending lawsuits, mergers and attempted takeovers.

The not-for-profit corporation or foundation

A non-profit organization is supposed to serve an important public function or service. In exchange, it pays no federal or state taxes on its revenues, which may come from donations, fees or grants. (However, the salaries of individuals working for such tax-exempt firms *are* taxable.) An example of such an organization is the Gannett Foundation, a philanthropic and educational group that funds various community services from non-taxable holdings in the Gannett Corporation, a media conglomerate and publicly traded corporation.

This type of firm receives great public scrutiny. The most important public document related to its operation is Internal Revenue Service Form 990 (see page 190), which lists all revenues and expenditures

---

*Richard Meeker. *Newspaperman: S. I. Newhouse and the Business of News.* New Haven: Ticknor & Fields, 1983.

annually. It was this document that revealed so much information about the fund-raising schemes of Boys Town.

DOCUMENTS AND SOURCES

Many sources are available to you, regardless of the type of business you are covering. This chapter considers both institutions and people as sources; reports, documents and personal interviews are the keys to your work.

As Chapter 8 showed, government plays a vital, unceasing role in our lives. Corporate directors no doubt would have other adjectives to describe the effect of government on the business world. Let's look at government activities and regulations and the information about business and the economy that their work generates.

Government agencies and documents

The Securities and Exchange Commission

The largest original information source about publicly held corporations comes from the Securities and Exchange Commission, formed in 1934. It has nine regional offices, complete with libraries of company files. Many SEC documents also are on file in the more than 1,000 depository libraries in the United States. (See Chapter 6.)

The SEC requires public corporations to file a number of reports. It monitors this information closely, as do the trade press and financial analysts. Some important reports are SEC forms 10, 8 and 13.

SEC Form 10. Form 10K is an annual, audited report of a public corporation's activities. This lengthy form will give you:

- A summary of company operations and the activities of its foreign subsidiaries
- The company's financial statement, including profit, loss, cash flow, working capital, debts and extraordinary items contributing to profits or losses
- Principal stockholders
- Remuneration of directors and officers
- Pending legal proceedings

■ Forecasts of the results of future operations and information about issues that may affect them

Form 10Q is a quarterly report detailing changes in the company since the last reporting period. Filed for the first three quarters of the company's fiscal year, this form is a good source of new information about legal proceedings by or against the company, as well as for updated financial information.

SEC Form 8K. The filing of an 8K is an important signal that significant changes are taking place in the firm. Any changes in ownership or assets, default in payment of securities, new auditing arrangements, or pending bankruptcy or litigation must be reported to the SEC within 15 days of the event.

SEC Form 13D. If a private party, group or corporation is attempting to purchase more than 5 percent of the stock of a publicly traded corporation (assuming the target firm has at least $1 million in assets and 500 shareholders), the acquiring party must submit a Form 13D. This form gives interesting details about the hopeful buyer—information that may not have been available before if the buyer is a privately held firm.

The SEC tries to inform shareholders and the public about the activities of public corporations—all 15,000 of them. SEC disclosure rules also require that companies make annual reports to stockholders and inform the media in a timely fashion about corporate activities. However, it is up to the information-gatherer to become familiar with the maze of SEC reports and filings. Here are some hints to aid in the search:

1. The SEC issues an annual report on corporations required to file forms under the Securities and Exchange Act. You can get this directory at most depository libraries or by contacting the SEC, 500 N. Capitol Street, Washington, DC 20549.

2. The SEC also issues the *Daily News Digest,* also available in microform, that lists recent administrative and criminal proceedings against firms, new securities registrations and recent 8K filings.

3. The regularly published *SEC Docket* lists commission opinions and interpretations of the Securities Exchange Act.

4. SEC information is available from other sources, too. You can purchase it from private firms like Q-Data of St. Petersburg, Florida, or Disclosure, Inc., of Los Angeles. You can see many of these materials in microform at larger libraries or in depository libraries.

You should also check which of the growing number of electronic databases (see Chapter 7) carries these forms and filings.

The state as corporate record-keeper

Businesses must register with corporation commissions in the state of their preference, if they choose to incorporate. For many corporations, the state of preference has been Delaware because of its hands-off manner of corporate regulation. But most states today have adopted the Model Business Corporation Act, which recognizes the rights and interests of shareholders.

Your state, through either the office of the secretary of state or the corporation commissioner, will have records of registered firms, publicly traded or not. At the very least, these public documents will contain the name, address and purpose of the company; the names and addresses of the incorporators and directors; and the value of the stock issued, if any.

The state corporation office also receives a brief annual report from firms registered there. The amount of information won't be overwhelming, but it could be a start.

In addition, the state also will hold records of partnership registrations, registrations of securities offered in that state, industrial health and safety inspections, product liability insurance claims, workmen's compensation claims and any wage complaints.

To discover what other records are available in your state, check with the secretary of state, corporation commissioner, wage and hour division, insurance commissioner and labor bureau.

The Internal Revenue Service

You won't learn much of corporate life from the IRS—unless a tax dispute forces parties into U.S. Tax Court. At that point both the claims and contested records will be in plain view. If a company has apparently defaulted on payment of personal, corporate or employee withholding taxes, that will also be a matter of public record because the IRS will go to court to seek a lien against assets and property to recover the money.

Most public IRS information comes from the Form 990 required annually of not-for-profit corporations (Form 990PF for private foundations). These forms are filed at the IRS regional office nearest the corporation's headquarters. Not-so-recent filings will be stored at regional federal record centers.

These documents show revenue sources, employee remuneration and all major expenditures. They are especially helpful in showing the ratio of administrative overhead to total revenue. For example, a media examination of relief agencies providing Ethiopian famine relief in 1985 revealed that a few of them had astonishingly high administrative costs. (The Foundation Center of New York City also monitors thousands of private foundations and publishes the *Foundation Directory*. (See page 196.)

In many cases, the not-for-profit organization will make its 990s available for your inspection. If so, you should also ask to see its Application for Recognition of Exemption, an IRS form in which the corporation or foundation seeks nonprofit status. This status is important because it means that donations to the organization are tax deductible. As a result, the IRS routinely reviews the 990s to see if the spirit of the organization's application is being maintained. You should review this application to get a sense of the history and purpose of the organization.

The IRS also has a large staff of investigators who track down tax fraud, money "laundering" (funneling illicitly obtained money through certain banks that won't report large transactions) and other illegal practices. The Criminal Investigation Division (CID) of the IRS regularly offers workshops in financial investigative techniques for law enforcement agencies and financial institutions. These workshops, say IRS investigators, would be ideal for journalists. For further information, contact either the CID chief or the public affairs officer at any regional IRS office.

Other government agencies and documents

Other government agencies regulate, investigate and provide records about American business, both public and private. Read these agencies' bulletins and documents, most of which can be found in depository libraries and in the agencies' regional offices:

- *Antitrust Division of the Department of Justice*. This agency monitors and prosecutes monopolistic trade activities, including price discrimination practices. The regional offices of the U.S. attorney are good contacts.

- *Federal Trade Commission*. The FTC also watches for anti-competitive behavior, but it focuses on deceptive business practices. Advertising is a particular focus of enforcement; claims are regularly investigated and certified by the FTC.

- *Consumer Products Safety Commission*. This agency sets product safety standards and conducts investigations and public hearings on hazardous products.

- *Occupational Safety and Health Administration.* This troubled office and its burdensome rules have been streamlined recently, but suspicions still abound about its effectiveness. However, OSHA maintains helpful records of occupationally related accidents and illnesses.

- *Interstate Commerce Commission.* It regulates the rates and routes of trucking companies, railroads, bus lines and domestic water carriers. The commission collects quarterly and annual reports from these public carriers, which reveal much of the firms' financial and operating histories.

- *Food and Drug Administration.* The FDA sets standards for foods, drugs and some medical devices.

- *Federal Communications Commission.* The FCC regulates activities of telegraph, telephone and broadcasting firms. It is also active in antitrust matters.

- *Equal Employment Opportunity Commission.* The EEOC investigates discrimination in hiring, promotion and compensation.

Other documents may be available from state agencies not already mentioned. State public utility commissions, for example, can provide related but more local information about matters regulated by the Interstate Commerce Commission. Check with the office of your state's attorney general to see what records are available. (See Chapter 3.)

Company-offered information

The annual report

Although the SEC requires publicly held corporations to file annual reports, the company also produces an annual "showcase" of its work for its stockholders. Even if the year has been bad, the company will use this report—often a thick, colorful brochure—to explain mitigating circumstances and to urge continued confidence.

These reports usually contain a summary letter from the president or board chair, and information on revenues, liabilities and net earnings; assets; long-term debt; and stock dividends. The company may also use this report to forecast new projects, employment trends and investments.

Keep reports of interest to you. (Simple requests to be put on a company's mailing list should provide you a hefty library.) They can provide story ideas. For example, four years of recent annual reports for the Boeing Company show that the work force of Seattle's largest private employer had dropped by more than 20 percent without any reported operating losses during that period. In fact, in the year of lowest employment, earnings had increased by more than 20 percent. Earnings and dividends looked strong, but Boeing's work force had decreased by more than 22,000. Why? What effect did this decline have on the community? Reporters need to ask.

The proxy request

If all the stockholders of a mammoth corporation like General Motors decided to come to the annual meeting, many Astrodomes would be needed to house them. Most stockholders don't attend these meetings, but their votes count. That's why in the event of a merger proposal, a change in the slate of directors, or other matters having an impact on the corporation, the "no-show" stockholders are contacted with a proxy request.

With this request, stockholder votes are solicited for the annual meeting. In the proxy statement, the party seeking the proxy must state what matters are up for vote and how the party will vote the proxy.

Because a form of civil war occasionally erupts on corporate boards, it is not always the current holders of power who seek the proxy. Shareholder meetings have become battlegrounds, where the forces with the most proxies (representing the most shares) are the victors.

An attempted takeover of Marathon Oil in tiny Fremont, Ohio, and of CBS in New York City pitted stockholders against one another as rivals bid up the price of the stock they needed to buy to gain control. Documents related to these takeover attempts and proxy fights are, of course, public records. The results of any proxy fight or election must be reported in the next quarterly filing (Form 10Q) with the SEC.

The prospectus

When a private company goes public, or when a publicly traded firm wants to issue new securities to raise capital, the SEC requires it to file a registration statement (Form S-1). This lengthy, complicated form is intensively reviewed by the SEC before it allows the sale of securities to proceed. When the offering is approved, the corporation issues a prospectus to the public, which then may make a purchase.

Although a corporation may have met all SEC requirements for securities registration, it must still meet all state rules. Together, the federal and state documents make revealing reading. Here you will find thorough financial records, summaries of legal proceedings, information about both subsidiaries of the corporation and major lines of business, how the money from the sale of the securities will be used, and future plans of operation.

The news release

For an institution with the reputation of being secretive and uncooperative with information-seekers, the modern corporation is a prodigious provider of information. The news it both chooses and is required to release—which daily floods media outlets—announces, explains and fortifies the company's position on many matters. Although the company may urge "immediate release" on its announcements, the media must carefully assess the timeliness and newsworthiness of this information. That task is more difficult today because many press releases now receive the same high-speed electronic treatment that news gets from the wire services.

Two companies, BusinessWire and PR Newswire, compete to send news releases from companies directly to media outlets around the world. BusinessWire, for example, transmits press releases to more than 600 media organizations in 200 U.S. cities using the Associated Press Satellite Network. With press releases coming over regular news circuits and with these releases getting a more "official" look, editors must learn to be more on guard than in the past. Better packaging and smoother transmission (no more dusty mailbags full of news releases on company letterheads) don't justify publication of that information with no questions asked.

However, one benefit of this growing system is the creation of a new library of information. These electronic releases now are being filed daily into DIALOG, Mead Data Central and CompuServe. They should provide an important reservoir of information about companies using this service. For more information on these databases, see Chapter 7.

Reporting in the trade press

More than 10,000 periodicals are published in the United States every month. The majority of them are quite specialized, and many deal with business matters. Most daily newspapers are putting more resources into their business and economic coverage, encouraged, no doubt, by the growing number of specialized weekly business newspapers around the country. To find out what is being researched and reported in the trade press, your first step should be to check through several indexes. Here are several good ones:

Predicasts (Funk and Scott Index). *Predicasts* is an excellent, comprehensive weekly list of articles in the business and financial press. It has been published since 1960.

Business Periodicals Index (H.W. Wilson Co.). *BPI* is an old standard, issued monthly.

The Business Index (Information Access Co.). This is a regularly updated index on microform. It indexes more than 800 specialized periodicals, including law reviews. Published since 1979.

The Wall Street Journal, published five days a week, is obviously an important source of business reportage. It publishes a bound index of its coverage. Other valuable business publications include *Forbes, Business Week* and *Barron's,* published weekly; *Fortune,* published biweekly; and *Nation's Business,* published monthly by the U.S. Chamber of Commerce. In May, *Forbes* issues a list of the top 500 corporations by revenue and net profits. *Fortune* also lists a top 500 in May, ranked by total sales. In July, *Fortune* lists the top 50 financial, retail, transportation and utility companies. Some of these magazines are available on databases. (See Chapter 7.)

Reference works, guides and directories

The number of business reference sources is too lengthy to permit even an annotated list; many of them are also too specialized for your use. The following list, however, is both helpful and manageable:

Poor's Register of Corporations, Directors and Executives (Standard and Poors). This volume gives a daily news report, with cumulative index, on earnings, mergers, SEC registrations and business failures. It has a good directory of personnel.

Moody's Manuals (Moody's Investor Service). Moody's publishes seven annual volumes, with supplements and indexes: *Bank and Finance, Public Utility, Transportation, Industrial, Municipal, Over the Counter* (OTC stocks) and *International.* Provides company histories and excerpts from annual reports. The *International* manual lists 5,000 international corporations.

· *Reference Book of Corporate Management* (Dun & Bradstreet). Lists major officers and directors, including the personnel, credit and data processing managers for more than 6,000 firms.

Million Dollar Directory and *Billion Dollar Directory* (Dun & Bradstreet). These directories list businesses according to assets and sales. Provides financial summary, number of employees and company functions.

America's Corporate Families (Dun & Bradstreet). Lists more than 8,000 "ultimate" parent companies and 44,000 subsidiaries; it has good cross-referencing. (Since 1981, Standard and Poors also has published a *Directory of Corporate Affiliations*.)

Principal International Businesses (Dun & Bradstreet). Lists 50,000 companies and officers in 133 countries.

Directory of American Firms Operating in Foreign Countries (World Trade Academy Press). Lists more than 3,000 American corporations with 21,000 subsidiaries.

Bibliography of Publications of University Bureaus of Business and Economic Research (University of Colorado, Boulder). Most major universities have such research bureaus, which many times are housed in the school of business. The Association for Bureaus of Business and Economic Research maintains a comprehensive list of all research done by these bureaus.

Encyclopedia of Business Information Sources (Gale Research Co., Detroit). Lists sources for more than 1,000 topics in business and economics.

Financial Analysts Federation Membership Directory (Financial Analysts Federation, New York City). An excellent list of firms and the 15,000 analysts working for them. Good source for finding industry experts and for discussions of trends and forecasts.

Foundation Directory (Foundation Center and Columbia University Press, New York City). Lists private foundations, directors, major donors, assets and expenditures. (The center also maintains a recent collection of IRS 990 returns.)

Encyclopedia of Associations (Gales Research Co.) A three-volume set that lists 18,000 national and international associations, with their principal work and publications.

National Trade and Professional Associations of the United States (Columbia Books, Washington, D.C.). Similar to the Gale book, but it has an extensive listing of unions and labor sources.

Don't overlook regional, state and local directories. Chambers of commerce, economic development associations and regional trade groups may publish directories and data books.

Industry and trade groups

Both companies and trade associations have become increasingly active in producing information about products and services. Look through such publications as *Quill, Columbia Journalism Review* and *Advertising Age* and you will see offers of information from various trade sources. Here, for example, is a pitch from the McKesson Corporation:

> Writing a wrap-up?... A trend story?... Need a quote?... An industry expert?... A photo?... On deadline? We can help. We can provide information and experts on the drug and health care industry... the beverage business... the chemical industry.

The insurance industry has been an acknowledged leader in providing information and sourcebooks for the media. Allstate and State Farm Insurance have produced two of the best media kits available.

One of the main benefits of industry sourcebooks and these offers of help is that they give the information-gatherer insight into the agenda and language of the industry. Like the press release, however, this information must be carefully screened and evaluated.

Industry analysts and observers

Industry experts make their living by accurately evaluating and forecasting business trends. In general, these people are not apologists for industry, and they are voracious in their appetite for information about business because they are asked to recommend investments for their clients.

Several types of experts are available:

1. *Financial analysts.* Many brokerage houses and large investment firms employ analysts, who prepare reports and forecasts on spe-

cific businesses for clients. The media routinely call on these analysts, as did the New York *Times* in 1985 about a predicted boom in the sales of disposable diapers. According to an analyst for Goldman, Sachs and Co., a forecast of 3.5 million births and seven diaper changes a day in 1985 translated into potential disposable diaper sales of $4 billion. This information made a good business "bright." See the *Financial Analysts Federation Membership Directory* for a comprehensive list of these experts.

2. *Trade and industry economists.* Many large banks and brokerage houses have staff economists, who analyze industry trends and general business conditions and prospects. Firms such as the Chemical Bank of New York and Paine, Webber Inc. have chief economists who are regularly interviewed. Large banks and brokerages in metropolitan areas also have staff economists who will share their research and forecasts with you. Like psychiatrists arguing over the sanity of a criminal defendant, these economists may not always agree; nevertheless, their statements make interesting copy.

3. *Local brokers.* You might be surprised at the information and expertise that local stockbrokers possess. Many do research in order to make a favorable impression on their clients—and gain commissioned sales. Many of these brokers subscribe to expensive reports from Dun & Bradstreet and Moody's, and they may also receive SEC filings from companies they monitor. They are a good local source, and they may be able to connect you with prominent analysts and economists.

Consumer action groups

Although they can be strident and evangelical at times, consumer groups are talkative sources with a lot of research, dedication and political connections behind them. Many of these watchdog associations publish journals and newsletters, which may tip you off to a developing story.

The Encyclopedia of Associations is the best source for finding consumer groups and their publications. Further information on these publications is in the annual *N.W. Ayer Directory of Publications,* listed by state and city.

Here is a brief list of helpful consumer groups:

Consumer Federation of America, 1314 14th St. NW, Washington, DC 20005. This is the largest consumer advocacy group in the United States. It publishes several periodicals and features a consumer product safety network.

Center for Science in the Public Interest, 1501 16th St. NW, Washington, DC 20036. It represents consumer concerns about nutrition, the environment and health.

Consumer Action Now, 110 W. 34th St., New York, NY 10001. This group concentrates on energy and conservation issues.

Consumer Union of the United States, 256 Washington St., Mt. Vernon, NY 10553. One of the most visible groups because of its monthly magazine *Consumer Reports,* this product-testing organization is well-respected and accessible.

Another valuable consumer resource may exist in your area. The Public Interest Research Group (PIRG), a subsidiary of Ralph Nader's Public Citizen organization, has been organized in most states, with student PIRGs created on many college campuses. Get on their mailing list and review their research on business, environmental, energy and health matters. They're as close as your phone book or university directory.

The PR spokesperson as a source

The public relations department always should be considered *a* source—but never *the* source. A PR spokesperson is valuable because he or she generally knows the truth of a situation. The concern of the media is, however, how much of the truth will be released?*

Release implies *control.* That's how you should view the PR function. So far as the corporation or institution is concerned, each piece of information and every story have parameters of control. Consider the interview. Here is the view of Jerr Boschee, PR director for the Control Data Corporation:

---

*For a fascinating analysis of the PR function, see *PR: How the Public Relations Industry Writes the News,* by Jeff and Marie Blyskal (New York: William Morrow Inc.), 1985.

At Control Data, and many other companies, employees are not allowed to be interviewed without a public relations person present.

Why? Because reporters are professionals. They conduct hundreds of interviews a year. They know what they are doing. When it comes to interviews, most business people do not, and this leads to something few journalists understand. As amateurs, business people are taking a significant risk. The stakes are much higher than the questioner may realize—a job, a reputation, a company's well-being. Amateurs make mistakes. They mis-speak, they contradict themselves, they release proprietary information, they speak with confidence about things they don't understand. In short, most of them are over-matched, and they know they need an equalizer—so they turn to their public relations people, many of whom are former journalists.*

What an amazing statement! It pictures the business person as the helpless, naive prey of the predatory journalist. The statement is helpful, however, because it shows the lines of control: Only certain information will be released, and even then, it will be carefully monitored. These "amateurs" are protecting information, not giving it. Keep that in mind when you go to a corporate source. What the source chooses (or is told) *not* to release should give you a clue about the importance of the information. Go find it.

Though the PR spokesperson may not offer open-ended information to you, he or she may be able to confirm or deny specific details that you have discovered. With solid research behind you, you may get corporate sources to open up when they understand you already know most of the information they had thought to be "proprietary."

The American corporation is not a secure fortress. Despite occasional attempts to build moats and install steel-fortified doors, a business institution *is* vulnerable to public scrutiny. It relents under the gaze of government, consumers and alert media organizations.

It is your responsibility to investigate and research in a thorough and fair manner. Professionalism, not antagonism, should characterize your work.

But ultimately, it is you who must secure information's release.

---

*"Anatomy of an interview," in the *Observer*, published by the Minnesota Newspaper Foundation, January 1985.

Experts and Where to Find Them

10

When three Portland *Oregonian* reporters started researching a series on the Hanford Nuclear Reservation across the Columbia River in Washington, they didn't know the difference between radiation and radioactivity. Like most people in the Pacific Northwest, they had no idea what went on at the $975 million-a-year facility. "I didn't really understand whether Hanford was a place or a building or quite what it was," confessed one of the reporters.

A few months later, they produced a 15-part series coherently examining the massive nuclear power institution from environmental, technological, political and economic perspectives. How did they do it?

They relied on experts. During the course of their research, the reporters compiled a source list of nearly 400 names, conducted hundreds of hours of interviews, attended special briefings and waded through a 20-foot high stack of reports. They became students in the best tradition: curious, inquiring, questioning, skeptical. Their expert sources were the teachers.

The *Oregonian* reporters may have had more time and a more complex assignment than most journalists, but the challenge they faced is basic to all journalism: tackling an unfamiliar subject and understanding it well enough to write a fair, accurate story.

Every day, journalists are put in the uncomfortable but exciting position of trying to make sense of an increasingly complicated and specialized world they themselves don't understand. True, some journalists are experts—economists hired to write about economic issues, political scientists chosen to report on politics—but most are not. Most are initially as unfamiliar with the subjects they cover as are their audiences. It is the ability of journalists to identify, locate and question experts that allows them to do their job with a degree of confidence. It is their healthy skepticism that allows them to use—and not be used— by the experts they consult. Experienced journalists know that experts can range from knowledgeable, helpful guides to self-serving and manipulative sources. That's why no serious journalist depends on any single source for information, and why no journalist goes unprepared to an interview.

General assignment reporters for print and broadcast media often face a daunting array of issues. Consider these stories covered by a first-year, just-out-of-journalism-school general assignment reporter for a small daily.

- Will a proposed change in approach patterns at the nearby airport have an adverse effect on the health of the community?

- What educational programs best prepare mentally retarded persons for productive lives?

- How will changes in zoning regulations affect the community's residential neighborhoods?

- Why can't the city balance its budget?

- Are police officers being adequately trained to deal with domestic violence?

- Why did a supposedly solid, 60-year-old local company go bankrupt?

And all these assignments came in the reporter's first two months on the job! She was able to handle the assignments by picking the brains of a variety of experts.

FINDING EXPERTS

The first and most important step in using experts is finding them. A journalist who can combine curiosity, resourcefulness, perseverance and common sense with solid researching skills will discover rich sources of information for every imaginable story.

Who are the experts?

The biggest mistake journalists make in looking for expert sources is misdefining them. With our penchant for inflated job titles and our abiding faith in formal education, it's no wonder we tend to define experts by the words and initials surrounding their names rather than by their actual knowledge.

Experts may or may not have elaborate titles and advanced degrees. It's possible that the executive director of the state Department of Fish and Wildlife—an impressively titled, multidegreed official—doesn't know as much about the effects of industrial pollution on fish as some untitled, lesser-degreed research assistant. The local Vietnam vets counselor may be able to answer questions about delayed stress with more clarity and precision than a top executive in the Veterans Administration.

It's possible, even likely, that the top person in an organization knows less about any specific area relating to the organization's activities than does an underling. That's because chief administrators, if they are effective, delegate authority. Their assistants and subordinates grapple with specifics daily. They know the ins and outs of the issues and problems in their domain. Perhaps once a week, they brief the boss. Some bosses have a good general feel for the organization's activities; others are isolated by their very power, distorting their perspective. Whatever the case, the person at the top of the hierarchy is often not the expert you're looking for.

Who are the experts? They are the people who have information on and experience with the issue you are researching. They exist in government and the private sector at all rungs on the bureaucratic ladder. They may be associated with well-known organizations, little-known groups or neither. They may be designated official spokespersons or people deep within some corporate labyrinth. It is their knowledge that makes them useful to you, not their titles, degrees and affiliations.

Digging for experts

Good journalists are rarely content to skim the top layer of officialdom for expert sources. They look elsewhere for people who can help them understand and report on complex issues. And they use all their research abilities to meet the challenge. Digging for experts means using the information-gathering skills and tools you have learned in previous chapters.

The federal government is one place journalists repeatedly turn to in their quest for specialized information, expert testimony and knowledgeable comment. Within the bowels of the bureaucracy, reporters can find experts on subjects from organized crime to organic fertilizers, from franchise practices to foreign travel. In addition to gathering information that is national and international in scope, the federal government is a key source of detailed local, state and regional data, either through main agency offices in the Washington, D.C., area or regional offices scattered throughout the country.

Chapter 7 takes you step-by-step through the federal labyrinth, using reference tools commonly found in depository, university or public libraries. The following guides, discussed fully in Chapter 7, will help you quickly locate federal government experts. By using these directories, you break your dependence on the top layer of officialdom, designated spokespersons and media flacks.

- *Congressional Quarterly's Washington Information Directory*
- *Congressional Quarterly's Federal Regulatory Directory*
- *The Congressional Staff Directory*
- *The Federal Staff Directory*
- *Washington Monitor's Congressional Yellow Book*
- *Washington Monitor's Federal Yellow Book*

City, county and state governments are also good hunting grounds. As discussed in Chapter 8, these entities are concerned with a variety of vital issues including public safety, corrections, education, social services, public works, employment, economics and the environment. Most governments publish directories of their services with the names and phone numbers of personnel. Many department numbers are published under city, county and state headings in local telephone directories. Additionally, a growing number of government units employ public information officers who can be helpful in directing the journalist to experts and specialists.

Private industry can also be a gold mine of experts, particularly if the journalist is savvy enough to use these sources in a way that avoids puffery. Calling a book publishing company business executive and asking for information on the future of that company invites meaningless self-promotion. Calling the same person and asking questions about the impact of computers on the publishing industry may get you detailed information from an expert.

To find the experts you're looking for, use your researching skills. Remember the following guides, all detailed in Chapter 4:

- *The Directory of Directories*
- *Encyclopedia of Associations*
- *Moody's Manual of Investments, American and Foreign*
- *Poor's Register of Corporations, Director and Executives*
- *Thomas Register of American Manufacturers*

Perusing trade magazines is another method of locating industry experts. Numbering in the tens of thousands, each devoted to the special interests of a particular trade or profession, these magazines regularly profile, quote and refer to industry experts. Trade magazines and professional journals are also good places to find the names of experts on particular issues or problems. Many of these publications are indexed.

Experts at the university

Like most things right under our noses, university experts are often overlooked. These men and women have invested years becoming knowledgeable in their fields and spend their days reading, researching, writing and talking about their subjects. They are accustomed to explaining complex subjects to novices and, compared with some government or industry experts, are often less interested in the outcome of a particular story. All these characteristics make academic experts attractive sources. Consider these stories. In each case, the journalist discovered valuable information from a university specialist:

- A nationally known religious cult establishes a community in the state. (A professor in the Department of Religion is an expert on cults.)
- A famous novelist sues one of the state's largest newspapers for libel. (A journalism professor is a specialist in libel law.)
- The state's wine industry takes off. (A business professor's special interest is the economics of the wine industry.)
- Herbicide spraying is contemplated in city and state parks. (A biochemistry professor is conducting an ongoing research project on herbicides and public health.)

How do you locate academic experts? Annually published university catalogs will tell you the names, academic backgrounds and teaching/research specialties of faculty members. University phone directories often publish both work and home numbers for all staff. These important research tools should be part of your reference library. But sometimes the descriptions of specialties are too vague or the university too immense to make reading the catalog an efficient way of locating sources.

You might want to contact the dean, director or chairperson of the relevant department or school. That person is generally quite familiar with the specialties, interests and current projects of faculty members and can give you referrals. If the university has a public information department or news bureau designed to handle such requests efficiently, use it. The department may maintain an updated list of all faculty members qualified to answer questions on certain subjects. Sometimes one phone call will get you a complete list of academic experts on the desired topic.

Using public information and public relations departments

PR departments are a fact of modern life. Most government units have them. So do virtually all corporations, foundations, universities, agencies, associations and major non-profit organizations. PR people have a well-defined mission: to tell the story of and promote the organizations that employ them. This mission may or may not conflict with the journalist's quest for information. As we discussed in Chapter 9, PR departments can act as either facilitators or obstacles in the research process, often depending on the kind of information the journalist is after.

Their helpfulness in locating experts is also often tied to the story the reporter is pursuing. Two recent dealings with a hospital PR department illustrate the point. In the first case, the journalist was looking for a medical expert on athletic injuries for a story on the risks of overexercising. The PR staff found the expert and returned the journalist's call within the hour. The second story involved the hospital's fight against the opening of an independent local clinic. The journalist wanted to talk with hospital business personnel about the potential economic effect of the clinic on the hospital. After five days and numerous phone calls, a PR staffer called to say that the business experts were unavailable, and the hospital would have no comment on the matter.

At their best, PR departments can be vital links between complex bureaucracies and information-hunting journalists. They can quickly locate experts, help set up interviews and even provide background reports, usable photos and other important material. At their worst, they can stonewall requests and construct a difficult-to-penetrate barrier between the organization and the media.

Getting referrals

An efficient, commonsense way of locating experts is to ask for referrals from any number of different people and organizations. When you are wracking your brains for names of specialists, ask yourself these questions:

- Would any of my colleagues, because of past assignments or personal interests, know of experts in this field?

- Could specialty reporters at my organization or elsewhere offer referrals?

- Is the subject I'm interested in covered by a trade publication or research journal? If so, would an editor be able to direct me to the specialists I need?

- Is there a society or association that can put me into contact with experts?

- Have I remembered to ask every expert I talk with for the names of others in the field?

Following up on any or all of these questions may net you just the expert you're after.

Calling hotlines

Usually set up as adjuncts to public affairs departments, industry hotlines are designed to answer specific questions quickly. They can also be important sources of experts. A recent issue of *Columbia Journalism Review*—an excellent place to find out about industry hotlines—contained hotline ads for a drug company (information on nutritional supplements versus diet quackery), a health care corporation (facts on alcohol, drug and mental health problems), a chemical company (information on its own activities), an insurance company (traffic accidents and the legal drinking age) and the Tobacco Institute (the ongoing smoking controversy). Obviously, some hotlines are more self-serving than others, but that doesn't necessarily diminish their use as locators of experts.

The federal government also operates a number of hotlines with free "800" numbers. Among the potentially useful ones for journalists are numbers to call for information on dangerous chemicals, runaway children, cancer, political fund-raising laws and energy conservation. These and other hotline numbers are listed in Matthew Lesko's *Information U.S.A.,* a reference tool discussed in Chapter 7. The 800 directory assistance operator (call 800–555–1212) can also be helpful.

One of the most important hotlines operating today, in terms of both its scope and credibility, is the Media Resource Service (MRS). Established by the Scientists' Institute for Public Information and funded primarily by foundations, MRS is a free referral service (800–223–1730) for all members of the media seeking reliable sources with scientific and technological expertise. Acting on your request, the MRS staff searches a computerized list of nearly 15,000 scientists and engineers who have agreed to participate in the program. Often within the hour, MRS returns your call with a list of experts. In the case of controversial issues, representatives of all sides are provided along with each person's position on the issue. Because of its large database, policy of providing experts with conflicting views, and lack of ties to industry, MRS is a highly trustworthy guide to sources.

Avoiding sexism

Many journalists are conscious of—and purposely avoid—sexist language in their writing. But few are conscious of inadvertent sexism in their choice of experts. When journalists consistently quote male experts in stories about the public sphere (politics, business, science and so forth) and confine female experts to stories about the private sphere (nutrition, child rearing, domestic affairs), they help perpetuate oppressive, restricting, out-of-date stereotypes.

If the mass media are a mirror of our society, then the reflection should show female scientists, lawyers, business executives, doctors and athletes. It should show men competent and interested in child rearing, family affairs and household management. That doesn't mean story after story about "the first woman/man who. . . ." It means integration of the sexes into all relevant stories. The balance of experts is one simple way journalists can help make journalism a truer reflection of reality.

This certainly does not mean choosing a less qualified source of one sex over an expert of another sex merely to achieve male-female balance in a story. It does mean being conscious of societal realities, being wary of stereotypes and making an effort to show in your choice of experts that both men and women are competent in a wide range of human affairs.

DEALING WITH EXPERTS

Now that you've tracked down the experts, how do you deal with them? On the one hand, because you are not an expert, you are dependent on information and guidance from your sources. On the other hand, because you are a journalist, you have the responsibility not to be duped, manipulated or overwhelmed by your sources. Thorough backgrounding and intelligent interviewing techniques are vital to sensible and sensitive handling of experts.

Backgrounding is essential

He was a well-published science writer with two advanced degrees—an expert compared with his general assignment colleagues—but when he readied himself to interview the Nobel laureate scientist Linus Pauling, he prepared as if cramming for a final exam.

"I read everything I could get my hands on," says Tom Hager, a magazine journalist whose medical specialty brings him into contact with a wide range of experts. "You don't want to be caught short talking with a man of his reputation. You want to be able to ask good questions and listen intelligently. At the very least, you don't want to embarrass yourself."

Not every journalist interviews big name experts, but all deal regularly with people who know more about their own field than the journalist does. That's the nature of working for the mass media. What allows the journalist to deal with these sources professionally and obtain quality information is solid backgrounding. At its most fundamental, this means:

- A reasonable understanding of the basics of the field
- Sufficient depth of knowledge specific to the story so that you know what questions to ask
- A working vocabulary of the special jargon related to the field

Without this background, communication is difficult and information gathering is, at best, inefficient. This doesn't mean you have to be a trained criminologist to talk intelligently with the local police chief. But it does mean that your eyes don't glaze over when the chief begins to talk about "class A misdemeanors" and "DWI citations."

How can you prepare yourself to get the most out of your interviews with experts?

- For basic background, skim general and specialty encyclopedias, almanacs and other reference tools. (See Chapter 4 for specific suggestions.)
- Read newspaper and magazine articles on the subject. (See Chapters 4 and 6 for how to locate them.)

- Read trade magazine and journal articles on the subject (Chapter 4).
- Check government documents for helpful material (Chapter 5).
- Ask sources for suggestions of relevant special reports and publications that you can read before the interview.
- Contact knowledgeable colleagues or dependable "background experts" (see page 213) for information.

You cannot become an "instant expert" by doing background research for a few hours or a few days, but you can create a solid basis for questioning experts. You can improve communication and increase the chances of performing your job intelligently and responsibly.

Setting the rules

You're interviewing a local legislator about a proposal to lower the legal drinking age. "Our committee is studying the plan carefully," she tells you in measured tones. Then she confides, "But off the record, I'm going to fight this one tooth and nail." What did she mean by "off the record"? Can you use her statement in any way in your story?

Journalists regularly face situations like this. Sources give you information in the strictest confidence. They talk only after you promise them complete anonymity. They answer your questions after assurances that their names will not be connected with the answers. These deals between journalists and their sources are commonplace. One study found that Washington, D.C., reporters conduct approximately 28 percent of their interviews off the record.* A recent analysis of *Time* and *Newsweek* found that anonymous sources were quoted in 81 percent of all national and international stories.†

Agreeing on the rules of the conversation is vital. Unless you and the source understand each other perfectly from past experience, do not take anything for granted. Your definition of terms may differ from that of your source. Here are some common ones:

- *Deep background.* When a source agrees to give you information for "deep background," it generally means the information is to be used only to help you understand an issue. The source does not want the information published or broadcast in any form. Often

*Stephen Hess, *The Washington Reporters*, (Washington: The Brookings Institution, 1981), 19–20.

†K. Tim Wulfemeyer, "How and Why Anonymous Attribution Is Used by *Time* and *Newsweek*," *Journalism Quarterly*, 62 (Spring 1985):81–86.

the source doesn't even want you to use the information in conducting interviews with other sources. Make sure you know the conditions.

- *Background.* Your source probably means the information is not to be used in a story in any form. However, the source may not object to your using the information to question others.

- *Off the record.* This confusing term may mean at least three things: You can't publish or broadcast the information in any form; you can weave the information into your story if you make no mention whatever of where you got it; you can use the information if you do not explicitly mention the source. Because the term *off the record* is both vague and commonplace, you need to discuss its meaning with the source.

- *Not for attribution.* Generally, the source will allow you to use the material in the story if you don't attribute it directly. How vague does the attribution have to be to satisfy the source?

- *Don't quote me.* Another hazy term, this can mean you can't use the quotation at all or you can use it, but you can't attribute it directly to the source. Make sure you know what interpretation you're consenting to.

Agreeing to one of these deals can help you get information that would otherwise be unavailable. Such agreements can encourage sources to talk more freely and candidly. They can lead to tips, leaks and sensitive information while protecting sources from retribution. On the other hand, it is a dangerous business that can lead to abuses. Fabricated, distorted or self-serving information can be transmitted more easily when the source is not publicly accountable for the remarks. The credibility of the story may suffer when important or controversial information is not attributed. As Charles Seib wrote in the Washington *Post* more than 10 years ago, "Concealment of news sources . . . is a game stacked against the public. The press and insiders usually know who is leaking what. . . . Only the customers are kept in the dark."

When you are faced with a demand from a source, first make sure you know what the source is asking for. Next, use every argument you can muster to get the material on the record and for attribution.

Interviewing tips

Interviewing experts is one important way to gather information. Whether the interview is 10 minutes or two hours, by phone or in person, its success depends on your ability to structure and focus the conversation. Skillful interviewing is no mystery. It is a combination of good questions, careful listening and decent social skills. These five tips will help you conduct successful interviews:

1. Prepare for the interview as thoroughly as time allows. In general, the less you walk in knowing, the less you'll walk out knowing. Solid preparation is essential to establishing basic rapport, asking good questions, and doing careful probing.

2. Ask straightforward questions. Avoid vague, equivocal or wordy questions. A question should ask for specific information and should be phrased so that the respondent is neither boxed in nor asked to make meaningless, sweeping statements. Never ask a question designed merely to showcase your own knowledge.

3. Remain flexible. No successful interviewer walks in with 10 questions, asks them and walks out. An interview is a dynamic conversation that changes in the making. Listening carefully, responding quickly to hints and leads dropped in the conversation, and rephrasing questions are essential to a successful interview.

4. Be a good journalist. Remembering your responsibility to your audience, be curious, probing and skeptical. Make sure you understand what your source is telling you well enough so that you can communicate it clearly to the public.

5. Be a skillful conversationalist. Some interviews are hurried; others are hostile. In these cases, the niceties of conversation have little place. But many interviews can progress more smoothly and net more and better information if you establish a basic rapport with your subject. Often that means making the subject feel comfortable by beginning the interview with non-threatening questions. In face-to-face interviews, eye contact and nonverbal cues (nodding, smiling) can create a simple bond. There's little mystery to all this. Most of us naturally adopt certain behaviors when we want to put strangers at ease. Watch yourself at the next gathering you attend.

USING EXPERTS IN YOUR WORK

Where do experts fit in the information-gathering process? What place do they have in your story? How can you help your readers or viewers understand what the experts are saying? Using experts in your work is a more complex process than you might imagine. Let's look at the function of different kinds of experts in the information-gathering process using this example: A journalist is about to start researching a story on a startling new diet aid just introduced locally and growing in popularity—a pill that supposedly allows dieters to eat all the carbohydrates they want without gaining an ounce. Does it work? Is it safe? The journalist, who is not a health, nutrition or science specialist, wants to find out.

The background expert

Where do you go for information when you know so little that you don't even know what questions to ask? You can depend on that invaluable person known as the background expert, the person who can give you a crash course and point you to helpful references and sources. She's the banker you can contact when you've been assigned a story on an increase in home foreclosures, but you have no idea what banking policies and procedures are. He's the contractor you can phone when you're doing a story on lax enforcement of building codes, but you can't even begin to decipher the jargon.

Background experts are behind-the-scenes sources you use early in the information-gathering process, not to amass quotes but to educate yourself and begin formulating questions. They are people you can trust to give you initial guidance. They are people in front of whom you can shamelessly parade your lack of knowledge. Generally, they are friends, acquaintances or people with whom you've already established rapport.

One of the best places to look for background experts is the university. Professors, as we've mentioned before, are generally good at explaining the basics, accustomed to talking to people who know little about their field and often less self-interested in the outcome of a story than those directly involved. Another obvious place to look is within your own professional and social circles. Wherever you find them, background experts can be exceptional frontline sources.

Who might serve as background experts for the journalist on the diet pill story? The journalist's own physician might be a likely candidate. Nutritional science teachers at the local college or university could be important sources.

The bull's-eye strategy

All of us are, from time to time, guided by self-interest. Your information sources may have their own agendas, regardless of the story you're pursuing: politicians who seek positive media coverage to boost their campaigns, business executives who believe good stories can lead to promotions, scientific researchers looking for publicity to help them secure grants. Others may be impelled by institutional loyalty: the college president who glosses over the resignation of an important faculty member or the hospital administrator who releases only those statistics that show cost containment. Journalists need not be suspicious or distrustful of the motives of all sources. But they must realize that the information flow can be affected by forces unrelated to the story itself.

Knowing this, careful, sensibly skeptical journalists will devise an information-gathering strategy that helps prevent them from being manipulated by the self-interest of others. This plan, called the bull's-eye strategy, is simple: Contact sources beginning with those least personally and professionally involved in the story (those with the least to gain or lose by it and therefore the least self-interested). The background expert is the natural first stop. Then, after establishing the outlines of the story, begin contacting people with increasing involvement (and potential self-interest). You will be better able to question the self-interested sources and evaluate their responses if you speak to them last. Thus, the information search follows the perimeter of the target, spiraling in to the bull's-eye.

Consider the *Oregonian* reporters researching the Hanford Nuclear Reservation story. Suppose they began their information quest by interviewing Hanford's chief administrator, a top scientist or the executive of one of the firms with a large financial investment in the facility? These are people whose careers and futures may be on the line. They have devoted their professional lives to making Hanford a success. It would be natural to find self-interest. Without the background information attained through research and "perimeter" interviews, the reporters would be ill-prepared to ask tough questions and evaluate the extent of the self-interest.

What about the journalist investigating the diet pill story? The perimeter sources would be uninvolved background experts (the journalist's own doctor plus the academic nutritionists). The intermediate sources could be any or all of the following: professional nutritionists and dieticians, scientific researchers doing work in the field, government experts in the Department of Health and Human Services, Food and Drug Administration investigators, physicians and clinics specializing in weight loss, and users of the diet pill. Those in the bull's-eye, the ones with the most to lose or gain by the story, would be the manufacturers and distributors of the pill.

Outsiders versus insiders

Outsiders are sources knowledgeable about but not directly involved in the issue you are researching. Insiders are in the thick of it. Both have their place in the information-gathering scheme, providing information and insights specific to their different positions. In general, insiders provide the intimate details only they can know, as well as the fiery quotations their involvement may dictate. Outsiders provide background, perspective and context, helping both you and your audience better understand an issue. Sometimes, but not always, outsiders will be less self-interested "perimeter" sources while insiders will be more self-interested "bull's eye" sources.

The insider-outsider lineup for the diet pill story is obvious. In-the-thick-of-it insiders include FDA investigators, the manufacturers and distributors of the product and its satisfied and dissatisfied users. Interested-but-not-directly-involved outsiders include nutrition experts and scientists.

Incidentally, this story—which was, in fact, researched using the sources mentioned—found that the carbohydrate blocking pill was probably not effective and definitely not safe. It disappeared from the market after the FDA announced a formal investigation.

Identifying experts

Good journalists always attribute a comment, opinion, inference or judgment to its source. (Even a reference to "a top State Department official" is an attribution of sorts.) But there is more to attribution than merely identifying a source as Senator So-and-so. Journalists have an obligation to give their audience identifying information that will help them evaluate the source's remarks and think independently about the story.

Consider the difference the additional information (italicized) makes in the following attributions:

"This is the most important, most powerful anti-arthritic medication ever invented," says Michael Dant, *president of the pharmaceutical company that will begin marketing the formula next month.*

"This is the most important, most powerful anti-arthritic medication ever invented," says Michael Dant, *a National Institutes of Health scientist involved in arthritis research for more than three decades.*

Full attribution can help put an expert's remarks in context, clarify an expert's position and identify the motivation for the comment. Identification is particularly useful to the public when experts disagree. Suppose you were to write:

> "The president's plan to do away with the federal tax deduction for state income tax is an abomination," said Sen. Tom Thompson, D-N.Y.

> "The president's plan will be the greatest boon to the hard-hit taxpayer since the introduction of the individual retirement account," said Sen. Roberta Roberts, R-Alaska.

Considering these two statements, readers or viewers might dismiss the conflicting remarks as typical party squabbling. But, depending on the information you've gathered for this story, the following might be more helpful:

> "The president's plan to do away with the federal tax deduction for state income tax is an abomination," said Sen Tom Thompson, *whose New York constituents pay the highest state income tax in the nation.*

> "The president's plan to do away with the federal tax deduction for state income tax is an abomination," said Sen. Tom Thompson, *whose New York constituents pay the highest state income tax in the nation.*

Help your audience make informed decisions about the comments of experts. Include all pertinent identification as part of the attribution. Also, when relevant, include information explaining the conditions under which the information was obtained. If you've spoken directly to a source, make that clear in your story. If you've culled a statement from a memo, press release, wire service story or other source, mention that too.

Jargon slaying

Experts often talk their own language. It's both a shorthand by which they communicate with each other and a barrier to their communication for those outside the profession. Be it the secret tongue of butchers or of bureaucrats, jargon has little place in mainstream journalism. On the contrary, the journalist's job is to cut through jargon to communicate clearly and effectively with the audience.

The journalist who interviews a banker and then writes about "downturns in commercial lending package applications" (jargon) instead of "fewer business loan applications" (translation) is doing no one a service. Jargon is not impressive; lucid explanations are.

There may be times when knowing a bit of jargon can help you establish rapport with a source or communicate more quickly. Specialty encyclopedias and dictionaries are particularly helpful tools. (See Chapter 4.) But regardless of your own mastery of the special language, you owe your readers or viewers a jargon-free story.

PROBLEM EXPERTS

In the best of all possible journalistic worlds, expert sources are co-operative, articulate, honest and accessible. Like reporters, they are interested in communicating complete, accurate, timely information that helps others understand and function in society.

But it doesn't always work that way. Some sources present problems.

- *The rehearsed spokesperson.* These sources are generally closed to two-way communication. They have a message to relate, most often dictated to them by a higher-up, and their job is to relate it. Their major concern is media coverage for that message. Presidential press secretaries and corporate media liaisons—especially during times of trouble or tension—are often good examples of this type. Although rehearsed spokespersons frequently must be contacted for "official comment," they are generally not good sources for anything other than their rehearsed message. The good journalist looks beyond them for complete information.

- *The well-used expert.* Journalists can be lazy. Instead of digging for information, they can wait for it to be handed to them. Instead of cultivating new sources, they return to the same ones time and again. A trusted expert is a person to hold on to, but the search for new sources of information should never stop. The well-used expert can quickly become the over-used expert, thus unintentionally narrowing the scope of the information the journalist gathers and the audience learns. Is Ralph Nader the only consumer affairs advocate in the nation? Is Sam Donaldson the only in-house network news critic? Is Chris Evert Lloyd the only person qualified to talk about women's tennis? Sometimes it seems so. Journalists who talk exclusively to the mayor about city affairs or to the police chief about crime are doing their audiences a similar disservice. The promise of American journalism is that it can be a forum for a wide range of voices. It can't begin to be that if journalists consistently rely on well-used experts.

- *The self-interested expert.* As discussed earlier in this chapter, the self-interested expert operates from a personal agenda that may get in the way of complete, accurate, honest communication. Journalists can protect themselves and their audience against potentially manipulative or deceptive information by recognizing self-interest (in themselves as well as in others), backgrounding themselves thoroughly before questioning sources and using the bull's-eye strategy.

- *Battling experts.* It's both exciting and frustrating to encounter experts who categorically disagree. Spirited debate can help crystallize the issues, and controversy certainly can create exciting copy. But conflict does not necessarily promote understanding, and journalists have a responsibility to do more than let experts battle it out within a story. Not all experts are equally knowledgeable or trustworthy. It is the journalist's job to confirm information and give the audience concrete ways to judge the value of various experts. (Much more on this problem follows in the next chapter.)

- *Equivocating experts.* Even more frustrating than experts who disagree are experts who do not offer straightforward responses. Some who respond to questions with ambiguous answers or what seems like double-talk may be acting out of self-interest. These people are truly problem experts and should be approached as such. But others may be responding honestly with no hidden agenda. Journalists often crave black-and-white answers to complex problems, and the mass media are in the habit of trumpeting simple, definitive statements (*the* cure for the common cold, *the* cause of teenage alcoholism). The truth is, few questions have simple answers, and the more expert an expert source really is, the less likely he or she is to offer an emphatic, unequivocal statement. Journalists should think of using experts to explore questions as well as answer them, to report on uncertainty as well as fact.

Whom Do You Trust?

11

This chapter is about precision *and* intuition, about airtight confirmation *and* anxious second-guessing. It looks, with some curiosity, at journalists' pursuit of the truth and their inevitable settling for the closest thing to it. It is more than a chapter about trust. It also is about confidence—that feeling the journalist gets when the story *appears* to be complete and well-rounded.

With this book, you have examined information sources and strategies. You have considered the process, rewards and pitfalls of the search for information. Now it is time to think about putting it all together in a coherent, useful form.

This entails a philosophical examination of validity and trust. It requires analysis of such issues as collecting and evaluating evidence, determining credibility of sources and resolving conflicting evidence. This philosophy is both pragmatic and spiritual, and a natural emphasis is on ideals—the way things *should* be.

VALIDITY AND TRUST

When sailors near land, they face new dangers as threatening as gales on the open sea; shallow water, riptides, reefs and confusing channels can spell an ironic end to a hard-fought voyage. They need to establish exactly where they are.

To do this, sailors take a navigational fix to determine their location. The most accurate fix is made by taking several lines of position using various navigational aids as reference points. Establishing these points against, for example, a lighthouse, day marker and mooring buoy gives them a reliable fix—if they follow directions and are precise. When a fix is plotted on a navigational chart, these three lines will intersect at the same point. That point is exactly where the sailors are—away from danger, they hope.

Establishing journalistic validity is much like taking a proper navigational fix. If a sailor's technique is poor and the charts aren't researched properly, the lines of position won't intersect at the same point. The point of position will instead be a large triangle (intersecting at three different points), leaving the sailors to guess where they are on that section of the chart. Similarly, journalists need to work precisely and thoroughly to validate where they are, and they need to be able to trust their own work. The lesson of this analogy, then, is to recognize your sources, learn how to evaluate and use them, and don't depend on just one to fix your position.

Joel Brinkley, Pulitzer Prize-winning reporter for the New York *Times*, believes that most journalists develop their concept of trust by *instinct.* He is quick to add, however, that

> the first and most important thing is to figure out what motivates the person, what he hopes to gain or fears he might lose as a result of the piece I am writing. For most people, everything they say to a reporter is run through that filter.
>
> As to when I trust a source, if it's a one-time interview with someone I don't know well, it is when I have been able to confirm with other sources large elements of what he said. If it is someone I use all the time, I begin trusting him and may not feel as compelled to confirm every little element, after we have worked on a few stories together and he had established a clean record of reliability.*

For Brinkley, trust is directly related to the validity of the information that emerges from his "filter." Like the navigator, he doesn't depend on a single source, though he may eventually rely on a source more because he or she has turned out to be reliable. He feels better about his story if the information received is in line with his previous research and documentation. He tries to detect bias and deceit; he tries to understand the backgrounds and positions of his sources in order to learn what motivates them to provide the information.

---

*Personal correspondence with the authors, September 7, 1985.

What is said about the source as a person applies equally to the source as a record, document or publication. People and institutions stand behind this intelligence. Assessing the background, motivation and track record of this collected information is as important as making judgments about the veracity of an interviewee.

It is clear that successful information gathering and constructing a complete story require solid research—digging and cross-checking—in order to validate information and to create the trust necessary to prepare a story with confidence.

COLLECTING AND EVALUATING EVIDENCE

Journalists face a dilemma that spawns criticism and self-doubt. In their watchdog role, they are expected to become instant experts on their assigned subject—even though they cannot possibly make infallible judgments about the motivations of the real experts (those who understand and control the information the journalists seek). On the other hand, journalists are expected to provide as timely and as complete a story as possible. If a story is incomplete; if it doesn't properly evaluate the evidence given by experts and other sources; if it doesn't help readers or viewers to make informed decisions about the sources and their material, then the journalist meets criticism and suspicion. A few examples illustrate this problem.

Publicity and public outcry about excessive military expenditures for "ordinary" items have almost become a national pastime. The $600 toilet seat cover and the $3,000 coffee maker are now entrenched in our folklore. However, *The National Review* magazine has complained about both the media focus on the original revelations concerning overspending and about the media's lack of attention to further investigation of these complaints:

> The $640 toilet seat cover was not a toilet seat cover at all but a heavily molded plastic cover for the entire toilet system of the P-3 aircraft. The toilet seats themselves cost only $9.37 each. . . .
> . . . there is the much-publicized case of the $3,046 coffee maker. This was for an airplane, the C-5, that can carry up to 365 troops. Delta and TWA buy similar coffee makers for $3,107 each.*

Because this editorial reflects new evidence, it is important for the reporter to ask some questions about it. For example,

*"Horror Stories," *The National Review,"* September 6, 1985, 19.

- Is this information true?
- If so, what sources did the *Review* use to obtain this information?
- What is the background of the sources who provided this information? If this information came from documents, who prepared and published them?
- Does the highly conservative reputation of *The National Review* make its information suspect in this defense-oriented issue?
- If these examples *are* true, do they show enough of a pattern to question common conceptions of military misspending? Why?

These are questions readers will ask. Reporters and editors need to ask them before the copy makes publication.

Consider the case of the school principal who is asked by the school board to resign because several parents had apparently accused him of making sexual advances toward their teenaged sons. However, the board does not identify the parents. No complaints are filed with the district attorney. The principal denies all allegations.

None of this information is discussed in public session because under its state law, the school board may meet in executive session to discuss personnel matters.*

Although the board can take action or vote on an issue only in a public meeting, the matter is apparently resolved when, under great pressure from the board, the principal agrees to resign. He cites personal and health reasons. The board agrees to pay off the remaining five months on the principal's contract. The unidentified parents, speaking through the board chair, agree not to press the issue.

At the board's next public meeting, the board votes to accept, "with regret," the resignation. The reporter, who attended the executive session under a customary promise to only report the board's public actions, is torn.

The reporter knows a cover-up has taken place. But nothing is on the record at this point. The reporter is concerned that (1) the principal may have been hounded out of his job and (2) if the principal had been taking sexual liberties with his students, his record remains unblemished.

If a story is written on what actually happened *before* the public announcement, the reporter may face official denials, lack of corroboration or even a libel suit. It is clear that this story needs more digging, but without the cooperation of the parents, students, board members or principal, nothing probably will come of it.

---

*For a discussion of open meeting laws, see Chapter 3.

In trying to collect as much evidence to get as close to the truth as possible, the reporter faces an important reality: Not all story leads turn into published stories. The reporter must understand when a story is incomplete and not rush it to an editor.

A story is complete when all its angles have been properly examined, when points likely to raise questions or conflict have been corroborated or explained. Here is a checklist reporters should follow when collecting and evaluating information:

1. What people and which institutions have an interest in, and are affected by, the story? (This question suggests whom to interview and what to research.)

2. Have the sources been properly evaluated and explained? (Readers want to know about your story research. Telling them about sources helps them understand the motivations of sources as well as their body of knowledge.)

3. What kinds of complaints can reporters expect to receive about their stories? (Publishing a truthful story that creates a "negative" impact in the community is not a valid complaint, but leaving out an important story element with the explanation that the source was "unavailable for comment" can rarely be justified.)

Perhaps *The National Review* was correct in chastizing the media for not following up stories about Defense Department misspending. Perhaps the contractors' explanations and subsequent actions were not properly reported. But the magazine did not instill much confidence by failing to reveal the sources of its newly acquired information. In this case, the reader was unable to judge the motives of those sources and the context of their messages.

Perhaps the story of the principal's resignation had so many dead-ends and was meeting so much resistance and silence that the reporter was unable to gather the truth. But the reporter could have focused on why the board paid off the principal's contract and allowed him to step down immediately. Wouldn't the public be asking that? And why shouldn't the reporter ask if something is terribly wrong with an open meetings law that permits withholding information vital to the public on a technicality? A story, told with some details withheld to protect innocent parties, could pull together several case studies to show the problems of this law.

In the end, the *best* evidence is that which has several sources standing behind it, *publicly* attesting to its truth. Dependence on unnamed sources will not take a reporter far down the road of credibility and confidence.

THE CREDIBLE SOURCE

Just as objectivity is a journalistic fairy tale, so is the unbiased source pure fantasy. Reporters cannot prevent their political, social, economic and religious interests from somehow affecting the way they interview people, select sources and arrange information in a story. This is not to say that reporters blatantly put their biases into stories. But they are human, and they must struggle constantly to select and present information in an evenhanded manner.

Likewise, reporters should not expect their sources to be plain-spoken, guileless and humanitarian founts of information. Knowing what motivates your sources will take you a long way in determining what kind of baggage is attached to the information you are receiving— whether it comes from an unusually talkative official or from a quiet, dusty document. The reporter must not only evaluate the credibility of information within the context of his or her own research but also within the context of the source's own attitudes and beliefs.

One of the first jobs of the reporter in compiling information, then, is to learn context. For example, what is the background of this source? What attitudes and beliefs characterize the source? The reporter thus creates a scale of credibility. The reporter learns when to seek more corroboration for the information of certain sources. And most important, the reporter is able to explain how sources were chosen—and who they are, exactly—to the audience.

When a source realizes that the reporter understands the context of the information, he or she is likely to speak more openly. *Ideally,* reporters should probe, and sources should explain:

- The sources' interest in the information they are dispensing
- The "turf" the sources are trying to protect
- Some background on the information sources are providing, including how they acquired it
- Why sources can't provide all the information they know at present

Let's examine the following cast of sources in an unhappy story. Less than 10 minutes after the start of a routine tonsillectomy, a 10-year-old boy dies on the operating table. The initial diagnosis is heart failure; an autopsy is scheduled.

Leading the list of the most *accessible* sources is the hospital's PR spokesperson. Note the emphasis on accessible; this in no way implies that the most accessible source has the most or the best information. Indeed, the reporter would be surprised if the PR spokesperson made any startling revelations, such as "the anesthesiologist made an error in computing the amount of anesthetic for the patient." More likely, the spokesperson will release basic information, such as the name and age of the patient, the suspected cause of death, and the fact that the hospital is cooperating in an autopsy.

The sources with the most information—the doctors, nurses and involved staff—probably will have been instructed not to talk to the media.

The parents may either be too shocked to comment or may make allegations about the care of their child.

In an emotional story like this, nothing will be resolved quickly, even though the time pressure the media puts on gathering the news may create an artificial sense of urgency. However, the reporter must continue to search for additional information and sources:

- Have there been enough other unexpected deaths at this hospital or with this physician in charge to raise suspicions?

- Have information or reports been withheld from relatives or appropriate agencies?

- Are some hospital personnel willing to comment on operating and care procedures? What is their interest?

- Are credible outside experts (other doctors, administrators, health care agency personnel) willing to comment?

Perhaps this tragic story is a simple one: The autopsy report and the medical examiner's investigation show flawless behavior on the part of the hospital and its personnel. The child's cardiac arrest resulted from an unexplained change in heart rhythm—an occurrence that has killed many apparently healthy people.

But such an outcome (or its prediction) should not have prevented the reporter from probing the potential of this story. Though the PR spokesperson may have a good reputation for providing information to the media, that fact alone doesn't ensure that the current information is complete, let alone accurate. (True, reputation can push information up on the credibility scale.) Remember that the PR person is *dispensing* information he or she is *directed* to give. The true source is the hospital administration, which quickly discovers what happened in its operating room but which is naturally eager to downplay any negative publicity and to avoid costly lawsuits. This account may appear cynical, but it merely presupposes that there is always more information beyond what is initially revealed.

It is the reporter's duty to find the real source and to search out evidence that either corroborates or challenges official pronouncements. In this case, a clean bill from the medical examiner, glowing reports from staff and acceptance by the grieving parents may end this story—maybe. More evidence may surface later.

When reporters investigate the motivations and allegiances of sources, they open themselves to criticism. The press is being arrogant, some will say. The answer is that audiences deserve as much information as journalists can find. They deserve vigorously checked, valid information.

To do a responsible job, the media *must* question the intentions and actions of other institutions. The media-government adversarial relationship is a case in point. The U.S. government's 1983 invasion of the Caribbean nation of Grenada reflects a natural conflict between the media and the government. Unfortunately, it also reveals deceit from a source and the public's acceptance of a limited source of information.

After U.S. armed forces invaded Grenada, the Reagan administration denied the press any access until the military operation was completed. Instead, the military released these "facts" to the media: Three thousand troops landed to protect the lives of 1,000 American citizens. Their lives were in danger from a Cuban occupation of more than 1,000 troops who were setting up a terrorist center. In the aftermath, the U.S. government called its Grenada operation a success. It claimed that only eight servicemen had been killed and that damage had been kept to a minimum.

What more was there to say after the government had given the public the *official* version? Plenty, said communications scholars Melvin DeFleur and Everette Dennis:

> There was a lot more. Reporters went to Grenada after the invasion and unearthed a number of discrepancies between what they saw and the government's reports. For instance, 6,000 American servicemen were on the island on October 25, not 3,000. On October 30, the State Department admitted there had been only about 700 Cubans there, all but 100 of whom were in fact construction workers. Similarly, the alleged cache of weapons was found to be much smaller than the president had indicated, and there was no evidence of a terrorist training base on the island. Papers released by the government did not show that any Cuban takeover had been planned or that the Soviets had been involved in any way with the prime minister's [Maurice Bishop's] murder. Some of the returning American citizens, while grateful to be safely at home, admitted that they had never been aware of any danger, and journalists found that the Cuban government had given assurances several times that they would not be harmed. American casualties were eventually listed at 18 dead and 89 wounded; most of these had been sustained on the first day of the inva-

sion. And a Canadian reporter discovered that a mental hospital had mistakenly been bombed, resulting in the deaths of 17 civilians, which the government never reported. . . . In the confusion over the facts, one point about press censorship became clear: Many Americans learned only what the government told them.*

The lessons here are that (1) sources will *never* reveal *all* they know; (2) they naturally will present information according to their attitudes and needs; and (3) reporters can change the outcomes of tendencies 1 and 2 if they confront those sources with other intelligence that shows defects in the original version. *One* source is a piece of the puzzle; many sources, cross-checked, can complete the picture.

DEALING WITH CONFLICTING INFORMATION

Theories, opinions and other statements often conflict, but facts rarely do. The key is to identify the facts and properly label other information as opinion, hypothesis or misstatement. Consider this brief wire service dispatch about actor Rock Hudson, who died of Acquired Immune Deficiency Syndrome in 1985:

> Rock Hudson may or may not have known whether his name was being used in the fight against AIDS, the disease that eventually killed him. Syndicated Hollywood columnist Marilyn Beck has reported that Hudson was unaware of a statement read in his name at a star-studded AIDS benefit in Los Angeles last month. She also quoted friends and associates of the actor as saying that during the final weeks Hudson was rarely lucid. Other friends and associates, however, are differing with those reports and are saying he was well aware of the statement made in his behalf and wanted the nature of his illness made public.

Although this is hardly a paragon of reporting, it is useful to show conflicting evidence. Some people claim Hudson knew that his name was used in the AIDS campaign; others dispute that. This dispatch contains no real supportive information or attribution to persuade the audience to accept one version over the other—unless a reader swears by the track record of a Hollywood columnist! The issue might have been resolved if a source produced a notarized document in which Hudson agreed to the use of his name. Or, two "sources" are identified,

*Melvin DeFleur and Everette Dennis, *Understanding Mass Communications*, 2nd. ed. (Boston: Houghton-Mifflin, 1985), 134.

call each other liars, and embroil themselves in a libel suit. A Solomon-like judge decides the issue.

However, it sometimes doesn't matter if a conflict of information exists because the story itself isn't that important. In these cases, it is sufficient to present the conflicting material and let readers decide for themselves.

In more significant stories, however, *how* the reporter presents conflicting information and sources affects the way readers evaluate the story. For example, even if you think one source is clearly superior to another, you should allow the audience to make that judgment by writing an even-handed story that doesn't denigrate the other source. Use sources with good track records, cross-check claims and let a story develop more slowly in the presence of conflicting evidence. You'll end up with a stronger story and give your audience more confidence in your work.

In the end, it is facts that will triumph over opinion and innuendo. While reporters feel bound to report all sides of an issue, they must dig deep to illuminate conflict and controversy with truth.

In 1985, the crisis in the farmbelt was one of the most keenly focused media issues in America. The Minneapolis *Star and Tribune* spent six months examining price supports and farm bankruptcies. Its series, with 22 stories and almost 50 charts, maps and graphs, told an amazing, compelling story. With an incredible array of sources backing it up, the paper highlighted its findings in a myth-versus-fact arrangement, amplifying that information with lengthy, well-researched stories. An excerpt:

> *Myth:* American farmers, as a group, are economically disadvantaged.
> *Fact:* The average American farm—house, buildings, land, machinery and other investments—today has an estimated net worth of $360,000, according to the U.S. Department of Agriculture. In 1983, the latest year for which figures are available, average net income for a farm family was $29,408—slightly higher than the average family income in the nation.
> *Myth:* Farming has become an enterprise dominated by corporations that someday may have enough power to dictate food prices.
> *Fact:* Only about 3 percent of the nation's farms are owned by non-family corporations.
> *Myth:* Farming doesn't get its fair share of government aid compared with other industries.
> *Fact:* By any financial gauge of their contribution to the public weal, farmers get more federal aid than any other sector of the economy. . . . Agriculture last year got about $8,700 in direct and indirect federal aid for

every full-time farm job—almost six times the $1,500 in federal subsidies for each manufacturing job.*

What the *Star and Tribune* did was exceptional. Granted, not many stories can command such time and resources. Even a scaled-down version of the paper's project shows the success of well-planned information gathering. The *Star and Tribune* reporters pored over official documents, found and interviewed experts, did computer searches for relevant articles and research papers, and used public records to trace the activities of farmers who had left agriculture. Their work shows that difficult, controversial topics are best examined with *intensive* research.

All media can shine, if journalists do their research well and give their audience enough information to help it form an educated opinion. The media gain credibility when journalists explain their sources and when their information answers more questions than it raises.

The media are in the business of information. They should produce a quality product. Sometimes, however, their work is rushed, crude and tinged with a "this-is-what-I've-decided-to-let-you-know" attitude. Such a lack of planning and polish caused *Harper's* magazine editor Lewis Lapham to observe that journalism was "a primitive form of psychoanalysis to help the patient judge the distance between fantasy and reality."

We have to do better than that.

Surely we can.

---

*John Ullmann, project editor, "Propping up the farm," Minneapolis *Star and Tribune*, Aug. 11–12, 1985.

Identifying and
Dealing with
Ethical Issues

As professional communicators search for and report information, they face a host of tough ethical issues. These issues, which involve moral codes and professional standards, go beyond the rigid proscriptions of our legal system.

All people need an ethical system to guide them. Approved conduct and values are the products of such a system. In mass communications, the need for an ethical system cannot be overstated; gathering and disseminating information have a profound impact on people and institutions. We must ensure that our work is done with a reasonable degree of fairness to, and concern for, our audiences. We must also be careful to extend that concern to the subjects of our search for information.

In an effort to stimulate a dialogue about ethical issues in journalism, we offer some topics in this appendix for personal reflection and class discussion. It is an attempt to persuade you to closely examine your values and your own perception of the media's values.

Two valuable books on this subject will provide you with perspective on contemporary issues in the ethics of journalism. Please review these books and then examine the following topics.

- John Hulteng. *The Messenger's Motives*. Englewood Cliffs, N.J.: Prentice-Hall, 1976.

- Tom Goldstein. *The News at Any Cost: How Journalists Compromise Their Ethics to Shape the News*. New York: Simon and Schuster, 1985.

1. Examining codes of ethics

Carefully read the published codes of ethics of the American Society of Newspaper Editors and the Society of Professional Journalists/SDX. Do you see a common theme? Do you detect any conflicts?

Consider, for example, these passages from two different sections of the SPJ/SDX Code:

> *Ethics:* Journalists must be free of obligation to any interest other than the public's right to know.

> *Fair Play:* Journalists at all times will show respect for the dignity, privacy, rights and well-being of people encountered in the course of gathering and presenting the news.

Do you see instances where the journalist's need to be "free of obligation" could interfere with the rights of people encountered in the course of gathering the news? How would you resolve such conflicts? Does it strike you as odd that the SPJ/SDX code has separate sections on ethics and fair play?

2. For the greater good

At what point do you think a journalist has a higher obligation to the profession than to the governing institutions of his or her society?

Consider, for example, a reporter's receipt of a stolen government document that purports to show official malfeasance, collusion and deceit. Is violating a law to bring important information to the public a justifiable breach of traditional standards of conduct?

Consider also a reporter's claim of privilege from testifying when he or she has information that could help a criminal defendant but would reveal important confidential sources of information.

Question journalists in your area about these all-too-real scenarios. Discover their attitudes and experiences. Do their explanations agree with your standards?

3. But it's a great photograph

Discuss this situation: A photojournalist makes a heart-wrenching image of a family mourning over the body of its youngest, just found drowned at the beach. The body is dominant in the picture's foreground. The managing editor knows there will be some protest, but decides to run the picture. In the face of overwhelming protest from outraged readers, the managing editor backs down and apologizes for running the picture. The photographer, however, still believes that use of the picture was valid. However, the managing editor also decides to enter that picture in the Pulitzer Prize competition for spot news photography. He says there is no conflict between his apology to readers and his desire to enter the competition. He claims the prize is not given for reader approval. Still, he now admits that the picture should never have been published.

If you are the publisher of this paper, what do you say to the photographer and the managing editor? Is what you say any different from what the average reader will say? Why?

What is the news value of such a picture? Do you think that value outweighs the "fair play" admonition of the SPJ/SDX code?

4. We're not in the fairness business

Consider this statement from an angry newspaper editor: "We have no business trying to make our stories fair to all concerned. . . . those types who urge us to be fair would have our newspapers become a gray morass of innocuous inanity." Can you think of an instance in which a desire to be fair and objective would interfere with news reporting? Does this editor's statement imply that newspapers, because of their nature and because of the pressures on them, *are* somewhat unfair? If so, what implications does this have for a code of ethics?

5. It sounded good, so I used it

Plagiarism is the appropriation of one's ideas or writings and passing them off as your own. It is not only a problem in academic settings; it affects journalism as well. The SPJ/SDX code makes this brief statement about plagiarism: "Plagiarism is dishonest and unacceptable."

Suppose a columnist working for you publishes a piece in which he blatantly uses material taken directly from a national magazine article published several years ago. Several readers call your attention to it. What will you do? Is suspension without pay sufficient? Should the columnist just get a warning? Or is termination of employment the answer?

Is the term "unacceptable" in the SPJ/SDX code too general? Does it make you wonder if codes of ethics should have more teeth?

6. This is where I get off, thanks

Now face the music and list the activities you would *not* engage in as a journalist. Also list how strongly you feel about certain "prohibited" activities. Present this list to students or colleagues and see if they agree.

Do you see a pattern in the types of things you wouldn't do? For example, does your "no" list have more to do with privacy rights than with media cooperation with the government or misrepresentation?

Do you see a sliding scale of values in your list and in those of others? If at the top of your list is not publishing the name of a rape victim or not participating in a police-inspired hoax to capture a criminal, then what is in the middle or toward the bottom? When absolute values are shaded, institutional pressures and peer judgments play a role in the decision-making process.

Do you know at what point your values will start to bend?

Index